A Handbook of

MANAGEMENT AND LEADERSHIP

A GUIDE TO MANAGING FOR RESULTS

Michael Armstrong • Tina Stephens

KOGAN PAGE

London and Philadelphia

Publisher's note
Every possible effort has been made to ensure that the information contained in this book is accurate at the time of going to press, and the publishers and authors cannot accept responsibility for any errors or omissions, however caused. No responsibility for loss or damage occasioned to any person acting, or refraining from action, as a result of the material in this publication can be accepted by the editor, the publisher or any of the authors.

First published in Great Britain and the United States in 2005 by Kogan Page Limited
Reprinted in 2006

120 Pentonville Road
London N1 9JN
United Kingdom
www.kogan-page.co.uk

525 South 4th Street, #241
Philadelphia PA 19147
USA

© Michael Armstrong and Tina Stephens, 2005

ISBN 0 7494 4344 8

British Library Cataloguing-in-Publication Data

A CIP record for this book is available from the British Library.

Library of Congress Cataloging-in-Publication Data

Armstrong, Michael, 1928-
   A handbook of management and leadership : a guide to managing for results / Michael Armstrong and Tina Stephens.
      p. cm.
   Includes bibliographical references and index.
   ISBN 0–7494–4344–8
   1. Management–Handbooks, manuals, etc. 2. Leadership–Handbooks, manuals, etc. I. Stephens, Tina. II. Title. III. Title: Management and leadership.
   HD38.15.A76 2005
   658.4–dc22
                                   2005001556

Typeset by Datamatics Technologies Ltd, Mumbai, India
Printed and bound in Great Britain by Bell & Bain, Glasgow

Contents

Preface   *ix*

PART I   THE PRACTICE OF MANAGEMENT

1   The nature of management   3
What management is about 3; Purpose of management and
leadership 4; The processes of management 4; Differences between
management and leadership 5; Management standards 7; Influences on
management 8; Summary 11; References 11

2   Leadership   13
Leadership roles 13; Leadership and management styles 14; Situational
leadership 14; Exercising leadership 15; Leadership characteristics 15;
Leaders and followers 17; Leadership checklist 18; Summary 19;
References 20

3   The role of the manager   21
What is a manager? 21; The contribution of the manager 22; Factors
affecting added value contribution 22; The characteristics of the
manager's role 24; The significance of strategic and visionary
thinking 26; The contribution of the line/middle manager 27;
Managerial qualities 28; Summary 29; References 30

4 **Managerial activities**   31
   Planning 31; Organizing 33; Setting objectives and targets 35;
   Communicating 39; Summary 43

5 **Approaches to management**   45
   Delegation 45; Motivating others 48; Feedback 49; Coaching 50;
   Facilitation 52; Networking 53; Understanding organizational
   policies 54; Influence 55; Authority 56; Power 57; Dealing with
   unsatisfactory situations 58; Summary 58; References 60

6 **Making things happen**   61
   How to make it happen: basic questions 61; What makes achievers
   tick? 62; What do achievers who make things happen do? 63; On being
   decisive 64; Analysing and improving how you make things happen 65;
   Summary 66; References 66

7 **Strategic management**   67
   Strategy 67; Developing strategy 68; The role of strategic
   management 69; Developing a shared vision and strategic plans 70;
   Summary 70; References 71

8 **Systems and process management**   73
   Managing systems 73; Managing processes 74; Examples of systems
   and process management 74; The conflict and challenges that
   managing systems and processes presents 79; Summary 79

9 **Self-development**   81
   The process of self-development 81; Other methods of management
   development 83; Self-management strategies 86; Summary 87;
   References 88

PART II   DELIVERING CHANGE

10 **The process of change**   91
   Types of change 91; How change happens 98; Organization dynamics –
   how organizations grow and change 98; Summary 100; References 101

11 **The context of change**   103
   The basis of organization 103; Types of organizations 105; Development
   and maintenance of organization structures and systems 108;
   Organization functions 113; Organizational culture 115; Power 115;
   Authority 116; Summary 116; References 117

12 Change management 119

Change models 119; How people change 121; The steps to effective change 122; Resistance to change 122; Developing and embracing a change culture 125; Identifying the need for change 125; The benefits and risks of change 126; Making the business case for change 127; Planning the change programme 127; Requirements for success in managing change 129; Elements leading to the successful implementation of change 130; Summary 131; References 133

PART III   ENHANCING CUSTOMER RELATIONS

13 Basis of customer service 137

The nature of customer service 137; Customer service activities 140; Elements of customer satisfaction 140; Summary 142; Reference 143

14 Approaches to customer service 145

Managing relationships with customers 146; Assess customer needs 148; Identify target customers 151; Communicate to customers 152; Measure customer satisfaction 153; Develop products and services to meet customer needs 155; Provide the infrastructure for customer service 157; Evaluate models of customer service 157; Set standards for customer service 159; Monitor the delivery of service standards 161; Build satisfaction and keep customers 161; Internal customers 161; Summary 163; References 164

15 Achieving high levels of customer service 165

The twelve pillars of world-class service excellence 165; Customer service strategy 167; Developing a customer-centric culture 167; Define required attitudes, skills, knowledge, behaviours and competencies 170; Developing attitudes, skills and behaviours 174; World-class customer service examples 176; Summary 180; References 181

PART IV   ENABLING CONTINUOUS IMPROVEMENT

16 Continuous improvement 185

The nature of continuous improvement 185; Fostering a culture of continuous improvement 188; The conditions and behaviour that promote continuous improvement 190; The framework for continuous improvement 192; Continuous improvement programmes 193; Examples of approaches to continuous improvement 201; Summary 204; References 205

17 Quality management   **207**
Quality defined 207; Quality management defined 208; Contribution of
the quality gurus 208; Quality management approaches 210; Quality
standards 214; Quality management issues 216; Summary 218;
References 219

Appendix   Guidelines for Managing for Results students   *221*
Index   *235*

Preface

This book is primarily about the practice of management — the art and science of getting things done. But it is also about leadership — how things get done through people. Management and leadership are different but complementary activities, as is explained in Chapter 1.

The activities of management and leadership take place in order to make things happen — to get results. The book therefore also examines the process of managing for results, a phrase first used by Peter Drucker in his book of that name (1).

The book is divided into the following four parts. These constitute the separate sections of the Managing for Results professional standards of the Chartered Institute of Personnel and Development which form part of the overall Leadership and Management professional standards:

1. The Practice of Management
2. Delivering Change
3. Enhancing Customer Relations
4. Enabling Continuous Improvement.

The practice of management

Managing for results takes place within a management framework and this is analysed in Chapter 1. To manage for results effectively means understanding the roles of managers and leaders — what they do and how they do it, which is considered in Chapters 2 and 3.

The 'how and what' of managerial activities is dealt with in Chapters 4 and 5. Chapter 4 is concerned with the specific managerial activities of planning, organizing, objective setting and communicating, while Chapter 5 covers more general approaches to management and leadership such as delegation, motivation, coaching, facilitation, feedback and working in organizations.

The next two remaining chapters in part 1 (7 and 8) describe strategic management, and systems and process management, and the part is rounded off with an examination of approaches to self-development.

Delivering change

Managing for results and leadership involve managing change and this part deals with how change happens (Chapter 10), the organizational context in which change takes place (Chapter 11) and models and techniques of change management (Chapter 12).

Enhancing customer relations

Many years ago Peter Drucker wrote in The Practice of Management (2) that the business of business is 'to create a customer'. This part of the book examines the different aspects of customer relations in terms of the basis of customer service (Chapter 13), approaches to customer service (Chapter 14) and how to achieve high levels of customer service (Chapter 15). We acknowledge the invaluable help and guidance on this important subject provided by Dr Ted Johns, Chair of the Institute for Customer Service and Chief Examiner (People Resourcing) for the CIPD.

Enabling continuous improvement

Managers are there to get results by exercising leadership, implementing change and looking after customers. But as discussed in Chapter 16, they must always be looking for continuous improvement in what they and their organizations do. Continuous improvement is associated with quality management, which impacts strongly on customer service and is dealt with in Chapter 17.

REFERENCES

1   Drucker, P (1963) Managing for Results, Heinemann, London
2   Drucker, P (1955) The Practice of Management, Heinemann, London

Part I

The practice of management

1

The nature of management

This is an introductory chapter which aims to set the scene for the rest of this book. The chapter starts with a general examination of what the processes of management and leadership are about, followed by a discussion of their aims and purposes. The chapter continues with a comparison of the processes of management and leadership and a description of management standards. It concludes with a description of influences on management in the shape of codes of practice and organizational and legal requirements.

WHAT MANAGEMENT IS ABOUT

Management has often been described as 'getting things done through people'. This makes the important point that it is a purposeful activity. It could be extended to include the concept that management is concerned with defining ends as well as achieving them. The basic definition should therefore be extended to read: 'Management is about deciding what to do and then getting it done through people.' But there is more. Correctly, the definition emphasizes that people are the most important resource available to managers. It is through this resource that other resources are managed. However, managers are ultimately accountable for the management of all other resources, including their own. The definition of management should therefore be amended to: 'Deciding what to do and then getting it done through the effective use of resources.'

PURPOSE OF MANAGEMENT AND LEADERSHIP

The Management Standards Centre states that the key purpose of management and leadership is to 'provide direction, facilitate change and achieve results through the efficient, creative and responsible use of resources'.

THE PROCESSES OF MANAGEMENT

The overall process of management is divided into a number of individual processes which are methods of operation specially designed to assist in the achievement of objectives. Their purpose is to bring as much system, order, predictability, logic and consistency to the task of management as possible in the ever-changing, varied and turbulent environment in which managers work.

   The main processes of management were defined by the classical theorists of management such as Henri Fayol (1) as:

1. *planning* – deciding on a course of action to achieve a desired result;
2. *organizing* – setting up and staffing the most appropriate organization to achieve the aim;
3. *motivating* – exercising leadership to motivate people to work together smoothly and to the best of their ability as part of a team;
4. *controlling* – measuring and monitoring the progress of work in relation to the plan and taking corrective action when required.

But this classical view has been challenged by the empiricists, such as Henry Mintzberg (2) and Rosemary Stewart (3) who studied how managers actually spend their time. They observed that the work of managers is fragmented, varied and subjected to continual adjustment. It is governed to a large degree by events over which managers have little control and by a dynamic network of interrelationships with other people. Managers attempt to control their environment but sometimes it controls them. They may consciously or unconsciously seek to plan, organize, direct and control, but their days almost inevitably become a jumbled sequence of events.

   To the empiricists, management is a process involving a mix of rational, logical, problem-solving, decision-making activities, and intuitive, judgmental activities. It is therefore both science and art. However, the classical theorists were defining the main *processes* of management; they were not attempting to describe how managers actually spend their time.

Table 1.1 Distinctions between management and leadership (Zaleznik)

Management involves:	Leadership involves:
• Emphasizing rationality and control.	• Opening issues to new options.
• Adopting impersonal attitudes towards goals, tending to be reactive and simply responding to ideas.	• Adopting a personal and active attitude towards goals, shaping ideas rather than responding to them.
• Acting to limit choices and shift the balance of power towards solutions acceptable as compromises amongst conflicting values.	• Influencing the thoughts and actions of other people.
• Being driven by narrow purposes.	• Visualizing purposes and generating value in work.
• Favouring the tried and proven ways of doing things. Tending to be risk averse, a survival instinct dominates the need to avoid risk.	• Adopting fresh approaches to long-standing problems. Work from high-risk positions.
• The ability to tolerate mundane, practical work.	• Reacting to mundane work as an affliction.

DIFFERENCES BETWEEN MANAGEMENT AND LEADERSHIP

Managers have to be leaders, and leaders are often, but not always, managers. But a distinction can be made between the processes of management and leadership.

Management is concerned with achieving results by effectively obtaining, deploying, utilizing and controlling all the resources required, namely people, money, facilities, plant and equipment, information and knowledge.

Leadership focuses on the most important resource, people. It is the process of developing and communicating a vision for the future, motivating people and gaining their commitment and engagement.

The distinction is important. Management is mainly about the provision, deployment and utilization and control of resources. But where people are involved – and they almost always are – it is impossible to deliver results without providing effective leadership. It is not enough to be a good manager of resources; you also have to be a good leader of people.

According to Bennis and Nanus (4): 'Managers do things right, leaders do the right things'. Zaleznik (5) and Kotter (6) make the distinctions between leaders and managers as summarized in Tables 1.1 and 1.2.

Table 1.2 Distinctions between management and leadership (Kotter)

Management involves:	Leadership involves:
● Focusing on managing complexity by planning and budgeting with the aim of producing orderly results, not change. ● Developing the capacity to achieve plans by creating an organization structure and staffing it – developing human systems that can implement plans as precisely and efficiently as possible. ● Ensuring plan accomplishment by controlling and problem solving – formally and informally comparing results to the plan, identifying deviations and then planning and organizing to solve the problems.	● Focusing on producing change by developing a vision for the future along with strategies for bringing about the changes needed to achieve that vision. ● Aligning people by communicating the new direction and creating coalitions that understand the vision and are committed to its achievement. ● Using motivation to energize people, not by pushing them in the right direction as control mechanisms do, but by satisfying basic human needs for achievement, a sense of belonging, recognition, self-esteem, a feeling of control over one's life and the ability to live up to one's ideals.

These analyses indicate that the key words describing leadership are: change, vision, communication, proactive, high risk, and aligning and motivating people. The key words describing management are: organizing, planning and budgeting, rationality and control, reactive and risk averse.

The differences in the roles are significant and there is scope for potential tension and conflict between them. Leaders are not necessarily managers but if they are in charge of resources, especially people, they have to act like managers to the extent that the use of those resources has to be organized, planned and controlled. But over-emphasis on these managerial aspects of the role may prejudice leadership imperatives, especially the visionary, proactive and motivational aspects of leadership and the requirement to initiate and deliver change. Conversely, there is tension in the role of managers as leaders where there is the risk of conflict between their search for order, conformity and detailed plans and their need to be imaginative, innovative and concerned about how to get better results from the way in which they relate to their people rather than the use of control mechanisms.

MANAGEMENT STANDARDS

Management standards define what professional managers need to know and be able to do. They therefore serve as guides on what is expected of managers, as checklists against which performance can be assessed, and as the basis for management qualifications. The following management standards have been produced by the Management Standards Centre:

- Providing direction
  - develop a vision for the future;
  - gain commitment and provide leadership;
  - provide governance – comply with values, ethical and legal frameworks and manage risks in line with shared goals.
- Facilitating change
  - lead innovations;
  - manage change.
- Achieving results
  - lead the business to achieve goals and objectives;
  - lead operations to achieve specific results;
  - lead projects to achieve specified results.
- Meeting customer needs
  - promote products and/or services to customers;
  - obtain contracts to supply products and/or services;
  - deliver products and/or services to customers;
  - solve problems for customers;
  - assure the quality of products and/or services.
- Working with people
  - build relationships;
  - develop networks and partnerships;
  - manage people.
- Using resources
  - manage financial resources;
  - procure products and/or services;
  - manage physical resources and technology;
  - manage information and knowledge.
- Managing self and personal skills
  - manage own contribution;
  - develop own knowledge, skills and competence.

INFLUENCES ON MANAGEMENT

The process of management is influenced by codes of practice (professional, industrial and official). These codes provide guidance on behaviour and the procedures to be followed and, in the case of professional codes and some industry codes, are supported by disciplinary sanctions. They usefully define expectations but the extent to which they can be enforced may be limited, except that contravention of some official codes is taken into account in Employment Tribunal cases. Management processes are also influenced by procedures and legal and corporate governance (organizational) requirements.

Professional codes of practice

Professional codes of practice lay down the behaviours expected of the members of a profession. They are supported by disciplinary procedures which hold members to account for serious contraventions of the code.

For example, the Chartered Management Institute has a code of professional management practice which sets out the professional standards required of members of the Institute as a condition of membership. It states in the introduction that: 'As a member, you must demonstrate high standards of professional conduct, competence, judgement and honesty in your actions as a practising manager. It is also an expectation that you will display integrity, probity and fairness.' The code has sections dealing with standards for individual managers, relationships with others, supporting policies and practices of the organization and dealing with external relationships and the wider community. The section dealing with individual managers states that: 'As a professional manager you will:

- Pursue managerial activities with integrity, accountability and competence.
- Disclose any personal interest which might be seen to influence managerial decisions.
- Practice an open style of management so far as it is consistent with business needs.
- Keep up to date with developments in best management practice and continue to develop personal competence.
- Adopt an approach to the identification and resolution of conflicts of values, including ethical values, which is reasonable and justifiable.
- Safeguard personal information and not seek personal advantage from it.
- Exhaust all available internal remedies for dealing with matters perceived as improper before resorting to public disclosure.
- Encourage the development of quality and continuous improvement in all management activities.'

The code of the Chartered Institute of Personnel and Development includes the statement that in all circumstances CIPD members 'must endeavour to enhance the standing of the profession; adherence to this professional code of conduct is an essential aspect of this'.

Industrial codes of practice

Industrial codes of practice lay down rules for how an industry should conduct its work. For example, The Recruitment and Employment Confederation (REC) has a code of practice, the aim of which is to ensure that employment and recruitment agencies meet ethical and legal requirements. Amongst its general provisions are:

● Members will comply with any REC guidance on ethical, commercial or statutory issues in the operation of their businesses.
● Members and their staff will deal with and represent themselves to work seekers, hirers and others fairly, openly, honestly and courteously at all times.
● Any selection tests used, including psychometric and personality questionnaires, should be relevant, properly validated and where appropriate conducted by trained or licensed personnel.

The British Computer Society has a Code of Good Practice, the purpose of which is defined as being to describe 'standards of practice relating to the contemporary multifaceted demands found in Information Technology (IT)'. Its provisions include the requirement to maintain technical competence, adhere to regulations, act professionally as a specialist, use appropriate methods and tools and respect the interests of your customers. Specific guidance is given on the whole range of work carried out by IT specialists; for example, the guidelines on designing software include the requirement to 'achieve well-engineered products that demonstrate fitness for purpose, reliability, efficiency, security, maintainability and cost effectiveness'.

Industrial codes of practice in the UK are also developed by official bodies such as OFTEL (the Office of Telecommunications). This has overseen the development of codes of practice for 78 (in 2004) communication service providers. OFTEL has stated that these codes are 'primarily aimed at providing consumers with a clear statement of the range of policies, services and support activities offered by individual communication suppliers. It should provide sufficient information for any consumer to understand the range of services available, how to contact the supplier in order to, for example, obtain a new service, clarify the provider's terms and conditions, obtain support, or make a complaint.'

Official codes

A large number of codes of practice have been issued by the government, government agencies or bodies sponsored by the government. Examples include the code on job evaluation schemes free of sex bias issued by the Equal Opportunities Commission, the code on disciplinary and grievance procedures issued by ACAS and various practice codes issued by the Health and Safety Authority.

Procedures

Procedures are formal statements of how particular issues should be dealt with. They affect the way in which people handle certain matters in organizations. Typical procedures are concerned with people management on such matters as discipline, grievances, redundancy and equal opportunities, although procedures can be produced for any aspect of administration such as handling customer complaints.

Legal requirements

Management takes place within a framework of employment, health and safety, company, commercial and other legislation. Necessarily, this places obligations and constraints on managements in general and individual managers in particular.

Organizational requirements and corporate governance

Organizational requirements are expressed in the concept of 'corporate governance' which refers to the system by which businesses are directed and controlled. The Organization for Economic Co-operation and Development (OECD) in the Preamble to its Principles, 2004 has defined corporate governance as follows:

> Corporate governance is one key element in improving economic efficiency and growth as well as enhancing investor confidence. Corporate governance involves a set of relationships between a company's management, its board, its shareholders and other stakeholders. Corporate governance also provides the structure through which the objectives of the company are set and the means of attaining these objectives and monitoring performance are determined. Good corporate governance should provide proper incentives for the board and management to pursue objectives that are in the interests of the company and its shareholders and should facilitate effective monitoring.

Corporate governance is regulated by The Companies Acts, 1985 and 1989. A Combined Code on Corporate Governance was produced by the Hampel Committee. The issues covered by the Hampel and other reports include:

- board structure and membership;
- board management;
- directors' remuneration;
- financial controls;
- accountability and audit;
- relations with shareholders.

SUMMARY

- Management is defined as deciding what to do and then getting it done through the effective use of resources.
- The key purpose of management and leadership is to provide direction, facilitate change and achieve results through the efficient, creative and responsible use of resources.
- The main processes of management are planning, organizing, motivating and controlling.
- Managers have to be leaders, and leaders are often, but not always, managers.
- Management is concerned with achieving results by effectively obtaining, deploying, utilizing and controlling all the resources required, namely people, money, information, facilities, plant and equipment.
- Leadership focuses on the most important resource, people. It is the process of developing and communicating a vision for the future, motivating people and gaining their commitment and engagement.
- The differences in the roles are considerable and there is scope for potential tension and conflict between them.
- Management standards define what professional managers are expected to know and be able to do. They therefore serve as guides to what is expected of managers, as checklists against which performance can be assessed and as the basis for management qualifications.
- The process of management is influenced by codes of practice (professional, industrial and official). These codes provide guidance on behaviour and the procedures to be followed and, in the case of professional codes and some industry codes, are supported by disciplinary sanctions.

REFERENCES

1 Fayol, H (1916) *Administration Industrielle et General*, translated by C Storrs as *General and Industrial Management*, Pitman, London, 1949
2 Mintzberg, H (1973) *The Nature of Managerial Work*, Harper & Row, New York

3   Stewart, R (1967) *Managers and Their Jobs*, Macmillan, London
4   Bennis, W G and Nanus, B (1985) *Leaders; The Strategies for Taking Charge*, Harper & Row, New York
5   Zaleznik, A (2004) Manager and leaders: are they different? *Harvard Business Review*, January, pp 74–81
6   Kotter, J P (1991) Power, dependence and effective management, in *Managing People and Organizations*, ed J J Gabarro, Harvard Business School Publications, Boston, MA

2

Leadership

To lead, according to the Oxford English Dictionary, is 'to cause to go with one... to provide guidance'. Leaders set the direction and get people to follow them. Leadership is about inspiring individuals to give of their best to achieve a desired result, gaining their commitment and motivating them to achieve defined goals. In this chapter the process of leadership is explored in terms of leadership roles, leadership styles, the impact of the situation, exercising leadership, leadership characteristics, leaders and followers, and leaders and managers.

LEADERSHIP ROLES

Leaders have three essential roles. They have to:

1. *Define the task* – they have to make it quite clear what the group is expected to do.
2. *Achieve the task* – that is why the group exists. Leaders ensure that the group's purpose is fulfilled. If it is not, the result is frustration, disharmony, criticism and, eventually perhaps, disintegration of the group.
3. *Maintain effective relationships* – between themselves and the members of the group, and between the people within the group. These relationships are effective if they contribute to achieving the task. They can be divided into those concerned with the team and its morale and sense of common purpose, and those concerned with individuals and how they are motivated.

John Adair (1) suggested some time ago that these demands are best expressed as three areas of need which leaders are there to satisfy. These are: (1) *task needs* – to get the job done, (2) *individual needs* to harmonize the needs of the individual with the needs of the task and the group and (3) *group needs* – to build and maintain team spirit.

LEADERSHIP AND MANAGEMENT STYLES

Leaders and managers may adopt different approaches when dealing with their staff. The approach a leader or manager adopts is called his or her management style. The following are examples of contrasting styles:

- *Charismatic/non-charismatic.* Charismatic leaders rely on their personality, their inspirational qualities and their 'aura'. They are visionary leaders who are achievement orientated, calculated risk takers and good communicators. Non-charismatic leaders rely mainly on their know-how (authority goes to the person who knows), their quiet confidence and their cool, analytical approach to dealing with problems.
- *Autocratic/democratic.* Autocratic leaders impose their decisions, using their position to force people to do as they are told. Democratic leaders encourage people to participate and involve themselves in decision taking.
- Enabler/controller. Enablers inspire people with their vision of the future and empower them to accomplish team goals. Controllers manipulate people to obtain their compliance.
- *Transactional/transformational.* Transactional leaders trade money, jobs and security for compliance. Transformational leaders motivate people to strive for higher-level goals.

SITUATIONAL LEADERSHIP

The situation in which leaders and their teams function will influence the approaches that leaders adopt. There is no such thing as an ideal leadership style. It all depends. The factors affecting the degree to which a style is appropriate will be the type of organization, the nature of the task, the characteristics of the group and, importantly, the personality of the leader.

A task-orientated approach (autocratic, controlling, transactional) may be best in emergency or crisis situations or when the leader has power, formal backing and a relatively well-structured task. In these circumstances the group is more ready to be directed and told what to do. In less well-structured or ambiguous situations, where results depend on the group working well together with a common sense of purpose, leaders who are more concerned with maintaining good relationships (democratic, enablers, transformational) are more likely to obtain good results.

However, commentators such as Charles Handy (2) are concerned that intelligent organizations have to be run by persuasion and consent. He suggests that the heroic leader of the past 'knew all, could do all and could solve every problem'. Now, the post-heroic leader who 'asks how every problem can be solved in a way that develops other people's capacity to handle it' has come to the fore.

EXERCISING LEADERSHIP

As noted above, the kind of leadership exercised will be related to the nature of the task and the people being led. It also depends on the context and, of course, on the leaders themselves. Analysing the qualities of leadership in terms of intelligence, initiative, self-assurance and so on has only limited value. The qualities required may be different in different circumstances. It is better to adopt a contingency approach and take account of the variables the leader has to deal with.

Fiedler (3) concentrated on leaders and their group and the structure of the task as determinants in the choice of the most effective style of leadership. His research indicated that the leaders of the most effective groups tended to maintain greater distance between themselves and their team than the leaders of less effective groups. He followed the terminology of Halpin and Winer (4) and distinguished between the leader's role of 'initiating structure' – specifying ways of achieving group goals and coordinating the activities of the group's members, and 'consideration' – motivating group members and maintaining internal harmony and satisfaction. Fiedler's findings were that an 'initiating structure' approach worked best when the situation was either very favourable or unfavourable to the leader, while 'consideration' was more appropriate when the situation was only moderately favourable. He also emphasized the 'situational' aspects of leadership:

> Leadership performance then depends as much on the organization as on the leader's own attributes. Except perhaps for the unusual case, it is simply not meaningful to speak of an effective leader and an ineffective leader; we can only speak of a leader who tends to be effective in one situation and not in another.

LEADERSHIP CHARACTERISTICS

The qualities required of leaders may vary somewhat in different situations, but research and analysis of effective leaders have identified a number of generic characteristics and competencies which good leaders are likely to have.

Leadership qualities

John Adair (1) lists the following qualities:

- *enthusiasm* – to get things done which they can communicate to other people;
- *confidence* – belief in themselves which again people can sense (but this must not be over-confidence, which leads to arrogance);
- *toughness* – resilient, tenacious and demanding high standards, seeking respect but not necessarily popularity;
- *integrity* – being true to oneself – personal wholeness, soundness and honesty which inspires trust;
- *warmth* – in personal relationships, caring for people and being considerate;
- *humility* – willingness to listen and take the blame; not being arrogant and overbearing.

Leadership competencies

Bennis and Thomas (5) suggest that leadership competencies are outcomes of their formative experiences. The key competencies are adaptive capacity, an ability to engage others in shared meanings, a compelling voice and integrity. They claim that one of the most reliable indicators and predictors of 'true leadership' is an individual's ability to find meaning in negative situations and to learn from trying circumstances.

Requirements for leadership behaviour

A survey conducted by the Industrial Survey, now the Work Foundation (6), showed that what good leaders do is to make the right space for people to perform well without having to be watched over. The top 10 requirements for leader behaviour as ranked by respondents were:

Rank	Factor
1	Shows enthusiasm
2	Supports other people
3	Recognizes individual effort
4	Listens to individuals' ideas and problems
5	Provides direction
6	Demonstrates personal integrity
7	Practises what he/she preaches
8	Encourages teamwork
9	Actively encourages feedback
10	Develops other people.

Leadership and emotional intelligence

Emotional intelligence has been defined by Goleman (7) as 'the capacity for recognizing our own feelings and that of others, for motivating ourselves, for managing emotions well in ourselves as well as others'. He went on to say that 'you act with emotional intelligence when you are aware of and regulate your own emotions and when you are sensitive to what others are feeling and handle relationships accordingly'. An emotionally intelligent person understands his or her strengths and weaknesses and knows that it is more productive to manage emotions rather than be led by them.

Emotional intelligence, according to Goleman, is a critical ingredient in leadership. His research showed that effective leaders are alike in one crucial way: they have a high degree of emotional intelligence which plays an increasingly important part at higher levels in organizations where differences in technical skills are of negligible importance.

The components of emotional intelligence identified by Goleman are:

1. *Self-awareness* – the ability to recognize and understand your moods, emotions and drives as well as their effect on others. This is linked to three competencies: self-confidence, realistic self-assessment, self-deprecating sense of humour.
2. *Self-regulation* – the ability to control or redirect disruptive impulses and moods and regulate own behaviour coupled with a propensity to pursue goals with energy and persistence. The three competencies associated with this component are trustworthiness and integrity, comfort with ambiguity, and openness to change.
3. *Motivation* – a passion to work for reasons that go beyond money and status and a propensity to pursue goals with energy and persistence. The three associated competencies are: strong drive to achieve, optimism, even in the face of failure, and organizational commitment.
4. *Empathy* – the ability to understand the emotional makeup of other people and skill in treating people according to their emotional reactions. This is linked to three competencies: expertise in building and retaining talent, cross-cultural sensitivity, and service to clients and customers.
5. *Social skills* – proficiency in managing relationships and building networks to get the desired result from others and reach personal goals and the ability to find common ground and build rapport. The three competencies associated with this component are: effectiveness in leading change, persuasiveness, and expertise in building and leading teams.

LEADERS AND FOLLOWERS

A report on Robert Graves by his CO in the First World War said that: 'The men will follow this young officer if only to know where he is going.' This is a good start but it is not enough. Successful leaders have followers who want to feel that they are being led in the right direction. They need to know where they stand, where they are going and what is in it for them. They want to feel that it is all worth while. They have three requirements of their leaders:

1. *Leaders must fit their followers' expectations* – they are more likely to gain the respect and cooperation of their followers if they behave in ways that people expect from their leaders. These expectations will vary according to the group and the context but will often include being straight, fair and firm – as a 19th-century schoolboy once said of his headmaster: 'He's a beast but a just beast.' They also appreciate leaders who are considerate, friendly and approachable but don't want them to get too close – leaders who take too much time courting popularity are not liked.
2. *Leaders must be perceived as the 'best of us'* – they have to demonstrate that they are experts in the overall task facing the group. They need not necessarily have more expertise than any members of their group in particular aspects of the task, but they must demonstrate that they can get the group working purposefully together and direct and harness the expertise shared by group members to obtain results.
3. *Leaders must be perceived as 'the most of us'* – they must incorporate the norms and values which are central to the group. They can influence these values by visionary powers but they will fail if they move too far away from them.

Kelley (8) suggests that the role of the follower should be studied as carefully as that of the leader. Leaders need effective followers and one of the tasks of leaders is to develop what Kelley calls 'followship' qualities. These include the ability to manage themselves well, to be committed to the organization, to build their competence and focus their efforts for maximum impact.

LEADERSHIP CHECKLIST

Task

- What needs to be done and why?
- What results have to be achieved and by when?
- What problems have to be overcome?
- To what extent are these problems straightforward?
- Is there a crisis situation?
- What has to be done now to deal with the crisis?
- What are these priorities?
- What pressures are likely to be exerted?

Individual

- What are their strengths and weaknesses?
- What are likely to be the best ways of motivating them?

- What tasks are they best at doing?
- Is there scope to increase flexibility by developing new skills?
- How well do they perform in achieving targets and performance standards?
- To what extent can they manage their own performance and development?
- Are there any areas where there is a need to develop skill or competence?
- How can I provide them with the sort of support and guidance which will improve their performance?

Teams

- How well is the team organized?
- Does the team work well together?
- How can the commitment and motivation of the team be achieved?
- What is the team good and not so good at doing?
- What can I do to improve the performance of the team?
- Are team members flexible – capable of carrying out different tasks?
- To what extent can the team manage its own performance?
- Is there scope to empower the team so that it can take on greater responsibility for setting standards, monitoring performance and taking corrective action?
- Can the team be encouraged to work together to produce ideas for improving performance?

SUMMARY

- Leaders set the direction and get people to follow them.
- Leadership is about inspiring individuals to give of their best to achieve a desired result, gaining their commitment and motivating them to achieve defined goals.
- Leaders have three essential roles; they have to: *define the task, achieve the task,* and *maintain effective relationships.*
- John Adair (1) suggested that there are three areas of need which leaders are there to satisfy: (1) task needs, (2) individual needs, (3) group needs – to build and maintain team spirit.
- Leaders can be classified as charismatic/non-charismatic, autocratic/democratic, enabler/controller or transactional/transformational.
- The situation in which leaders and their teams function will influence the approaches that leaders adopt.
- Analysing the qualities of leadership in terms of intelligence, initiative, self-assurance and so on has only limited value. The qualities required may be different in different circumstances.
- John Adair (1) lists the following qualities: enthusiasm, confidence, toughness, integrity, warmth and humility.

- Bennis and Thomas (5) suggest that the key leadership competencies are adaptive capacity, an ability to engage others in shared meanings, a compelling voice and integrity.
- The top 10 requirements for leader behaviour as ranked by respondents to an Industrial Society survey (6) were: shows enthusiasm, supports other people, recognizes individual effort, listens to individuals' ideas and problems, provides direction, demonstrates personal integrity, practises what he/she preaches, encourages teamwork, actively encourages feedback, develops other people.
- Goleman's (7) research showed that effective leaders have a high degree of emotional intelligence, which is defined as 'the capacity for recognizing our own feelings and that of others, for motivating ourselves, for managing emotions well in ourselves as well as others'.
- Leaders must fit their followers' expectations and be perceived as the 'best of us' and 'the most of us'.
- Analyses of leaders and managers by Zaleznik (9) and Kotter (10) indicate that the key words describing leadership are: delivering change, developing a vision, communicating the vision and the direction, proactive, high risk, and aligning and motivating people. The key words describing management are: organizing, planning and budgeting, rationality and control, reactive and risk averse.
- The differences in these roles are considerable and there is scope for potential tension and conflict between them.

REFERENCES

1 Adair, J (1973) *The Action-Centred Leader*, McGraw-Hill, London
2 Handy, C (1994) *The Empty Raincoat*, Hutchinson, London
3 Fiedler, F E (1967) *A Theory of Leadership Effectiveness*, McGraw-Hill, New York
4 Halpin, A W and Winer, B J (1957) *A Factorial Study of the Leadership Behavioural Descriptions*, Ohio State University
5 Bennis, W G and Thomas, R J (2002) *Geeks and Geezers: How era, values and defining moments shape leaders*, Harvard University Press, Boston, MA
6 Industrial Society (1997) *Leadership – Steering a new course*, London
7 Goleman, D (2001) 'What makes a leader?', in *What Makes a Leader*, Harvard Business School Press, Boston, MA
8 Kelley, R E (1991) 'In praise of followers', in *Managing People and Organizations*, ed J J Gabarro, Harvard Business School Publications, Boston, MA
9 Zaleznik, A (2004) Manager and leaders: are they different? *Harvard Business Review*, January, pp 74–81
10 Kotter, J P (1991) Power, dependence and effective management, in *Managing People and Organizations*, ed J J Gabarro, Harvard Business School Publications, Boston, MA

3

The role of the manager

In this chapter the role of the manager is examined under the following headings:

- what is a manager?
- the contribution of the manager;
- factors affecting 'added value' contribution;
- the characteristics of the manager's role;
- the significance of strategic and visionary thinking;
- the contribution of the line/middle manager;
- managerial qualities.

WHAT IS A MANAGER?

Managers ensure that their organizational function or department operates effectively and are accountable for attaining the required results, having been given authority over those working in that unit or function. Accountability means that they are responsible (held to account) for what they do and what they achieve. Authority means having the right or power to get people to do things. Authority is exercised through leadership and personal influence arising from position or knowledge. However, managers may have no staff; for example, an investment manager could be solely responsible for controlling investments without any help. And managers are, of course, also responsible for managing other resources – finance, facilities, knowledge, information, time and themselves.

THE CONTRIBUTION OF THE MANAGER

Managers contribute to organizational success by getting the best out of other people but also by getting the best out of themselves. Specifically, effective managers:

- get the things done that they are expected to get done;
- exercise visionary leadership;
- plan the effective use of the resources allocated to them;
- set the direction and ensure that everyone knows what is expected of them;
- initiate and manage change designed to improve performance;
- adapt and respond rapidly to changing demands and circumstances;
- anticipate problems but deal promptly with those that arise unexpectedly;
- monitor performance so that swift corrective action can be taken when necessary.

FACTORS AFFECTING ADDED VALUE CONTRIBUTION

The term 'added value' was originally used in accountancy where it is defined as the difference between the income of the business arising from sales (output) and the amount spent on materials and other purchased goods and services (input). This technical use of the term has been expanded and it is now frequently adopted to indicate the development and use of any resource in such a way as to ensure that it yields a substantial and sustainable higher return on whatever has been invested in it. A value added approach to management means the creation of more out of less.

Added value is created by managers and the people they manage. It is managers at various levels who create visions, define values and missions, set goals, develop strategic plans, and implement those plans in accordance with the underpinning values. Added value will be enhanced by anything that is done to obtain and develop the right sort of people, to motivate and manage them effectively, to gain their commitment to the organization's values and to build and maintain stable relationships with them based on mutual trust.

Managers make an added value contribution when they make the best use of their resources to produce better results. They are concerned with productivity, which is the relationship between the input of resources and the output of goods or services. A productivity index can be formulated as a series of ratios:

$$\text{Productivity index} = \frac{\text{Output}}{\text{Input}} = \frac{\text{Performance achieved}}{\text{Resources consumed}} = \frac{\text{Effectiveness}}{\text{Efficiency}}$$

The difference between efficiency and effectiveness is important. Efficiency is doing things right, effectiveness is doing the right things. Managers who concentrate on the former at the expense of the latter solve problems rather than producing creative alternatives, safeguard resources rather than optimize the use of resources and reduce costs rather than increase profit.

Clearly managers need to adopt the most efficient way of doing things, which means that they make good use of their time and resources, ensure that systems and procedures run smoothly and minimize errors. It is desirable that they should behave like 'the efficient Baxter' in P G Wodehouse's *Summer Lightning*. Wodehouse explains:

> We have called Rupert Baxter efficient and efficient he was. The word as we interpret it, implies not only a capacity for performing the ordinary things in life with a firm smoothness of touch, but in addition a certain alertness of mind, a genius for opportunism, a genius for seeing clearly, thinking swiftly and Doing it Now.

But it is even more important to remember that it is the end that counts, not the means. The danger of laying too much emphasis on efficiency is that the objective of the exercise becomes obscured by the bureaucratic machinery set up to achieve it. Managers need to adopt Peter Drucker's (1) precept and 'manage for results'. Drucker (2) also pointed out forcibly that to concentrate on efficiency rather than effectiveness could be limiting and therefore prejudice the achievement of added value. He wrote:

> Management we are usually told, should concern itself with efficiency, that is doing better what is already being done. It should therefore focus on costs. But the entrepreneurial approach focuses on effectiveness, that is on the decision what to do. It focuses on opportunities to produce revenue, to create markets and to change the existing characteristics of products and markets. It asks not: how do we do this or that? It asks: which of the products really produce extraordinary economic results or are capable of producing them? It then asks: to what results should the resources and efforts of the business be allocated so as to produce extraordinary results rather than the 'ordinary' ones which are all efficiency possibly can produce.

Drucker writes about managers running a business but what he is saying applies equally well to any managers who are concerned, as they must be, with adding value.

THE CHARACTERISTICS OF THE MANAGER'S ROLE

Managerial roles

A role is the part people play in fulfilling their responsibilities. A role is not the same as a job, as set out in a job description, which is a list of duties and, perhaps, a statement of the overall purpose of the job. The role someone plays describes how they carry out their job. Roles, especially managerial roles, can therefore be fluid, and managers have to adapt rapidly – they cannot remain within the rigid confines of a prescribed set of duties. Managers may have to work in conditions of role ambiguity, when they are not sure of what they are expected to do, or role conflict, when what they feel they should do is not in accord with what others believe they should do.

In carrying out their roles:

- Managers are engaged in activities and tasks. Activities comprise what managers do – their behaviour. Tasks are what managers are expected or seek to achieve.
- Managers are there to get things done. They plan ahead, maintain momentum and make things happen. They have to deal with immediate issues, responding to demands, but they are also proactive in developing new ways of doing things which anticipate problems.
- Managers deal with programmes, processes, events and eventualities. They do this through people by the exercise of leadership, but in managing programmes, processes and events, managers have to be personally involved. They manage themselves as well as other people. They cannot delegate everything. They frequently have to rely on their own resources to get things done. These resources include skill, know-how, competences, time, and their own reserves of resilience and determination. All of these have to be deployed, not only in directing and motivating people but also in understanding situations and issues, problem analysis and definition, decision making, and taking action themselves as well as through others. They get support, advice and assistance from their own staff and specialists, but in the last analysis they are on their own. They have to make the decisions and they have to initiate and sometimes take the action. A chief executive fighting a takeover bid will get lots of advice, but he or she will personally manage the crisis, talking directly to the financial institutions, merchant banks, financial analysts, City editors and the mass of shareholders.

The classical view of managers as people who divide their time neatly into the management activities of planning, organizing, motivating and controlling is misleading. Managers may carry out their work on a day-to-day basis in conditions of variety, turbulence and unpredictability. Managers may have to be specialists in ambiguity, with the ability to cope with conflicting and unclear requirements.

The role of the manager in a variety of different contexts

What managers do varies according to the context in which they work. The roles of managers will be dependent on their function, level, organization (type, structure, culture, size) and their working environment generally (the extent to which it is turbulent, predictable, settled, pressurized, steady). Individual managers will adapt to these circumstances in different ways and will operate more or less successfully in accordance with their perceptions of the behaviour expected of them, their experience of what has or has not worked in the past, and their own personal characteristics.

What managers actually do

There are, however, some typical characteristics of managerial work as described below.

Response to circumstances

Managers are largely reactive. They respond to circumstances and seldom spend much time adopting a systematic approach to problem solving and decision making. They spend a lot of their time troubleshooting.

Choice

Managers do not generally operate within strictly prescribed boundaries. The results they have to achieve may be well defined but they make choices about how these results should be obtained within the framework of organizational policies and procedures.

Communication

Managers spend most of their time talking to other people, usually in short bursts.

How managers work

Little time is spent on any one activity or on planning systematically. Plans tend to be made as part of the normal day's activities. Managers spend a lot of time explaining what they do and maintaining informal relationships.

The fragmentary nature of managerial work

The activities of managers are characterized by fragmentation, brevity and variety. This arises for the following four reasons:

1. They spend most of their working days dealing with people who behave unpredictably and, from the manager's point of view, irrationally. This includes their team members and colleagues. It also means being at the beck and call of their own managers.
2. Managers are subject to constant interruptions; they have little chance to settle down. Sudden demands, which limit their ability to control their work and time, are constantly being made on them. Crises can occur which they are unable to predict.
3. Managers have to deal with situations as they arise and this means that any plans they have made are likely to be disrupted.
4. In turbulent conditions managers may not be clear about what is expected of them when new situations arise. They therefore tend to deal with immediate problems in an ad hoc way rather than trying to anticipate them.

THE SIGNIFICANCE OF STRATEGIC AND VISIONARY THINKING

Managers may find that they are overwhelmed by events and have little time for strategic and visionary thinking. But the attempt must be made, especially at higher levels of management, otherwise the organization will stagnate.

Strategic thinking

Strategic thinking ensures that a sense of purpose exists. Strategies evolve – they cannot be preserved on tablets of stone – but they provide a framework for defining intentions and future directions which can be modified as new situations arise. Strategic thinking needs strategic capability, which is the ability people possess to think imaginatively about where they want to go and how they are going to get there. It is concerned with taking a longer-term view of what needs to happen in the future to ensure continued success. People with strategic capability recognize that while they have to be successful now in order to succeed in the future, it is always necessary to think ahead and decide what direction to take.

Visionary thinking

Visionary thinking sets out a broad picture of what can and should be attained – a state of future being which is significantly superior to the present state. It is imaginative, inspirational and insightful. It defines and describes goals. It is significant because if carried out and presented convincingly, it can enhance, indeed drive, commitment to the achievement of what the organization or an individual manager believes to be important.

THE CONTRIBUTION OF THE LINE/MIDDLE MANAGER

Line or middle managers form the essential link between top managers who are concerned with broad strategic issues and the overall direction of the organization, and the employees who carry out the detailed work. Line managers are intermediaries and this can make their life difficult. They have to interpret and apply corporate strategies, plans and policies and ensure that these are implemented by their teams on whom they depend to get results.

The research conducted by Professor John Purcell and his colleagues (3), which was completed in 2003, showed that the role of line managers is crucial: 'The way line managers implement and enact policies, show leadership in dealing with employees and in exercising control come through as a major issue.' It is line managers who bring organizational policies to life. Further work by Sue Hutchinson and John Purcell (4) found that the responsibilities of line managers covered a wide range of duties, ranging from traditional supervisory duties – such as work allocation and monitoring quality – to newer management activities, such as people management. In some cases it included cost control/budgeting. The role typically included a combination of the following activities:

● people management;
● managing operational costs;
● providing technical expertise;
● organizing, such as planning work allocation and rotas, monitoring work processes;
● checking quality;
● dealing with customers/clients;
● measuring operational performance.

In addition, managers promote appropriate behaviours by serving as role models and exemplars, influencing the activities of their team members by what they do and how they do it. They are there to provide guidance and support to their staff through leadership and performance management processes (agreeing roles and expectations, providing feedback and reviewing performance in order to formulate improvement and personal development plans). They promote development by acting as coaches and mentors – advising and helping people to learn by doing and complementing learning on the job by functioning as mentors (experienced and trust advisors).

The variety of these activities demonstrates the complexity of the role and why the work of line managers is often fragmented.

MANAGERIAL QUALITIES

Attributes of successful managers

Pedler, Boydell and Burgoyne (5) suggest, on the basis of their research, that there are 11 attributes or qualities which are possessed by successful managers:

1. command of basic facts;
2. relevant professional knowledge;
3. continuing sensitivity to events;
4. analytical, problem-solving and decision/judgement-making skills;
5. social skills and abilities;
6. emotional resilience;
7. proactivity;
8. creativity;
9. mental agility;
10. balanced learning habits and skills;
11. self-knowledge.

Competency frameworks

Many organizations have developed competency frameworks which define what they believe to be the key competencies required for success. These consist of generic behavioural competencies describing how people are expected to behave in their roles and, for individual roles, technical or functional competencies which define what people are expected to know and be able to do to perform their work well.

Such frameworks are used to inform decisions on selection, management development and promotion. Importantly, they can provide the headings under which the performance of managers and other staff is assessed. Managers who want to get on need to know what the framework is and the types of behaviour expected of them in each of the areas it covers.

The following is an example of a competence framework:

- *Achievement/results orientation.* The desire to get things done well and the ability to set and meet challenging goals, create own measures of excellence and constantly seek ways of improving performance.
- *Business awareness.* The capacity continually to identify and explore business opportunities, understand the business opportunities and priorities of the organization and constantly to seek methods of ensuring that the organization becomes more businesslike.

- *Communication.* The ability to communicate clearly and persuasively, orally or in writing.
- *Customer focus.* The exercise of unceasing care in looking after the interests of external and internal customers to ensure that their wants, needs and expectations are met or exceeded.
- *Developing others.* The desire and capacity to foster the development of members of his or her team, providing feedback, support, encouragement and coaching.
- *Flexibility.* The ability to adapt to and work effectively in different situations and to carry out a variety of tasks.
- *Leadership.* The capacity to inspire individuals to give of their best to achieve a desired result and to maintain effective relationships with individuals and the team as a whole.
- *Planning.* The ability to decide on courses of action, ensuring that the resources required to implement the action will be available and scheduling the programme of work required to achieve a defined end-result.
- *Problem solving.* The capacity to analyse situations, diagnose problems, identify the key issues, establish and evaluate alternative courses of action and produce a logical, practical and acceptable solution.
- *Teamwork.* The ability to work cooperatively and flexibly with other members of the team with a full understanding of the role to be played as a team member.

SUMMARY

- Managers ensure that their organizational function or department operates effectively and are accountable for attaining the required results having been given authority over those working in that function or department.
- Managers contribute to organizational success by getting the best out of other people but also by getting the best out of themselves.
- Added value is created by managers and the people they manage. It is managers at various levels who create visions, define values and missions, set goals, develop strategic plans, and implement those plans in accordance with the underpinning values.
- Managers make an added value contribution when they make the best use of their resources to produce better results.
- Managers are there to get things done. They plan ahead, maintain momentum and make things happen. They have to deal with immediate issues, responding to demands, but they are also proactive in developing new ways of doing things which anticipate problems.

- The classical view of managers as people who divide their time neatly into the management activities of planning, organizing, motivating and controlling is misleading. Managers may carry out their work on a day-to-day basis in conditions of variety, turbulence and unpredictability.
- What managers do varies according to the context in which they work.
- Managers are largely reactive.
- Managers make choices about how their results should be obtained within the framework of organizational policies and procedures.
- Managers spend most of their time talking to other people, usually in short bursts.
- Little time is spent by managers on any one activity or on planning systematically.
- The activities of managers are characterized by fragmentation, brevity and variety.
- Strategic thinking by managers ensures that a sense of purpose exists.
- Visionary thinking by managers sets out a broad picture of what can and should be attained.
- Line or middle managers form the essential link between top managers who are concerned with broad strategic issues and the overall direction of the organization and the employees who carry out the detailed work.
- Pedler, Boydell and Burgoyne (5) suggest that the following attributes are possessed by successful managers: command of basic facts, relevant professional knowledge, continuing sensitivity to events, analytical, problem-solving and decision/judgement-making skills, social skills and abilities, emotional resilience, proactivity, creativity, mental agility, balanced learning habits and skills, self-knowledge.
- Many organizations have developed competency frameworks which define what they believe to be the key competencies required for success.

REFERENCES

1 Drucker, P (1963) *Managing for Results*, Heinemann, London
2 Drucker, P (1962) *The Effective Executive*, Heinemann, London
3 Purcell, J, Kinnie, K, Hutchinson, S, Rayton, B and Swart, J (2003) *Understanding the People and Performance Link: Unlocking the black box*, CIPD, London
4 Hutchinson, S and Purcell, J (2003) *Bringing Policies to Life: The vital role of front line managers in people management*, CIPD, London
5 Pedler, M, Boydell, T and Burgoyne, J (1986) *A Manager's Guide to Self-development*, McGraw-Hill, Maidenhead

4

Managerial activities

The managerial activities described in this chapter are concerned with planning, organizing, setting objectives and targets, and communicating.

PLANNING

Planning is the process of deciding on a course of action, ensuring that the resources required to implement the action will be available and scheduling and prioritizing the work required to achieve a defined end-result.

Managers normally plan ahead over a relatively short period of time – up to one or, at most, two years. Their objectives, targets and budgets will probably have been fixed by the corporate plan or company budget.

The aim of planning is to enable managers to complete tasks on time without using more resources than they are allowed. They need to avoid crises and the high costs that they cause; to have fewer 'drop everything and rush this' problems. Planning warns managers about possible crises and gives them a chance to avoid them. Contingency or fall-back plans are prepared if there is any reason to believe that the initial plan may fail for reasons beyond the manager's control.

When managers plan, they may choose certain courses of action and rule out others; that is to say, they lose flexibility. This will be a disadvantage if the future turns out differently from what was expected – which is only too likely. Managers should try to make plans that can be changed without undue difficulty or if it is unavoidable. It is a bad plan that admits no change.

Planning ingredients

Most of the planning you do as a manager is simply a matter of thinking systematically and using your common sense. Every plan contains four key ingredients:

1. *the objective* – what is to be achieved;
2. *the action programme* – the specific steps required to achieve the objective;
3. *resource requirements* – what resources in the shape of money, people, facilities and time will be required;
4. *impact* – the impact made on the organization by achieving the plan (assessed in terms of costs and benefits).

Planning activities

As a manager, there are eight planning activities you need to carry out:

1. *Forecasting*
   - what sort of work has to be done, how much and by when;
   - how the workload might change;
   - the likelihood of the department being called on to undertake specialized or rush jobs;
   - possible changes within or outside the department which might affect priorities, the activities carried out, or the workload.
2. *Programming* – deciding the sequence and timescale of operations and events required to produce results on time.
3. *Staffing* – deciding how many and what type of staff are needed and considering the feasibility of absorbing peak loads by means of overtime or temporary staff.
4. *Setting standards and targets* – for output, sales, times, quality, costs or for any other aspect of the work where performance should be planned, measured and controlled.
5. *Procedure planning* – deciding how the work should be done and planning the actual operations by defining the systems and procedures required.
6. *Materials planning* – deciding what materials, bought-in parts or subcontracted work are required and ensuring that they are made available in the right quantity at the right time.
7. *Facilities planning* – deciding on the plant, equipment, tools and space required.
8. *Budgeting*.

ORGANIZING

An effective enterprise ensures that collective effort is organized to achieve specific ends. Organizing involves dividing the overall management task into a variety of processes and activities and then establishing means of ensuring that these processes are carried out effectively and that the activities are coordinated. It is about differentiating activities in times of uncertainty and change, integrating them – grouping them together to achieve the organization's overall purpose – and ensuring that effective information flows and channels of communication are maintained.

Organization design

Organization design is based on the analysis of activities, processes, decisions, information flows and roles. It produces a structure which consists of positions and units between which there are relationships involving cooperation, the exercise of authority and the exchange of information.

Within the structure there will be line managers who are responsible for achieving results in the organization's key areas of activity by managing teams and individuals, and specialists who provide support, guidance and advice to the line.

The structure must be appropriate to the organization's purpose, technology and the environment in which it exists. It must be flexible enough to adapt itself easily to new circumstances – organization design is a continuous process of modification and change, it is never a one-off event. It must also be recognized that, although the formal organization structure may define who is responsible for what, and the ostensible lines of communication and control, the way in which it actually operates will depend on informal networks and other relationships which have not been defined in the design process and arise from people's daily interaction.

The approach to organization design

Organization design aims to clarify roles and relationships so far as this is possible in fluid conditions. It is also concerned with giving people the scope and opportunity to use their skills and abilities to better effect – this is the process of empowerment. Jobs should be designed to satisfy the requirements of the organization for productivity, operational efficiency and quality of product or service. But they must also meet the needs of individuals for interest, challenge and accomplishment. These aims are inter-related and an important aim of organization and job design is to integrate the needs of the individual with those of the organization.

When it comes to designing or modifying the structure a pragmatic approach is necessary. It is first necessary to understand the environment, the technology and the existing systems of social relationships. An organization can then be designed which is *contingent* upon the circumstances. There is always some choice, but designers should try to achieve the best fit they can. And in making their choice, they should be aware of the structural, human, process and system factors that will influence the design, and of the context within which the organization operates.

Organization design is ultimately a matter of ensuring that the structure, processes and methods of operation fit the strategic requirements of the business and its technology within its environment. Disruption occurs if internal and external coherence and consistency are not achieved.

Organization guidelines

There are no absolute principles of organization but there are certain guidelines which are worth bearing in mind.

Allocation of work

The work that has to be done should be defined and allocated to functions, units, departments, work teams, project groups and individual positions. Related activities should be grouped together. There will be a choice between dividing work by product, process, market or geographical area.

Differentiation and integration

It is necessary to differentiate between the activities that have to be carried out, but it is equally necessary to ensure that these activities are integrated so that everyone in the organization is working towards the same goals.

Teamwork

Jobs should be defined and roles described in ways that facilitate and underline the importance of teamwork. Areas where cooperation is required should be emphasized. The organization should be designed and operated in such a way as to facilitate cooperation across departmental or functional boundaries. Wherever possible, self-managing teams and autonomous work groups should be set up and given the maximum amount of responsibility to run their own affairs, including planning, budgeting and exercising quality control. Networking should be encouraged in the sense of people communicating openly and informally with one another as the need arises. It is recognized that these informal processes can be more productive than rigidly 'working through channels' as set out in the organization chart.

Flexibility

The organization structure should be flexible enough to respond quickly to change, challenge and uncertainty. Flexibility should be enhanced by the creation of core groups and using part-time, temporary and contract workers to handle extra demands. At top management level and elsewhere, a 'collegiate' approach to team operation should be considered in which people share responsibility and are expected to work with their colleagues in areas outside their primary function or skill.

Role clarification

People should be clear about their roles as individuals and as members of a team. They should know what they will be held accountable for and be given every opportunity to use their abilities in achieving objectives which they have agreed and to which they are committed. Job/role descriptions should define key result areas but should not act as straitjackets, restricting initiative and unduly limiting responsibility.

Decentralization

Authority to make decisions should be delegated as close to the scene of action as possible, subject to provisions for proper coordination and control. Profit centres should be set up as strategic business units which operate close to their markets and with a considerable degree of autonomy. A multi-product or multi-market business could develop a federal organization with each federated entity running its own affairs, although they will be linked together by the overall business strategy.

Delayering

Organizations should be 'flattened' by stripping out superfluous layers of management and supervision in order to promote flexibility, facilitate swifter communication, increase responsiveness, enable people to be given more responsibility as individuals or teams and reduce costs. But delayering can be carried too far, leaving the organization bereft of the middle management needed to provide direct leadership to teams.

SETTING OBJECTIVES AND TARGETS

One of your most important tasks as a manager is to make sure that the members of your team understand what is expected of them. Each individual and the team as a whole must know what they have to do and achieve. This is the management of expectations aspect of your role.

Your task is to ensure that performance requirements expressed as objectives are defined and agreed. You will then be in a position to review achievements in relation to agreed objectives.

What are objectives?

An objective describes something which has to be accomplished – a point to be aimed at. Objectives or goals (the terms are interchangeable) define what organizations, functions, departments, teams and individuals are expected to achieve. There are two main types of objective: work and personal.

Work objectives

Work or operational objectives refer to the results to be achieved or the contribution to be made to the accomplishment of team, departmental and corporate objectives. At corporate level they are related to the organization's mission, core values and strategic plans. At departmental or functional level they are related to corporate objectives, spelling out the specific mission, targets and purposes to be achieved by a function or department. At team level they will again be related specifically to the purpose of the team and the contribution it is expected to make to achieving departmental and corporate goals. At individual level they are role-related, referring to the principal accountabilities, main activity areas or key tasks which constitute the individual's role. They focus on the results individuals are expected to achieve and how they contribute to the attainment of team, departmental and corporate goals and to upholding the organization's core values.

Personal objectives

Personal or learning objectives are concerned with what individuals should do and learn to improve their performance (performance improvement plans) and/or their knowledge, skills and overall level of competency (training and personal development plans).

How are individual work objectives expressed?

Individual objectives define the results to be achieved and the basis upon which performance in attaining these results can be measured (performance measures). They can take the form of target objectives, project objectives or standing objectives.

Targets

Individual objectives can be expressed as quantified output or improvement targets (open 24 new accounts by 30 November, reduce cost per unit of output by 2.5 per cent by 30 June) or in terms of projects to be completed (open distribution depot in Northampton by 31 October). Targets may be reset regularly, say once a year or every six months, or be subject to frequent amendments to meet new requirements or changed circumstances.

Project objectives

Project objectives define what has to be achieved by an individual who is managing or contributing to a project. They will define the purpose of the project and the success criteria – how the impact of the project will be measured.

Standing objectives

Objectives for some aspects of a role (or for all aspects of some roles) can be what might be described as 'standing objectives'. These are concerned with the permanent or continuing features of a job. They incorporate or lead to defined standards of performance as discussed later.

Qualitative standing objectives may also be defined for behaviour which will contribute to upholding the core values of the organization. For example, if one of the core values relates to the development of the skills and competences of employees, a performance standard for employee development could be one of the objectives agreed for all managers and team leaders.

What is a good work objective?

Good work or operational objectives are:

- *Consistent* with the values of the organization and departmental and organizational objectives.
- *Precise* – clear and well defined, using positive words.
- *Challenging* – to stimulate high standards of performance and to encourage progress.
- *Measurable* – they can be related to quantified or qualitative performance measures.
- *Achievable* within the capabilities of the individual. Account should be taken of any constraints which might affect the individual's capacity to achieve the objectives; these could include lack of resources (money, time, equipment, support

from other people), lack of experience or training, external factors beyond the individual's control, etc.

- *Agreed* by the manager and the individual concerned. The aim is to provide for the ownership, not the imposition, of objectives, although there may be situations where individuals have to be persuaded to accept a higher standard than they believe themselves capable of attaining.
- *Time-related* – achievable within a defined timescale (this would not be applicable to a standing objective).
- *Teamwork orientated* – emphasize teamwork as well as individual achievement.

The acronym SMART is often used to define a good objective:

    S = stretching
    M = measurable
    A = agreed
    R = realistic
    T = time related

Defining work objectives

The process of agreeing objectives need not be unduly complicated. It starts from an agreed list of the principal accountabilities or main tasks of the job. It is then simply a matter of jointly examining each area and agreeing targets and standards of performance as appropriate. Agreement can also be reached on any projects to be undertaken which might be linked to a specific accountability, or maybe more general projects which fall broadly within the remit of the jobholder. Defining objectives involves agreeing targets and standards of performance.

Defining targets

Targets are quantified and time based – they always define specific and measurable outputs and when they have to be reached. The target may be to achieve a specified level of output or to improve performance in some way. Targets may be expressed in financial terms such as profits to be made, income to be generated, costs to be reduced or budgets to be worked within. Or they may be expressed in numerical terms as a specified number of units to be processed, sales volume to be achieved, responses to be obtained or clients or customers to be contacted over a period of time.

Output targets are expressed in financial or unitary terms, for example:

- Achieve sales of £1.6 million by 30 June.
- Maintain inventory levels at no more than £12 million.
- Maintain throughput at the rate of 800 units a day.

Performance improvement targets may be expressed in terms such as:

- Increase sales turnover for the year by 8 per cent in real terms.
- Reduce the overhead to sales ratio from 22.6 per cent to 20 per cent over the next 12 months.
- Increase the ratio of successful conversions (enquiry to sales) from 40 per cent to 50 per cent.

Define performance standards

A performance standard definition should take the form of a statement that performance will be up to standard if a desirable specified and observable result happens.

Performance standards should have been broadly defined in outcome terms in the why part of the accountability/task definition. But the broad definition should be expanded and, as far as possible, particularized. They should preferably be quantified in terms, for example, of level of service or speed of response. Where the standard cannot be quantified, a more qualitative approach may have to be adopted, in which case the standard of performance definition would in effect state: 'this job or task will have been well done if… (these things happen)'. Junior or more routine jobs are likely to have a higher proportion of standing objectives to which performance standards are attached than senior and more flexible or output-orientated jobs. A qualitative standard could be expressed as:

Performance will be up to standard if requests for information are dealt with promptly and helpfully on a can do/will do basis and are delivered in the form required by the user. The following are some examples of performance standards which spell out the end results required in quantitative terms:…

It is often assumed that qualitative performance standards are difficult to define. But all managers make judgements about the standards of performance they expect and obtain from their staff, and most people have some idea of whether or not they are doing a good job. The problem is that these views are often subjective and are seldom articulated. Even if, as often happens, the final definition of a performance standard is somewhat unspecific, the discipline of working through the requirements in itself will lead to greater mutual understanding of performance expectations.

COMMUNICATING

The manager's role can be said to be 20 per cent doing and 80 per cent putting it across, that is, communicating. People recognize the need to communicate but find it difficult. Like Schopenhauer's hedgehogs, they want to get together, it's only their prickles that keep them apart.

Words may sound or look precise, but they are not. All sorts of barriers exist between the communicator and the receiver. Unless these barriers are overcome the message will be distorted or will not get through. It will fail to persuade or convince.

Barriers to communication

Hearing what we want to hear

What we hear or understand when someone speaks to us is largely based on our own experience and background. Instead of hearing what people have told us, we hear what our minds tell us they have said. We have preconceptions about what people are going to say and if what they say does not fit into our framework of reference we adjust it until it does.

Ignoring conflicting information

We tend to ignore or reject communications that conflict with our own beliefs. If they are not rejected, some way is found of twisting and shaping their meaning to fit our preconceptions. When a message is inconsistent with existing beliefs, the receiver rejects its validity, avoids further exposure to it, easily forgets it and, in his or her memory, distorts what has been heard.

Perceptions about the communicator

It is difficult to separate what we hear from our feelings about the person who says it. Non-existent motives may be ascribed to the communicator. If we like people we are more likely to accept what they say – whether it is right or wrong – than if we dislike them.

Influence of the group

The group with which we identify influences our attitudes and feelings. What a group hears depends on its interests. People are more likely to listen to their colleagues, who share their experiences (their reference group), than to outsiders such as managers or union officials.

Words mean different things to different people

Essentially language is a method of using symbols to represent facts and feelings. Strictly speaking, we can't convey *meaning*, all we can do is to convey *words*. Do not assume that because something has a certain meaning to you, it will convey the same meaning to someone else.

Non-verbal communication

When we try to understand the meaning of what people say we listen to the words but we use other clues which convey meaning. We attend not only to *what* people say but to *how* they say it. We form impressions from what is called body language – eyes, shape of the mouth, the muscles of the face, even posture. We may feel that these tell us more about what someone is really saying than the words he or she uses. But there is enormous scope for misinterpretation.

Emotions

Our emotions colour our ability to convey or to receive the true message. When we are insecure or worried, what we hear seems more threatening than when we are secure and at peace with the world. When we are angry or depressed, we tend to reject what might otherwise seem like reasonable requests or good ideas. During heated argument, many things that are said may not be understood or may be badly distorted.

Noise

Any interference to communication is 'noise'. It can be literal noise which prevents the message being heard, or figurative in the shape of distracting or confused information which distorts or obscures the meaning.

Size

The larger and more complex the organization, the greater the problem of communication. The more levels of management and supervision through which a message has to pass, the greater the opportunity for distortion or misunderstanding.

Overcoming barriers to communication

Adjust to the world of the receiver

Try to predict the impact of what you are going to write or say on the receiver's feelings and attitudes. Tailor the message to fit the receiver's vocabulary, interests and values. Be aware of how the information might be misinterpreted because of prejudices, the influence of others and the tendency of people to reject what they do not want to hear.

Use feedback

Ensure that you get a message back from the receiver which tells you how much has been understood.

Use face-to-face communication

Whenever possible, talk to people rather than write to them. That is how you get feedback. You can adjust or change your message according to reactions. You can also deliver it in a more human and understanding way – this can help to overcome prejudices. Verbal criticism can often be given in a more constructive manner than written reproof, which always seems to be harsher.

Use reinforcement

You may have to present your message in a number of different ways to get it across. Re-emphasize the important points and follow up.

Use direct, simple language

This seems obvious. But many people clutter up what they say with jargon, long words and elaborate sentences.

Suit the actions to the word

Communications have to be credible to be effective. There is nothing worse than promising the earth and then failing to deliver. When you say you are going to do something, do it. Next time you are more likely to be believed.

Use different channels

Some communications have to be in writing to put the message across promptly and without any variations in the way they are delivered. But, wherever possible, supplement written communications with the spoken word. Conversely, an oral briefing should be reinforced in writing.

Reduce problems of size

If you can, reduce the number of levels of management. Encourage a reasonable degree of informality in communications. Ensure that activities are grouped together to ease communication on matters of mutual concern.

Communicating persuasively and convincingly

Communications are often required to persuade or convince people that a proposed course of action is a good thing. To do this you first need to bear in mind the barriers to communication and how to overcome them set out above. You also have to hone your persuading skills along the lines described in Chapter 5 (pages 55–56). To be convincing you have not only to express well what you are trying to convey but also believe in what you are saying. People are quick to spot an insincere message.

SUMMARY

- Planning is the process of deciding on a course of action, ensuring that the resources required to implement the action will be available and scheduling and prioritizing the work required to achieve a defined end-result.
- The aim of planning for managers is to complete tasks on time without using more resources than they are allowed.
- Planning is mainly a matter of thinking systematically and using your common sense.
- Every plan contains four key ingredients: the objective, the action programme, resource requirements, impact.
- Organizing involves dividing the overall management task into a variety of processes and activities and then establishing means of ensuring that these processes are carried out effectively and that the activities are coordinated.
- Organization design is based on the analysis of activities, processes, decisions, information flows and roles. It produces a structure which consists of positions and units between which there are relationships involving cooperation, the exercise of authority and the exchange of information.
- An objective describes something which has to be accomplished – a point to be aimed at.
- Work or operational objectives refer to the results to be achieved or the contribution to be made to the accomplishment of team, departmental and corporate objectives.
- Personal or learning objectives are concerned with what individuals should do and learn to improve their performance.
- Good work or operational objectives are consistent, precise, challenging, measurable, achievable, agreed, time related and teamwork orientated.
- The acronym SMART is often used to define a good objective: S = stretching, M = measurable, A = agreed, R = realistic, T = time related.

- The process of agreeing objectives starts from an agreed list of the principal account-abilities or main tasks of the job and continues with a joint examination of each area and an agreement on targets and standards of performance as appropriate.
- Many barriers exist between the communicator and the receiver. Unless these barriers are overcome the message will be distorted or will not get through.
- To overcome the barriers it is necessary to adjust to the world of the receiver, use feedback, use face-to-face communication, use reinforcement, use direct, simple language, suit the actions to the word, use different channels and reduce problems of size.
- To be convincing you have not only to express well what you are trying to convey but also believe in what you are saying. People are quick to spot an insincere message.

5

Approaches to management

In this chapter the following approaches to management are described: delegation, motivating others, coaching, facilitation, giving and acting on feedback and networking. The chapter also covers understanding organizational policies and influence, power and authority, and the assessment of working conditions and remedies to address unsatisfactory situations.

DELEGATION

Delegation takes place when individuals are allocated duties or tasks in order to achieve outcomes for which their managers have overall responsibility but which the managers for a variety of reasons cannot or do not want to undertake themselves.

You can't do everything yourself, so you have to delegate tasks to your team or its individual members for them to do. This relieves you of routine and less critical tasks, frees you for more important work, extends your capacity to manage, reduces delay in decision making and allows decisions to be taken at the level where the details are known. Delegation is also one of the best ways to enable people to extend their skills and develop their careers.

At first sight delegation looks simple. Just tell people what you want them to do and then let them do it. But there is more to it than that.

It may be that you would wish to delegate everything except what your team members cannot do. But you cannot then withdraw. You have arranged for someone else to do the job, but you have not passed on the responsibility for it. You are always accountable to your superior for what your people do. Hence, as is often said, you can't delegate responsibility.

Delegation is difficult. It is perhaps the hardest task that managers have to do. The problem is achieving the right balance between delegating too much or too little and between over- or under-supervision. When you give people a job to do you have to make sure that it is done. And you have to do that without breathing down their necks, wasting your time and theirs and getting in the way. There has to be trust as well as guidance and supervision.

The process of delegation

Delegation is a process which can follow a sequence from total control (no freedom of action for the individual to whom work has been allocated) to full devolution (the individual is completely empowered to carry out the work), as illustrated in Figure 5.1.

When to delegate

You should delegate when you have more work than you can effectively carry out yourself, you cannot allocate sufficient time to your priority tasks, the task can be done well by your team member and you want to develop your team member.

How to delegate

You delegate tasks that you don't need to do yourself. You are not just ridding yourself of the difficult, tedious or unrewarding tasks. Neither are you trying to win for

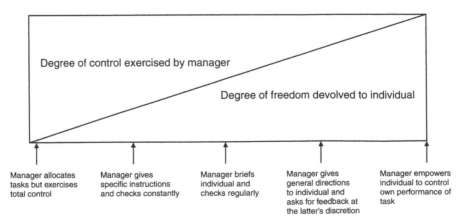

Figure 5.1 The delegation sequence

yourself an easier life. Delegation will, in fact, make your life more difficult, but also more rewarding.

Clearly, you delegate routine and repetitive tasks which you cannot reasonably be expected to do – as long as you use the time you have won productively. You also delegate specialist tasks to those who have the skills and know-how to do them. You cannot do it all yourself. Nor can you be expected to know it all yourself. You have to know how to select and use expertise. There will be no problem as long as you make it clear what you want from the experts and get them to present it to you in a usable way. As a manager you must know what specialists can do for you and you should be knowledgeable enough about the subject to understand whether or not what they produce is worth having.

Ideally the person you choose to do the work should have the knowledge, skills, motivation and time needed to get it done to your complete satisfaction. Frequently, however, you will have to use someone who has less than ideal experience, knowledge or skills. In these cases you should try to select an individual who has intelligence, natural aptitude and, above all, willingness to learn how to do the job with help and guidance. This is how people develop, and the development of your staff should be your conscious aim whenever you delegate.

You are looking for someone you can trust. You don't want to over-supervise, so you have to believe that the person you select will get on with it and have the sense to come to you when stuck or before making a bad mistake. How do you know whom you can trust? The best way is to try people out first on smaller and less important tasks, increasingly giving them more scope so that they learn how far they can go and you can observe how they do it. If they get on well, their sense of responsibility and powers of judgement will increase and improve and you will be able to trust them with more demanding and responsible tasks.

When you delegate you should ensure that people to whom you delegate understand:

- why the work needs to be done;
- what they are expected to do;
- the date by which they are expected to do it;
- the authority they have to make decisions;
- the problems they must refer back;
- the progress or completion reports they should submit;
- how you propose to guide and monitor them;
- the resources and help they will have to complete the work.

People may need guidance on how the work should be done. The extent to which you spell it out will clearly depend on how much they already know about how to do the work. You don't want to give directions in such laborious detail that you run the risk of stifling initiative. As long as you are sure they will do the job without breaking the law, exceeding the budget, embarrassing you or seriously upsetting people, let them get on with it.

You can make a distinction between *hard* and *soft* delegation. *Hard delegation* takes place when you tell someone exactly what to do, how to do it and when you want the results. You spell it out, confirm it in writing and make a note in your diary of the date when you expect the job to be completed. And then you follow up regularly.

Soft delegation takes place when you agree generally what has to be achieved, and leave the individual to get on with it. You should still agree limits of authority, define the decisions to be referred to you and say what exception reports you want (an exception report is one that simply sets out any deviances from the norm – focusing on the exception rather than the norm enables you to concentrate on what matters). You should indicate when and how you will review progress. Then you sit back until the results are due and observe from afar, only coming closer for periodic progress meetings, or when the exception reports suggest that something needs looking into, or when a problem or decision is referred to you.

You should always delegate by the results you expect. Even if you do not need to specify *exactly* how the results should be achieved, it is a good idea when delegating a problem to ask the individual how she or he proposes to solve it. You then have the opportunity to provide guidance at the outset; guidance at a later stage may be seen as interference.

MOTIVATING OTHERS

Motivating other people is about getting them to move in the direction you want them to go in order to achieve a result. Well-motivated people are those with clearly defined goals who take action which they expect will achieve those goals. Such people may be self-motivated, and as long as this means they are going in the right direction to achieve what they are there to achieve, then this is the best form of motivation.

Most of us, however, need to be motivated to a greater or lesser degree. The organization as a whole can provide the context within which high levels of motivation can be achieved by providing incentives and rewards and opportunities for learning and growth. But managers still have a major part to play in using their motivating skills to get people to give of their best and to make good use of the motivational processes provided by the organization.

The following are 10 steps to achieving high levels of motivation:

1. Agree demanding but achievable goals.
2. Clarify expectations on how people should behave in carrying out their work.
3. Provide feedback on performance.
4. Provide appropriate financial rewards for achievement.
5. Provide appropriate non-financial rewards such as recognition for achievement.

6. Communicate the links between performance and rewards.
7. Design roles which give people a sense of accomplishment and the opportunity to use their skills and abilities and to exercise their decision-making powers.
8. Select and develop team leaders who will exercise leadership and have motivating skills.
9. Give people the experience and training that will develop the knowledge and skills needed to improve performance.
10. Show people what they have to do to develop their careers.

FEEDBACK

People need to know how well they are doing in order to carry on doing it to good effect or to understand what they need to do to improve. They take action, they learn through feedback information how effective that action has been and they complete the feedback loop by making any corrections to their behaviour on the basis of the information they have received.

Ideally, feedback should be built into the job. Individuals should be able to keep track of what they are doing so that they can initiate speedy corrective action. But that is not always feasible and the manager has the responsibility of providing the feedback. This can and should be done regularly, and especially after a particular task has been carried out or a project has been completed. But it can also be provided in more formal performance review meetings.

Aim of feedback

The aim of feedback is to provide information to people which will enable them to understand how well they have been doing and how effective their behaviour has been. Feedback should promote this understanding so that appropriate action can be taken. This can be corrective action where the feedback has indicated that something has gone wrong or, more positively, action can be taken to make the best use of the opportunities the feedback has revealed. In the latter case, feedback acts as a reinforcement, and positive feedback can be a powerful motivator because it is a recognition of achievement.

Giving feedback

Feedback should be based on fact, not subjective judgement. The following are some guidelines on giving feedback:

● *Build feedback into the job.* To be effective, feedback should be built into the job. Individuals or teams should be able to find out easily how they have done from the control information readily available to them. If it cannot be built into the job it should be provided as quickly as possible after the activity has taken place, ideally within a day or two.

- *Provide feedback on actual events.* Feedback should be provided on actual results or observed behaviour, not based on subjective opinion.
- *Describe, don't judge.* The feedback should be presented as a description of what has happened. It should not be accompanied by a judgement.
- *Refer to specific behaviours.* The feedback should be related to specific items of behaviour; it should not transmit general feelings or impressions.
- *Ask questions.* Ask questions rather than make statements: 'Why do you think this happened?', 'On reflection, is there any other way in which you think you could have handled the situation?', 'What are the factors that influenced you to make that decision?'
- *Get people to work things out for themselves.* Encourage people to come to their own conclusions about what they should do or how they should behave. Ask questions such as: 'How do you think you should tackle this sort of problem in the future?', 'How do you feel you could avoid getting into this situation again?'
- *Select key issues.* Select key issues and restrict the feedback to them. There is a limit to how much criticism anyone can take. If it is overdone, the shutters will go up and the discussion will get nowhere.
- *Focus.* Focus on aspects of performance the individual can improve. It is a waste of time to concentrate on areas that the individual can do little or nothing about.
- *Show understanding.* If something has gone wrong, find out if this has happened because of circumstances beyond the individual's control and indicate that this is understood.

Receiving and acting on feedback

Managers both give and receive feedback. When they are on the receiving end they have to be prepared to take an objective view of what they are hearing. It is easy enough to take in positive feedback but negative feedback – however carefully or tactfully it is delivered – can easily provoke resentment and failure to act, even when it is pointing the way to an area for improvement. Receivers of feedback have the right to seek clarification about the basis on which it is given. This is why objective evidence is so important. But having obtained and accepted the evidence, it is necessary to discuss and agree with the manager what needs to be done to overcome the problem.

COACHING

Coaching is a personal (usually one-to-one), on-the-job approach used by managers and trainers to help people develop their skills and levels of competence. As a manager you are there to get results through people; this means that you have a personal responsibility for ensuring that they acquire and develop the skills they need. Other people in the shape of learning and development specialists may help, but because by far the best way of learning is on the job, the onus is mainly on you.

The need for coaching may arise from formal or informal performance reviews but opportunities for coaching will emerge during normal day-to-day activities. Every time you delegate a new task to someone, a coaching opportunity is created to help the individual learn any new skills or techniques which are needed to do the job. Every time you provide feedback to an individual after a task has been completed, there is an opportunity to help that individual do better next time. Methods of giving feedback are described later in this chapter.

Aims of coaching

The aims of coaching are to:

- help people to become aware of how well they are doing, where they need to improve and what they need to learn;
- put controlled delegation into practice; in other words, managers can delegate new tasks or enlarged areas of work, provide guidance as necessary on how the tasks or work should be carried out and monitor performance in doing the work;
- get managers and individuals to use whatever situations arise as learning opportunities;
- enable guidance to be provided on how to carry out specific tasks as necessary, but always on the basis of helping people to learn rather than spoon-feeding them with instructions on what to do and how to do it.

The coaching sequence

Coaching can be carried out in the following stages:

1. Identify the areas of knowledge, skills or capabilities where learning needs to take place to qualify people to carry out the task, provide for continuous development, enhance transferable skills or improve performance.
2. Ensure that the person understands and accepts the need to learn.
3. Discuss with the person what needs to be learnt and the best way to undertake the learning.
4. Get the person to work out how they can manage their own learning while identifying where they will need help from you or someone else.
5. Provide encouragement and advice to the person in pursuing the self-learning programme.

6. Provide specific guidance as required where the person needs your help.
7. Agree how progress should be monitored and reviewed.

Effective coaching

Coaching will be most effective when the coach understands that his or her role is to help people to learn, individuals are motivated to learn and are given guidance on what they should be learning and feedback on how they are doing, the coach listens to individuals to understand what they want and need and adopts a constructive approach, building on strengths and experience. It should be remembered that learning is an active, not a passive, process – individuals need to be actively involved with their coach.

Planned coaching

Coaching may be informal but it has to be planned. It is not simply checking from time to time on what people are doing and then advising them on how to do it better. Nor is it occasionally telling people where they have gone wrong and throwing in a lecture for good measure. As far as possible, coaching should take place within the framework of a general plan of the areas and direction in which individuals will benefit from further development. Coaching plans can and should be incorporated into the general development plans set out in performance management discussions.

The manager as coach

Coaching enables you to provide motivation, structure and effective feedback as long as you have the required skills and commitment. As coaches, good managers believe that people can succeed and that they can contribute to their success. They can identify what people need to be able to do to improve their performance. They have to see this as an important part of the role – an enabling, empowering process which focuses on learning requirements.

FACILITATION

Facilitation is defined in the *Oxford English Dictionary* as to 'make easy, promote, help move forward'. Managers act as facilitators in relation to their team members when they make it easier for them to develop by promoting their skills and capabilities, thus helping them to move forward. Managers may also be involved in facilitating the work of groups of people assembled to carry out a task jointly.

Facilitating individual learning

The process of facilitating individual learning involves focusing on the learners and helping them to achieve agreed learning objectives. Facilitators work alongside learners – they do not act like 'trainers' delivering learning on a plate. Working with people means encouraging learners to participate in the learning process so that it becomes largely self-managed learning with the manager as facilitator providing support, guidance and help, but only as required. Facilitators ask questions but do not provide ready-made answers to them. They help people to learn from their experience, listen to them and respond encouragingly. Facilitators may use coaching skills but always take account of the learner's views on what to learn and how best to learn it.

Facilitating groups

A group facilitator is there to help the group reach conclusions in the shape of ideas and solutions. Facilitators do not exist to 'chair' the meeting in the sense of controlling the discussion and pressurizing the group to agree to a course of action. The group is there to make up its own mind and the facilitator helps it to do so. The help is provided by asking questions which encourage the group members to think for themselves. These can be challenging and probing questions but the facilitator does not provide the answers – that is the role of the group. Neither do facilitators allow their own opinions to intrude – they are there to help the group marshal its opinions, not to enforce their own ideas. However, by using questioning techniques carefully, facilitators can ensure that the group does thoroughly discuss and analyse the issues and reaches conclusions by consensus rather than allowing anyone to dominate the process.

Facilitators ensure that everyone has their say and that they are listened to. They step in quickly to defuse unproductive arguments. They see that the group defines and understands its objectives and any methodology they might use. They summarize from time to time the progress made in achieving the objectives without bringing their own views to bear. Facilitators are there to ensure that the group makes progress and does not get stuck in fruitless or disruptive argument. But they encourage the group rather than drive it forward.

NETWORKING

Increasingly in today's more fluid and flexible organizations people get things done by networking. Networks are loosely organized connections between people with shared interests. People taking part in networks exchange information, enlist support and create alliances – getting agreement with other people on a course of action and joining forces to make it happen. Networks inside organizations are often fluid and informal. They exist to meet a need but they can be dispersed if that need no longer exists, only to be re-formed when it reappears. Networks may just consist of people with similar aims or interests who communicate with one another or get together as required. Networks are sometimes set up formally in organizations, for example the 'communities of interest' which are created to exchange and share knowledge and experience as part of a 'knowledge management' programme.

Networks can also exist outside the organization. Again they may consist of like-minded individuals exchanging information and meeting informally, or they may be set up formally with regular meetings and newsletters.

To network effectively, here are 10 steps you can take:

1. Identify people who may be able to help.
2. Seize any opportunity that presents itself to get to know people who may be useful.
3. Have a clear idea of why you want to network – to share knowledge, to persuade people to accept your proposal or point of view, to form an alliance.
4. Know what you can contribute – networking is not simply about enlisting support, it is just as much if not more concerned with developing knowledge and understanding and joining forces with like-minded people so that concerted effort can be deployed to get things done.
5. Show interest – if you engage with people and listen to them they are more likely to want to network with you.
6. Ask people if you can help them as well as asking people to help you.
7. Put people in touch with one another.
8. Operate informally but be prepared to call formal meetings when necessary to reach agreement and plan action.
9. Make an effort to keep in touch with people.
10. Follow up – check with members of the network on progress in achieving something, refer back to conversations you have had, discuss with others how the network might be developed or extended to increase its effectiveness.

UNDERSTANDING ORGANIZATIONAL POLICIES

Policies exist to provide guides to action and set limits to decision making – what should be done in certain circumstances, how particular requirements or issues should be dealt with. Organizational policies can be set up in such areas as marketing (eg what products should be sold, what markets should be developed, what price levels should be set, what levels of service should be provided for customers), operations (eg make or buy products, how to achieve high quality, what stock levels should be maintained, outsourcing), finance (eg treatment of depreciation, inflation accounting, capital budgeting, cash flow) and human resources (eg pay levels compared with market rates, equal opportunity, promote from within or external recruitment, work/life balance, security of employment).

Organizational policies may be expressed formally in manuals, and it is clearly necessary for managers to familiarize themselves with relevant policies and how they should be interpreted (however carefully expressed, policies almost always leave room for interpretation). Policies may also be informal and have grown by custom and practice over the years. Not knowing what is expected of them in the areas covered by such policies can make the life of managers more difficult. It is up to more senior managers to communicate policies if they have not been set out in writing but it is the job of all managers to find out what policies do impinge on their work, even when they are not recorded in a manual, and act accordingly.

INFLUENCE

Exerting influence is an important part of the role managers play. They may be given power and authority as discussed below, but this will not necessarily ensure that they will be able to get things done the ways they want them done, especially when it involves their own managers and their colleagues. And although managers are in a position of authority over their own staff, the extent to which that authority will force people to do something may be limited. They, like other people in the organization, may only move in the direction managers want if the managers are effective persuaders.

The 10 rules for effective persuasion are:

1. *Define the problem.* Determine whether the problem is a misunderstanding (a failure to understand each other accurately) or a true disagreement (a failure to agree even when both parties understand one another). It is not necessarily possible to resolve a true disagreement by understanding each other better. People generally believe that an argument is a battle to understand who is correct. More often, it is a battle to decide who is more stubborn.
2. *Define your objective and get the facts.* Decide what you want to achieve and why. Assemble all the facts you need to support your case. Eliminate emotional arguments so that you and others can judge the proposition on the facts alone.
3. *Find out what the other party wants.* The key to all persuasion is to see your proposition from the other person's point of view. Find out how they look at things. Establish what they need and want.
4. *Accentuate the benefits.* Present your case in a way that highlights the benefits to the other party or at least reduces any objections or fears.

5. *Predict the other person's response.* Everything we say should be focused on that likely response. Anticipate objections by asking yourself how the other party might react negatively to your proposition and thinking up ways of responding to them.
6. *Create the person's next move.* It is not a question of deciding what we want to do but what we want the other person to do. Your goal is to get results.
7. *Convince people by reference to their own perceptions.* People decide on what to do on the basis of their own perceptions, not yours.
8. *Prepare a simple and attractive proposition.* Make it as straightforward as possible. Present the case 'sunny side up', emphasizing its benefits. Break the problem into manageable pieces and deal with them one step at a time.
9. *Make them a party to your ideas.* Get them to contribute. Find some common ground so that you can start with agreement. Don't try to defeat them in an argument – you will only antagonize them.
10. *Clinch and take action.* Choose the right moment to clinch the proposal – don't prolong the discussion and risk losing it. But follow up promptly.

AUTHORITY

Managers are given the authority to get things done. They are expected to ensure that their teams follow their leadership, although this should not necessarily mean *telling* them what to do. It can involve motivating, empowering and persuading. Effective managers give the lead and their teams will follow without being forced to do so by the use of authority in a 'command and control' mode.

Charles Handy (1) advocates the development of a 'culture of consent' and the emphasis is on the virtues of decentralization, empowerment and self-managed teams. Authority is best exercised in the form of management by agreement rather than management by control. Managers who rely entirely on what is called authority based on position are less likely to succeed than those whose authority rests on the respect they have earned from their team on the basis of their abilities to lead and get results and their expertise.

But managers still have to be authoritative. As such, they are listened to. They get things done and others take note of what they say and act on it. Good managers demonstrate that they are authoritative by the way they behave. They rely on the authority of expertise and wisdom rather than the authority of power. Managers may be 'drest in a little brief authority' but they have to earn respect for that authority and keep on earning it.

To be authoritative you have to:

1. Be good at what you are doing as a leader, a manager, an expert or all three.
2. Be able to define what you expect people to do clearly, concisely and persuasively.

3. Demonstrate that you know where you are going, what you are doing and why you are doing it.
4. As necessary, explain the course of action you are taking.
5. Lead by example.
6. Accept that your authority is not absolute – it only exists if others recognize it.
7. Be decisive but avoid rushing into decisions without careful thought.
8. Get people to accept that there will be occasions when what you say goes – you are accountable and the final decision is always yours.
9. Be self-confident and convey that to everyone concerned.
10. Be a good communicator, ensuring that people know exactly what is expected of them.

POWER

Power is the capacity to get other people to do what you want them to do. There are five ways in which it can be exercised:

- by exercising leadership;
- by demonstrating that you are the expert – 'power goes to the one who knows';
- by using managerial position and authority;
- by offering rewards for compliance;
- by making it plain that non-compliance will bring punishment.

The responsible use of power means that managers do their best to gain acceptance through the use of leadership and expertise. This may be backed up by the trappings of authority but managerial position is not enough. Bribing people through rewards will only work, if it works at all, in the short term. Coercing people may again work in the short term but is a highly unsatisfactory basis for a long-term productive relationship.

John Kotter (2) interviewed over 250 managers who were in a position to use power. He found that the successful ones had the following characteristics:

1. They use power openly and legitimately. They are seen as genuine experts in their field and constantly live up to the leadership images they build for themselves.
2. They are sensitive to what types of power are most effective with different kinds of people. For example, experts respect expertise.
3. They develop all their sources of power and do not rely on any particular technique.
4. They seek jobs and tasks which will give them the opportunity to acquire and use power. They constantly seek ways to invest the power they already have to secure an even higher positive return.

5. They use their power in a mature and self-controlled way. They seldom if ever use power impulsively or for their own aggrandizement.
6. They get satisfaction from influencing others.

DEALING WITH UNSATISFACTORY SITUATIONS

Managers are often confronted with unsatisfactory situations which they have to resolve. They can do this by applying their expertise and experience to assess the circumstances – the working situation – in which the problem has arisen. To do this they need to use their problem-solving skills. Effective problem solving requires the following steps:

1. *Analyse the situation* – establish what has gone wrong or is about to go wrong.
2. *Get the facts* – find out what is happening or is likely to happen.
3. *Develop hypotheses* – identify the cause(s) of the problem.
4. *Specify objectives* – define what you would like to happen, compare this with what is happening and decide what you need to achieve to fill the gap.
5. *Identify and assess alternative courses of action* – weigh and decide between the options available and choose the one most likely to succeed without using too many resources.
6. *Produce an action plan* – the programme of work required to implement the preferred course of action.
7. *Implement action plan* – manage the programme of work and ensure that resources are being used properly to achieve the planned result.
8. *Evaluate* – assess the degree to which the objectives have been achieved and institute further action if necessary.

SUMMARY

- Delegation takes place when individuals are allocated duties or tasks in order to achieve outcomes for which their managers have overall responsibility but which the managers for a variety of reasons cannot or do not want to undertake themselves.
- Motivating other people is about getting them to move in the direction you want them to go in order to achieve a result.
- Managers have a major part to play in using their motivating skills to get people to give of their best.

- Coaching is a personal (usually one-to-one), on-the-job approach used by managers and trainers to help people develop their skills and levels of competence. As a manager you are there to get results through people.
- The main aims of coaching are to help people to become aware of how well they are doing, where they need to improve and what they need to learn.
- Coaching will be most effective when the coach understands that his or her role is to help people to learn, individuals are motivated to learn and are given guidance on what they should be learning and feedback on how they are doing, the coach listens to individuals to understand what they want and need and adopts a constructive approach, building on strengths and experience.
- Managers act as facilitators in relation to their team members when they make it easier for them to develop by promoting their skills and capabilities, thus helping them to move forward. The process of facilitating individual learning involves focusing on the learners and helping them to achieve agreed learning objectives.
- Managers may also be involved in facilitating the work of groups of people assembled to carry out a task jointly, where the aim is to help the group reach conclusions in the shape of ideas and solutions.
- People need feedback. They have to know how well they are doing in order to carry on doing it to good effect or to understand what they need to do to improve.
- Increasingly in today's more fluid and flexible organizations people get things done by networking. Networks are loosely organized connections between people with shared interests.
- Policies exist to provide guides to action and set limits to decision making – what should be done in certain circumstances, how particular requirements or issues should be dealt with.
- Exerting influence is an important part of the role managers play.
- Managers are given the authority to get things done. They are expected to ensure that their teams follow their leadership.
- Power is the capacity to get other people to do what you want them to do. There are five ways in which it can be exercised: by exercising leadership; by demonstrating that you are the expert – 'power goes to the one who knows'; by using managerial position and authority; by offering rewards for compliance, and by making it plain that non-compliance will bring punishment.
- Managers are often confronted with unsatisfactory situations which they have to resolve. They can do this by applying their expertise and experience to assess the circumstances – the working situation – in which the problem has arisen. To do this they need to use their problem-solving skills.

REFERENCES

1   Handy, C (1994) *The Empty Raincoat*, Hutchinson, London
2   Kotter, J P (1992) 'Power, dependence, and effective management', in *Managing People and Organizations*, ed J J Gabarro, Harvard Business School Publications, Boston, MA

6

Making things happen

Making things happen, managing for results, getting things done – this is what management is all about. Managers have to be achievers, taking personal responsibility for achieving objectives. John Harvey-Jones (1), in *Making it Happen,* said of the approaches used by successful business managers:

- Nothing will happen unless everyone down the line knows what they are trying to achieve and gives of their best to achieve it.
- The whole of business is taking an acceptable risk.
- The process of deciding where you take the business is an opportunity to involve others, which actually forms the motive power that will make it happen.

This chapter first poses and answers three basic questions on how to make it happen. An analysis is then conducted of what makes achievers tick and what achievers do. The chapter continues by considering a key quality required to make things happen, namely decisiveness, and concludes with a discussion of how to analyse and improve your capacity to get things done.

HOW TO MAKE IT HAPPEN: BASIC QUESTIONS

It is said that there are three sorts of managers: those who make things happen, those who watch things happening, and those who don't know what is happening. Before finding out how to get into the first category, there are three questions to answer:

1. Is making things happen simply a matter of personality – characteristics like drive, decisiveness, leadership, ambition, a high level of achievement motivation – which some people have and others haven't?
2. And if you haven't got the drive, decisiveness and so forth that it takes, is there anything you can do about it?
3. To what extent is an ability to get things done a matter of using techniques which can be learnt and developed?

The significance of personality

Personality is important. Unless you have will power and drive nothing will happen. But remember that your personality is a function of both nature and nurture. You may be born with genes which influence certain characteristics of your behaviour, but upbringing, education, training and, above all, experience develop you into the person you are.

Doing something about it

We may not be able to change our personality which, according to Freud, is formed in the first few years of our life. But we can develop and adapt it by consciously learning from our experience and analysing other people's behaviour.

Using techniques

Techniques for achieving results such as setting objectives, planning, organizing, delegating, motivating and monitoring performance can be learnt. But these techniques are only as effective as the person that uses them. They must be applied in the right way and in the right circumstances. And you still have to use your experience to select the right technique for your personality to make it work.

WHAT MAKES ACHIEVERS TICK?

People who make things happen have high levels of achievement motivation – a drive to get something done for the sheer satisfaction of achieving it. David McClelland (2) of Harvard University identified through his research three needs which he believed were key factors in motivating managers. These were:

1. the need for achievement;
2. the need for power (having control and influence over people);
3. the need for affiliation (to be accepted by others).

All effective managers need to have each of these needs to a certain degree but by far the most important is achievement. This is what counts, and achievers, according to McClelland, have these characteristics:

- They set themselves realistic but achievable goals with some 'stretch' built in.
- They prefer situations which they can influence rather than those which are governed by chance.
- They are more concerned with knowing that they have done well than with the rewards that success brings.
- They get their rewards from their accomplishment rather than from money or praise. This does not mean that high achievers reject money, which can in fact motivate them as long as it is seen as a realistic measure of their performance.
- High achievers are most effective in situations where they can get ahead by their own efforts.

WHAT DO ACHIEVERS WHO MAKE THINGS HAPPEN DO?

High achievers do many, if not all, of these things:

- They define to themselves precisely what they want to do.
- They set demanding but not unattainable timescales and deadlines to do it, which they meet.
- They convey clearly what they want done and by when.
- They are single-minded about getting where they want to go, showing perseverance and determination in the face of adversity.
- They demand high performance from themselves and equally expect high performance from everyone else.
- They work hard and well under pressure; in fact, it brings out the best in them.
- They tend to be dissatisfied with the status quo.
- They are never completely satisfied with their own performance and continually question themselves.
- They take calculated risks.
- They snap out of setbacks and quickly regroup their forces and ideas.
- They are enthusiastic about the task and convey their enthusiasm to others.
- They are decisive in that they are able quickly to sum up situations, define alternative courses of action, determine the preferred course, and convey to the members of their team what needs to be done.
- They continually monitor their own performance and that of their team so that any deviation can be corrected in good time.

ON BEING DECISIVE

To make things happen you have to be decisive. This means being prepared to make decisions and live with the consequences. A consultant in a New York hospital promoted a registrar because he was a good decision-maker. When asked why she had promoted someone whose decisions were not always right, the consultant replied: 'I said he was a good decision-maker, not that he made good decisions.' Being decisive means that you sometimes have to take risks. They may be calculated but they do not always work. But indecisiveness is even worse. As long as you learn from your mistakes and avoid repeating them, the occasional and inevitable poor decision need not matter unduly.

Here are 10 approaches to being decisive:

1. *Make decisions faster* – Jack Welch, when heading General Electric, used to say: 'In today's lightning paced environment, you don't have time to think about things. Don't sit on decisions. Empty that in-basket so that you are free to search out new opportunities… Don't sit still. Anybody sitting still, you are going to guarantee they're going to get their legs knocked from under them.'
2. *Avoid procrastination* – it is easy to put an e-mail demanding a decision into the 'too difficult' section of your actual or mental in-tray. Avoid the temptation to fill your time with trivial tasks so that the evil moment when you have to address the issue is postponed. Make a start. Once you have got going, you can deal with the unpleasant task of making a decision in stages. A challenge often becomes easier once we have started dealing with it. Having spent five minutes on it we don't want to feel it was wasted so we carry on and complete the job.
3. *Expect the unexpected* – you are then in the frame of mind needed to respond decisively to a new situation.
4. *Think before you act* – this could be a recipe for delay but decisive people use their analytical ability to come to swift conclusions about the nature of the situation and what should be done about it.
5. *Be careful about assumptions* – we have a tendency to leap to conclusions and seize on assumptions that support our case and ignore the facts that might contradict it.
6. *Learn from the past* – build on your experience in decision making; what approaches work best. But don't rely too much on precedents. Situations change. The right decision last time could well be the wrong one now.
7. *Be systematic* – adopt a rigorous problem-solving approach. This means specifying objectives – what you want to achieve, defining the criteria for judging whether it has been achieved, getting and analysing the facts, looking for causes rather than focusing on symptoms, developing and testing hypotheses and alternative solutions, and evaluating possible causes of action against the objectives and criteria.

8. *Talk it through* – before you make a significant decision talk it through with some-one who is likely to disagree so that any challenge they make can be taken into account (but you have to canvass opinion swiftly).

9. *Leave time to think it over* – swift decision making is highly desirable but you must avoid knee-jerk reactions. Pause, if only for a few minutes, to allow yourself time to think through the decision you propose to make. And confirm that it is logical and fully justified.

10. *Consider the potential consequences* – McKinsey, the management consultants, calls this 'consequence management'. Every decision has a consequence and you should consider very carefully what that might be and how you will manage it. This is called 'working through the decision'. When making a decision it is a good idea to start from where you mean to end – define the end-result and then work out the steps needed to achieve it.

ANALYSING AND IMPROVING HOW YOU MAKE THINGS HAPPEN

Improving your ability to make things happen means analysing how you get things done, identifying areas for improvement and taking action. It is no good trying to assess your performance as a doer unless you have criteria against which you can measure that performance. You have to set standards for yourself and if you don't meet them, ask yourself why. The answer should tell you what to do next time.

The questions you should ask yourself are:

- What did I set out to do?
- Did I get it done?
- If I did, why and how did I succeed?
- If not, why not?

The aim is to make the best use of your experience in getting things done.

Use the list of what high achievers do to check your own behaviour and actions. If your performance has not been up to scratch under any of these headings, ask yourself what went wrong and decide how you are going to overcome this difficulty next time. This is not always easy. It is hard to admit to yourself, for example, that you have not been sufficiently enthusiastic. It may be even harder to decide what to do about it. You don't want to enthuse all over the place, indiscriminately. But you can consider whether there are better ways of displaying and conveying your enthusiasm to others in order to carry them with you.

SUMMARY

- People who make things happen have high levels of achievement motivation – a drive to get something done for the sheer satisfaction of achieving it.
- The three needs that motivate managers were listed by David McClelland as (1) the need for achievement, (2) the need for power (having control and influence over people) and (3) the need for affiliation (to be accepted by others).
- To make things happen you have to be decisive. This means being prepared to make decisions and live with the consequences.
- Improving your ability to make things happen means analysing how you get things done, identifying areas for improvement and taking action.

REFERENCES

1 Harvey-Jones, J (184) *Making It Happen*, Collins, Glasgow
2 McClelland, D C (1961) *The Achieving Society*, Van Norstrand, New York

7

Strategic management

In this chapter the concepts of strategy and strategic management are defined and consideration is given to the development of shared vision and providing direction, gaining support for the vision and strategy and refining strategy and gaining support for plans.

STRATEGY

Strategy consists of a statement or an understanding of what the organization or a part of it wants to become, where it wants to go and, broadly, how it means to get there. Business strategy in a commercial enterprise answers the questions: 'What business are we in?' and 'How are we going to make money out of it?' Strategy determines the direction in which the enterprise is going in relation to its environment in order to achieve sustainable competitive advantage. The emphasis is on focused actions that differentiate the firm from its competitors. It is a declaration of intent which defines means to achieve ends, and is concerned with the long-term allocation of significant resources and with matching those resources and capabilities to the external environment. Strategy is a perspective on the way in which critical issues or success factors can be addressed, and strategic decisions aim to make a major and long-term impact on the behaviour and success of the organization.

Individual managers develop strategies for the accomplishment of their longer-term objectives. Again these are directions of intent and definitions of how it is proposed those intentions should be put into effect.

Strategies are developed to provide for the realization of visions – views on what the future should be. Shared visions can be inspirational.

DEVELOPING STRATEGY

The formulation of strategy can be defined as a process for developing a sense of direction. It has often been described as a logical, step-by-step affair, the outcome of which is a formal written statement which provides a definitive guide to the organization's or the manager's long-term intentions. Many people still believe and act as if this were the case, but it is a misrepresentation of reality. This is not to dismiss completely the ideal of adopting a systematic approach – it has its uses as a means of providing an analytical framework for strategic decision making and a reference point for monitoring the implementation of strategy. But in practice the formulation of strategy can never be as rational and linear a process as some managers attempt to make it.

Strategy formulation can best be described as 'problem solving in unstructured situations' (Digman (1)) and strategies will always be formed under conditions of partial ignorance. The difficulty is that strategies are often based on the questionable assumption that the future will resemble the past. Robert Heller (2) had a go at the cult of long-range planning: 'What goes wrong,' he wrote, 'is that sensible anticipation gets converted into foolish numbers: and their validity always hinges on large loose assumptions.' Faulkner and Johnson (3) have said of long-term planning that it:

> was inclined to take a definitive view of the future, and to extrapolate trend lines for the key business variables in order to arrive at this view. Economic turbulence was insufficiently considered, and the reality that much strategy is formulated and implemented in the act of managing the enterprise was ignored. Precise forecasts ending with derived financials were constructed, the only weakness of which was that the future almost invariably turned out differently.

Strategy formulation is not necessarily a rational and continuous process, as was pointed out by Mintzberg (4). He believes that, rather than being consciously and systematically developed, strategy reorientation happens in what he calls brief 'quantum loops'. A strategy, according to Mintzberg, can be deliberate – it can realize the intentions of management, for example to attack and conquer a new market. But this is not always the case. In theory, he says, strategy is a systematic process: first we think, then we act; we formulate then we implement. But we also 'act in order to think'. In practice, 'a realized strategy can emerge in response to an evolving situation' and the strategic planner is often 'a pattern organizer, a learner if you like, who manages a process in which strategies and visions can emerge as well as be deliberately conceived... Strategy is a pattern in a stream of activities.' Mintzberg (5) contends that 'the failure of systematic planning is the failure of systems to do better than, or nearly as well as, human beings'. He went on to say that: 'real strategists get their hands dirty digging for ideas, and real strategies are built from the nuggets they discover'. And 'sometimes strategies must be left as broad visions, not precisely articulated, to adapt to a changing environment'.

THE ROLE OF STRATEGIC MANAGEMENT

Strategic management means that managers are looking ahead at what they need to achieve in the middle or relatively distant future. Although, as Fombrun, Tichy and Devanna (6) put it, they are aware of the fact that businesses, like managers, must perform well in the present to succeed in the future, they are concerned with the broader issues they are facing and the general directions in which they must go to deal with these issues and achieve longer-term objectives. They do not take a narrow or restricted view.

The purpose of strategic management has been expressed by Rosabeth Moss Kanter (7) as being to: 'elicit the present actions for the future' and become 'action vehicles – integrating and institutionalizing mechanisms for change'. She goes on to say: 'Strong leaders articulate direction and save the organization from change by drift... They see a vision of the future that allows them to see more clearly what steps to take, building on present capacities and strengths.'

Strategic management deals with both ends and means. As an end it describes a vision of what something will look like in a few years' time. As a means, it shows how it is expected that the vision will be realized. Strategic management is therefore visionary management, concerned with creating and conceptualizing ideas of where the organization should be going. But it is also empirical management which decides how in practice it is going to get there.

The focus is on identifying the organization's mission and strategies, but attention is also given to the resource base required. It is necessary to remember that strategy is the means to create value. Managers who think strategically will have a broad and long-term view of where they are going. They will also be aware that they are responsible, first, for planning how to allocate resources to opportunities which contribute to the implementation of strategy, second, for managing these opportunities in ways which will significantly add value to the results achieved by the firm, and third, for refining the strategy to meet new demands.

DEVELOPING A SHARED VISION AND STRATEGIC PLANS

Visionary management is much more than a process in which managers sit in their offices and indulge in pipe dreams about the future. A vision can only be realized if it is shared with those who have to act upon it in order to obtain their commitment and engagement. To gain support for the vision it is necessary to present it in language that people can understand and to discuss with those concerned its implications in terms of the part they will play and the benefits that will ensue for themselves as well as the organization. They need to be given a voice in deciding what needs to be done so that they become parties to the vision rather than simply being at the receiving end. They should be regarded as stakeholders who have a legitimate interest in what the vision means and their role in making it real.

A vision provides a broad picture of what the future might look like. It provides the basis for formulating and implementing strategic plans. Sharing the vision provides the basis for providing direction. Again, it is important to involve people in the process of strategic planning so they understand what is to be accomplished, why it needs to be accomplished and the part they will play in accomplishing it. A stakeholder approach is required. Everyone involved should be treated as stakeholders in the strategy because they are interested in its outcome as it affects not only the organization but also themselves. As stakeholders they have the right to comment on proposals and put forward their own ideas. In this way the original strategic concept can be refined so that it becomes more achievable with the participation of the stakeholders.

SUMMARY

- Strategy consists of a statement or an understanding of what the organization or a part of it wants to become, where it wants to go and, broadly, how it means to get there.
- Strategies are developed to provide for the realization of visions – views on what the future should be. Shared visions can be inspirational.
- The formulation of strategy can be defined as a process for developing a sense of direction.
- Strategy formulation can best be described as 'problem solving in unstructured situations'.
- Strategy consists of a pattern in a stream of activities.
- Strategic management is visionary management, concerned with creating and conceptualizing ideas of where the organization should be going.

- Managers who think strategically will have a broad and long-term view of where they are going.
- A vision can only be realized if it is shared with those who have to act upon it in order to gain their commitment and engagement.
- Sharing the vision provides the basis for providing direction.
- People should be involved in the process of strategic planning. A stakeholder approach is required.

REFERENCES

1   Digman, L A (1990) *Strategic Management – Concepts, Decisions, Cases*, Irwin, Georgetown, Ontario
2   Heller, R (1972) *The Naked Manager*, Barrie & Jenkins, London
3   Faulkner, D and Johnson, G (1992) *The Challenge of Strategic Management*, Kogan Page, London
4   Mintzberg, H (1987) Crafting strategy, *Harvard Business Review*, July–August, pp 66–74
5   Mintzberg, H (1994) The rise and fall of strategic planning, *Harvard Business Review*, January–February, pp 107–14
6   Fombrun, C J, Tichy, N M and Devanna, M A (1984) *Strategic Human Resource Management*, Wiley, New York
7   Kanter, R M (1984) *The Change Masters*, Allen & Unwin, London

8

Systems and process management

This chapter deals with an important aspect of managerial activities, namely, the management of the systems and processes which exist in organizations to get work done. A system consists of formally interconnected activities which together are managed to achieve certain defined ends. A process is a series of operations which are carried out in order to produce something, provide a service or carry out a complex task. In this chapter, the first two sections examine the approach to managing systems and processes. Examples are then given of system and process management. The chapter concludes with an assessment of the conflict and challenges that managing systems and processes presents.

MANAGING SYSTEMS

Systems can be complex and their management means that it is necessary to know how each part of the system contributes to the whole result. It is then essential to see that the different parts of the system work smoothly together so that each contributes to satisfactory performance. Complications arise when the parts do not fit together. The design and development of systems has to be based on a thorough analysis of requirements, with close attention being paid to who will use it and how the system will perform in different circumstances.

Systems need to be maintained and updated to ensure that they continue to function effectively and deliver the required results. Their performance has to be monitored and corrective action taken as necessary. The purpose of the system has to be explained to those who use it and people will have to be trained in its operation.

MANAGING PROCESSES

The management of processes starts with process definition. This involves specifying what the process is, how it operates, and what results it is expected to achieve in terms of output levels or levels of service, speed of operation, quality standards and cost. The process specification defines the process and sets out its inputs and outputs and the internal and external customers it serves. It is necessary to clarify the inputs required at each stage. Flow charts are produced to represent diagrammatically the events and stage of the process with a view to defining how it functions and allocating responsibilities for its operation and management.

Managing the process involves ensuring in the first place that the resources in the form of facilities and equipment required are available and trained and capable people are there to operate the process. The technique of process capability analysis may be used to examine variables in the process to establish the extent to which it is doing the job properly and, if not, what should be done about it. Control information needs to be generated to monitor the performance of the process and the people who operate it. This will analyse variations as a basis for further investigation.

EXAMPLES OF SYSTEMS AND PROCESS MANAGEMENT

The following examples of systems and process management are given below: health and safety, information technology (IT), reward systems and computer-integrated manufacturing.

Health and safety

A health and safety system is based on the organization's health and safety policies and consists of the arrangements for conducting health and safety audits and risk assessments and accident investigations.

Policy statement

The policy statement should set out the intention of the employer to safeguard the health and safety of employees. It should emphasize four fundamental points: (1) that the safety of employees and the public is of paramount importance, (2) that safety takes precedence over expediency, (3) that every effort will be made to involve all managers, team leaders and employees in the development and implementation of health and safety procedures, and (4) that health and safety legislation will be complied with in the spirit as well as the letter of the law.

Health and safety audits

Health and safety audits provide for a comprehensive review of all aspects of the health and safety system to assess the extent to which its objectives have been achieved with particular reference to procedures and practices and their outcome as measured by the health and safety performance of the organization. The audit will examine how effectively the procedures support the implementation of health and safety policies, check that accidents are investigated thoroughly and find out if health and safety considerations are given proper weight when designing systems of work or manufacturing and operational processes. It will also establish the extent to which health and safety legislation requirements are being met.

Risk assessments

Risk assessments are concerned with the identification of hazards and the analysis of the risks attached to them. A *hazard* is anything that can cause harm (eg working on roofs, lifting heavy objects, chemicals, electricity etc). A *risk* is the chance, large or small, of harm being actually done by the hazard. Risk assessments are concerned with looking for hazards and estimating the level of risk associated with them. The purpose of risk assessments is to initiate preventive action. They enable control measures to be devised on the basis of an understanding of the relative importance of risks.

Accident prevention

The prevention of accidents is achieved by:

- identifying the causes of accidents and the conditions under which they are most likely to occur;
- taking account of safety factors at the design stage – building safety into the system;

- designing safety equipment and protective devices and providing protective clothing;
- carrying out regular risk assessment audits, inspections and checks and taking action to eliminate risks;
- investigating all accidents resulting in damage to establish the cause and to initiate corrective action.

Organizing health and safety

Health and safety concerns everyone in an establishment, although the main responsibility lies with management in general and individual managers in particular. Management develops and implements health and safety policies and ensures that procedures for carrying out risk assessments, safety audits and inspections are implemented. Importantly, management has the duty of monitoring and evaluating health and safety performance and taking corrective action as necessary. Managers can exert the greater influence on health and safety. They are in immediate control and it is up to them to keep a constant watch for unsafe conditions or practices and to take immediate action. They are also directly responsible for ensuring that employees are conscious of health and safety hazards and do not take risks.

Information technology

Managing an IT system involves, in the first place, planning the system, analysing and agreeing with users their requirements and specifying how the system will meet them. Processors, operating systems and software have to be obtained and networks and databases developed, installed and maintained. Outsourcing to application service providers who run applications at their own data centres will need to be considered.

Managing an IT system within an organization means delivering to internal customers the information processing services they require. This involves managing support services which, as defined by the British Computer Society, means that the IT department must:

- establish the level of support that may reasonably be expected and provide the tools, documentation and suitably trained staff to meet this expectation;
- respond swiftly to support requests and satisfy internal customers that their needs are being met;
- identify to internal customers any changes to business procedures that will improve the efficiency of the service provided;

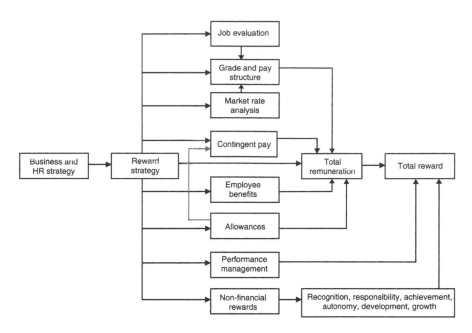

Figure 8.1 Reward management: elements and interrelationships

● keep internal customers informed of the steps being taken to maintain agreed service levels;
● maintain records of the services provided and take the actions needed to achieve target service levels.

Reward systems

A reward system is an example of a different type of system which is designed and operated to achieve the reward management objectives of an organization. A reward system consists of:

● *policies* which provide guidelines on approaches to managing rewards;
● *practices* which provide financial and non-financial rewards;
● *processes* which are concerned with evaluating the relative size of jobs (job evaluation) and assessing individual performance (performance management);
● *procedures* which are operated in order to maintain the system and to ensure that it operates efficiently and flexibly and provides value for money;
● *grade and pay structures* which provide the framework for managing relativities and pay.

The elements and interrelationships in a reward system are illustrated in Figure 8.1. The task of reward management is to ensure that all these elements are properly pro-

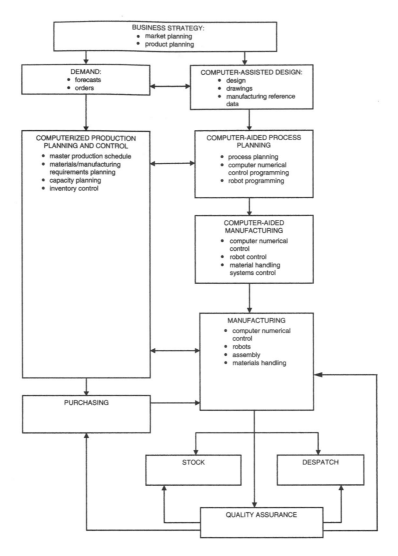

Figure 8.2 A computer-integrated manufacturing system

vided for, that they operate effectively in relation to one another and that the system achieves the reward objectives of the organization.

Computer-integrated manufacturing

A computer-integrated manufacturing (CIM) system uses information technology to integrate the various processes which together comprise the total manufacturing process. These processes can include design, production engineering, production planning and control, production scheduling, material requirements planning, manufacturing, material handling and inventory control. Such a system is illustrated in Figure 8.2.

THE CONFLICT AND CHALLENGES THAT MANAGING SYSTEMS AND PROCESSES PRESENTS

Conflict in managing systems and processes arises when they do not deliver to users what they are expected to deliver. Users expect an appropriate design and full support. If either of these are lacking they are rightly angry.

The main challenges presented by the management of systems and processes are:

- their design does not take sufficient account of user needs and is not user-friendly;
- they no longer serve their original purpose;
- their managers pay insufficient attention to developing them to meet new demands;
- support from technicians is inadequate;
- line managers find them difficult to use;
- they may rely heavily on a computer system which is prone to failures;
- they are clumsy, time-consuming and wasteful.

All these problems can be resolved if sufficient care is taken over the design and maintenance of the system or process and if proper training and support are given to users.

SUMMARY

- A system consists of formally interconnected activities which together are managed to achieve certain defined ends.
- A process is a series of operations which are carried out in order to produce something, provide a service or carry out a complex task.
- It is then necessary to see that the different parts of the system work smoothly together so that each contributes to satisfactory performance.
- Systems need to be maintained and updated to ensure that they continue to function effectively and deliver the required results.
- The process specification defines the process and sets out its inputs and outputs and the internal and external customers it serves. It is necessary to clarify the inputs required at each stage, including the internal customers who need outputs from the process.

- Conflict in managing systems and processes arises when they do not deliver to users what they are expected to deliver. Users expect an appropriate design and full support.
- There are a number of challenges arising from the need to design and maintain systems and processes which function well and provide the support that users need.

9

Self-development

As Peter Drucker (1) wisely said: 'Development is always self-development. Nothing could be more absurd than for the enterprise to assume responsibility for the development of a person. The responsibility rests with individuals, their abilities, their efforts.' This chapter expands on this statement by examining the processes of self-development and self-managed learning, discussing the use of personal development plans and examining the various ways in which organizations can help people to develop. The chapter concludes with comments on self-management strategies and the evaluation of one's own performance.

THE PROCESS OF SELF-DEVELOPMENT

The best way to get on is to rely on yourself while seeking and benefiting from any support you can get from your manager or the organization. Self-development takes place through self-managed or self-directed learning. This means that you take responsibility for satisfying your own learning needs to develop skills, improve performance and progress your career. It is based on processes which enable you to identify what you need to learn by reflecting on your experience and analysing what you need to know and be able to do to increase your effectiveness now and in the future.

Self-managed learning

The case for self-managed learning is that people learn and retain more if they find things out for themselves. But they may still need to be helped to identify what they should look for. Self-managed learning is about self-development and this will be furthered by self-assessment (evaluating the impact of your own performance), which leads to better self-understanding. Pedler and his co-writers (2) recommend the following four-stage approach:

1. *self-assessment* based on analysis by individuals of their work and life situation;
2. *diagnosis* derived from the analysis of learning needs and priorities;
3. *action planning* to identify objectives, helps and hindrances, resources required (including people) and timescales;
4. *monitoring and review* to assess progress in achieving action plans.

Identifying development needs

You can use performance management processes to identify self-development needs on your own or in discussion with your manager. These will include reviewing performance against agreed plans and assessing the levels of competence displayed in carrying out your work. The analysis is therefore based on an understanding of what you are expected to do, the knowledge and skills you need to carry out your job effectively, what you have achieved, and what knowledge and skills you have. If there are any gaps between the knowledge and skills you need and those you have, then this defines a development need. The analysis is always related to work and the capacity to carry it out effectively.

Defining the means of satisfying development needs

When deciding how to satisfy development needs you should remember that it is *not* just about selecting suitable training courses. These may form part of your development plan but probably only a minor part; other learning activities are much more important. Examples include:

- seeing what others do (good practice);
- project work;
- adopting a role model (mentor);
- networking – discussing with other people management issues and learning from them in the process – organizations concerned with knowledge management (enhancing the availability and effective use of knowledge relevant to the

organization) may set up 'communities of interest' which formalize networks by bringing people together to discuss ideas and enhance knowledge;
- involvement in other work areas;
- planned use of internal training media, including e-learning (use of electronic learning materials) and learning libraries;
- input to policy formulation;
- increased professionalism on the job;
- involvement in the community;
- coaching others;
- guided reading;
- special assignments;
- distance learning – learning in your own time from material prepared elsewhere, eg correspondence courses;
- training courses within or outside the organization.

Personal development plans

A personal development plan sets out the actions you propose to take to learn and to develop yourself. You take responsibility for formulating and implementing the plan but you may receive support from the organization and your manager in doing so. Personal development planning aims to promote learning and to provide you with the knowledge and portfolio of transferable skills which will help to progress your career.

A personal development action plan sets out what needs to be done and how it will be done under headings such as:

- development needs;
- outcomes expected (learning objectives);
- development activities to meet the needs;
- responsibility for development – what individuals will do and what support they will require from their manager, the HR department or other people;
- timing – when the learning activity is expected to start and be completed;
- outcome – what development activities have taken place and how effective they were.

OTHER METHODS OF MANAGEMENT DEVELOPMENT

To complement and support self-development the other methods of management development discussed below are coaching, mentoring and action learning.

Coaching

Coaching is a person-to-person technique designed to develop individual skills, knowledge and attitudes. It can take place informally as part of the normal process of management or team leadership. This type of coaching consists of:

- helping people to become aware of how well they are doing and what they need to learn;
- controlled delegation;
- using whatever situations arise as learning opportunities;
- providing guidance on how to carry out specific tasks as necessary, but always on the basis of helping individuals to learn rather than force-feeding them with instructions on what to do and how to do it.

Executive coaching can be provided by specialist consultants. They usually concentrate on helping people to develop more productive ways of behaving and to change dysfunctional management styles. Coaching is often based on the information provided by personality questionnaires such as the Myers Briggs Types Indicator.

Mentoring

Mentoring is the process of using specially selected and trained individuals to provide guidance and advice which will help to develop the careers of the people allocated to them (sometimes called 'protégés').

Mentoring is aimed at complementing learning on the job, which must always be the best way of acquiring the particular skills and knowledge the jobholder needs. Mentoring also complements formal training by providing those who benefit from it with individual guidance from experienced managers who are 'wise in the ways of the organization'.

Mentors provide for the person or persons assigned to them:

- advice in drawing up self-development programmes or learning contracts;
- general help with learning programmes;
- guidance on how to acquire the necessary knowledge and skills to do a new job;
- advice on dealing with any administrative, technical or people problems individuals meet, especially in the early stages of their careers;
- information on 'the way things are done around here' – the corporate culture and its manifestations in the shape of core values and organizational behaviour (management style);
- coaching in specific skills;

- help in tackling projects – not by doing it for people but by pointing them in the right direction, that is – helping people to help themselves;
- a parental figure with whom the people they are dealing with can discuss their aspirations and concerns and who will lend a sympathetic ear to their problems.

There are no standard mentoring procedures. Typically, however, a mentor is allocated one or more people and given a very general brief to carry out the functions described above having been carefully trained in mentoring techniques.

Action learning

Action learning, as developed by Revans (3), is a method of helping managers develop their talents by exposing them to real problems. They are required to analyse them, formulate recommendations, and then take action. It accords with the belief that managers learn best by doing rather than being taught.

Revans produced the following formula to describe his concept:

L (learning) = P (programmed learning) + Q (questioning, insight).

He suggested that the concept is based on six assumptions:

1. Experienced managers have a huge curiosity to know how other managers work.
2. We learn not as much when we are motivated to learn, as when we are motivated to learn something.
3. Learning about oneself is threatening and is resisted if it tends to change one's self-image. However, it is possible to reduce the external threat to a level which no longer acts as a total barrier to learning about oneself.
4. People learn only when they do something, and they learn more the more responsible they feel the task to be.
5. Learning is deepest when it involves the whole person – mind, values, body, emotions.
6. The learner knows better than anyone else what he or she has learnt. Nobody else has much chance of knowing.

A typical action learning programme brings together a 'set', or group, of four or five managers to solve the problem. They help and learn from each other, but an external consultant, or 'set adviser', sits in with them regularly. The project may last several months, and the set meets frequently, possibly one day a week. The adviser helps the members of the set to learn from one another and clarifies the process of action learning. This process involves change embedded in the web of relationships called 'the client system'. The web comprises at least three separate networks: the power network, the information network, and the motivational network (this is what Revans refers to as 'who can, who knows, and who cares'). The forces for change are already there within the client system and it is the adviser's role to point out the dynamics of this system as the work of diagnosis and implementation proceeds.

The set has to manage the project like any other project, deciding on objectives, planning resources, initiating action and monitoring progress. But all the time, with the help of their adviser, they are learning about the management processes involved as they actually happen.

SELF-MANAGEMENT STRATEGIES

Self-management strategies should be based on self-assessment, which means assessing your own performance and identifying how you can improve. To assess your own performance you need to:

1. Ensure that you are clear about what your job entails in terms of the main tasks or key result areas. If in doubt, ask your manager for clarification.
2. Find out what you are expected to achieve for each of the key result areas. Expectations should be definable as objectives in the form of quantified targets or standards of performance (qualitative statements of what constitutes effective performance). Ideally they should have been discussed and agreed as part of the performance management process but if this has not happened, ask your manager to spell out what he or she expects you to achieve.
3. Refer to the organization's competency framework. Discuss with your manager how he or she interprets these as far as you are concerned.
4. At fairly regular intervals, say once a month, review your progress by reference to the objectives, standards and competency headings. Take note of your achievements and, if they exist, your failures. Ask yourself why you were successful or unsuccessful and what you can do to build on success or overcome failure. You may identify actions you can take or specific changes in behaviour you can try to achieve. Or you may identify a need for further coaching, training or experience.
5. At the end of the review period and prior to the appraisal discussion with your manager, look back at each of your interim reviews and the actions you decided to take. Consider what more needs to be done in any specific area or generally. You will then be in a position to answer the following questions that might be posed by your manager before or during the performance review discussion:

   ● How do you feel you have done?
   ● What are you best at doing?
   ● Are there any parts of your job which you find difficult?

- Are there any aspects of your work in which you would benefit from better guidance or further training?

Self-management strategies can be derived from this assessment which should identify specific areas for development or improvement. The strategy can be based on the following 10 steps which you can take to develop yourself:

1. *Create a development log* – record your plans and action.
2. *State your objectives* – the career path you want to follow and the skills you will need to proceed along that path.
3. *Develop a personal profile* – what sort of person you are, your likes and dislikes about work, your aspirations.
4. *List your strengths and weaknesses* – what you are good at and what you are not so good at, with examples.
5. *List your achievements* – what you have done well so far and why you believe these were worthwhile achievements.
6. *List significant learning experiences* – recall events when you have learnt something worthwhile (this can help you to understand your learning style).
7. *Ask other people* about your strengths and weaknesses and what you should do to develop yourself.
8. *Focus on the present* – what is happening to you now: your job, your current skills, your short-term development needs.
9. *Focus on the future* – where you want to be in the longer term and how you are going to get there (including a list of the skills and abilities you need to develop).
10. *Plan your self-development strategy* – how you are going to achieve your ambitions.

SUMMARY

- Self-development takes place through self-managed or self-directed learning.
- People learn and retain more if they find things out for themselves.
- Performance management processes can be used to identify self-development needs.
- Development needs can be satisfied by a number of learning activities other than formal training.
- Personal development plans can be used as the basis for learning and development plans.
- To complement and support self-development, other methods of management development can be used, such as coaching, mentoring and action learning.
- Self-management strategies should be based on self-assessment, which means assessing your own performance and identifying how you can improve or do even better.

REFERENCES

1 Drucker, P (1955) *The Practice of Management*, Heinemann, London
2 Pedler, M, Burgoyne J and Boydell, T (1986) *A Manager's Guide to Self Development*, McGraw Hill, Maidenhead
3 Revans, R W (1989) *Action Learning*, Blond and Briggs, London

Part II

Delivering change

10

The process of change

Everything flows and nothing abides; everything gives way and nothing is fixed.

Heraclitus, 513 BC

This is the first of three chapters examining a key aspect of managing for results, namely the effective management of change. Change, it is often said, is the only thing that remains constant in organizations. As A P Sloan wrote in *My Years with General Motors* (1), 'The circumstances of an ever-changing market and an ever-changing product are capable of breaking any business organization if that organization is unprepared for change.' This chapter is concerned with an initial analysis of the process of change, covering the types of change, how change happens, the concepts of equilibrium, stability and disequilibrium and how organizations grow and change (organizational dynamics).

TYPES OF CHANGE

There are seven types of change: incremental, transformational, strategic, organizational, systems and processes, cultural, and behavioural.

Incremental change

Incremental change is gradual change. It takes place in small steps. At the strategic level, James Quinn (2) coined the phrase 'logical incrementalism' to describe how organizations developed their change strategies. He suggested that organizations go through an iterative process which leads to incremental commitments that enable the enterprise to experiment with, and learn about, an otherwise unknowable future. He observed that:

> Top managers seeking change often consciously create forums and allow slack time for their organizations to talk through threatening issues, work out the implications of new solutions, or gain an improved information base that will permit new options to be evaluated objectively in comparison with more familiar alternatives. In many cases strategic concepts which are strongly resisted gain acceptance and support simply by the passage of time.

Incremental change takes place at the operational as distinct from the strategic level. Continuous improvement as discussed in Chapter 16 is not about making sudden quantum leaps in response to crisis situations; it *is* about adopting a steady, step-by-step approach to improving the ways in which the organization goes about doing things. Innovations can be tried and tested and the people affected by them can progressively get used to new processes, systems or procedures without being startled and upset by a sudden, unexpected and dramatic change.

Transformational change

Transformation, according to Webster's dictionary, is: 'A change in the shape, structure, nature of something'. Transformational change is the process of ensuring that an organization can develop and implement major change programmes so that it responds strategically to new demands and continues to function effectively in the dynamic environment in which it operates. Organizational transformation activities may involve radical changes to the structure, culture and processes of the organization – the way it looks at the world. This may be in response to competitive pressures, mergers, acquisitions, investments, disinvestments, changes in technology, product lines, markets, cost reduction exercises and decisions to downsize or outsource work. Transformational change may be forced on an organization by investors or government decisions. It may be initiated by a new chief executive and top management team with a remit to 'turn round' the business.

Transformational change means that significant and far-reaching developments are planned and implemented in corporate structures and organization-wide processes. The change is neither incremental (bit by bit) nor transactional (concerned solely with systems and procedures). Transactional change, according to Pascale (3), is merely concerned with the alteration of ways in which the organization does business and people interact with one another on a day-to-day basis and 'is effective when what you want is more of what you've already got'. He advocates a 'discontinuous improvement in capability' and this he describes as transformation.

As Jack Welch said when CEO of General Electric: 'Shun the incremental: go for the leap.' He also stated that: 'We want to be a company that is constantly renewing itself, shedding the past, adapting to change.'

A distinction can also be made between first-order and second-order transformational development. First-order development is concerned with changes to the ways in which particular parts of the organization function. Second-order change aims to make an impact on the whole organization.

Strategic change

Strategic change is concerned with broad, long-term and organization-wide issues. It is about moving to a future state which has been defined generally in terms of strategic vision and scope. It will cover the purpose and mission of the organization, its corporate philosophy on such matters as growth, quality, innovation and values concerning people (employees and customers), and the technologies employed. This overall definition leads to specifications of competitive positioning and strategic goals for achieving competitive advantage and for product-market development. These goals are supported by policies concerning marketing, sales, customer service, product and process development and human resource management.

Strategic change takes place within the contexts of the external competitive, economic and social environment and the organization's internal resources, capabilities, culture structure and systems. Its successful implementation requires thorough analysis of those factors in the formulation and planning stages.

Organizational change

Organizational change deals with how organizations are structured and, in broad terms, how they function. It will involve identifying the need to reconsider the formal structure of organizations which Child (4) has defined as comprising 'all the tangible and regularly occurring features which help to shape their members' behaviour'. Organizational change programmes address issues of centralization and decentralization, how the overall management task should be divided into separate activities, how these activities should be allocated to different parts of the organization, and how they should be directed, controlled, coordinated and integrated. They will be concerned with 'organizational process' – how the organization should function. This may mean trying to free up the ways things are done to ensure that there is more flexibility in the system to enable the organization to respond and adapt to change. In the words of Ghoshal and Bartlett (5):

> managers are beginning to deal with their organizations in different ways. Rather than seeing them as a hierarchy of static roles, they think of them as a portfolio of dynamic processes. They see core organizational processes that overlay and often dominate the vertical, authority-based processes of the hierarchical structure.

Those interested in organizational change need to take account of what Pascale (3) describes as 'the new organizational paradigm'. He suggests that organizations should move:

- *from* the image of organizations as machines, with the emphasis on concrete strategy, structure and systems, *to* the idea of organizations as organisms, with the emphasis on the 'soft' dimensions – style, staff and shared values;
- *from* a hierarchical model with step-by-step problem solving, *to* a network model, with parallel nodes of intelligence which surrounds problems until they are eliminated;
- *from* the status-driven view that managers think and workers do as they are told, *to* a view of managers as 'facilitators', with workers empowered to initiate improvements and change;
- *from* an emphasis on 'vertical tasks' within functional units, *to* an emphasis on 'horizontal tasks' and collaboration across units;
- *from* a focus on content and the prescribed use of specific tools and techniques, *to* a focus on 'process' and a holistic synthesis of techniques;
- *from* the military model, *to* a commitment model.

Systems and processes

Changes to systems and processes affect operations and impact on working arrangements and practices in the whole or part of an organization. They take place when operating methods are revised, new technology is introduced or existing technology is modified. The technology may consist of computer systems (information technology) which is concerned with such activities as electronic data interchange, enterprise resource planning, customer relationship management (CRM), computer-based supply chain automation, mechanized manufacturing processes, automated manufacturing processes, eg computer-integrated manufacturing, and distribution systems.

New or changed systems may be concerned with various aspects of administration such as financial and management accounting, material requirements planning, scheduling, procurement, order processing and distribution. Changes affecting individuals may also be made to terms and conditions of employment, working arrangements, the content of their jobs, employment procedures and the reward system.

Changes to systems and processes affect the daily lives of people in the organization – the jobs they do, how they are required to do them and how they are treated. Their immediate impact may therefore be as high if not higher than strategic or organizational change and they have to be handled just as carefully. This is an area where getting change management processes right, as described in Chapter 12, is vital.

Cultural change

Cultural change aims to change the existing culture of an organization. Organizational or corporate culture is the system of values (what is regarded as important in organizational and individual behaviour) and accepted ways of behaviour (norms) which strongly influence 'the way things are done around here'. It is founded on well-established beliefs and assumptions.

Organizational culture is significant because it conveys a sense of identity and unity of purpose to members of an organization, facilitates the generation of commitment and helps to shape behaviour by providing guidance on what is expected. It can work for an organization by creating an environment which is conducive to high performance. It can work against an organization by encouraging unproductive behaviour. Strong cultures will have been formed over a considerable period of time and have more widely shared and more deeply held beliefs than weak ones. Strong cultures are only appropriate if they promote desirable behaviour. If they don't, they are inappropriate and must be changed.

A deeply rooted culture may be difficult to change – old habits die hard. Deal and Kennedy (6) said that there are only five reasons to justify large-scale cultural change:

1. If the organization has strong values that do not fit a changing environment.
2. If the industry is very competitive and moves with lightning speed.
3. If the organization is mediocre or worse.
4. If the company is about to join the ranks of the very largest companies.
5. If the company is small but growing rapidly.

They say that if none of these reasons apply, don't do it. Their analysis of 10 cases of attempted cultural change indicated that it will cost between 5 and 10 per cent of what you already spend on the people whose behaviour is supposed to change and even then you are likely to get only half the improvement you want. They warn that it costs a lot in effort and money and will take a long time.

Cultural change may mean ensuring that the organization has what John Purcell and his colleagues at Bath University (7) called 'the big idea'. Their research established that this is what the most successful companies possessed. They had a clear vision and a set of integrated values which were embedded, enduring, collective, measured and managed. They were concerned with sustaining performance and flexibility.

Cultural change involves developing a more appropriate set of the values which influence behaviour and ensuring that people 'live the values'. The problem is that there may be a large difference between the values espoused by an organization and the ways in which they are or are not applied – values in use. Gratton and Hailey (8) found through their research that there was generally a wide divergence between the rhetoric of managements about core values and the reality of their application – the 'rhetoric–reality gap'. Managements may start off with good intentions but the realization of them – theory in use – is often very difficult. This arises because of contextual and process problems: other business priorities, short-termism, lack of support from line managers, an inadequate infrastructure of supporting processes, lack of resources, resistance to change, and a climate in which employees do not trust management, whatever they say. It is therefore advisable to be cautious about 'big bang' cultural change projects. An incremental, gradualist approach which focuses on behavioural change (see below) may be more realistic. The aim is to close or at least reduce the rhetoric–reality gap.

If it is believed that a major cultural change programme is required it should not be too ambitious. However, it can be conducted systematically in the following sequence of activities:

1. *Analysis* of the current situation in terms of environment, strategy, performance, culture, structure, systems and processes, and the availability and quality of resources – human, financial and material.
2. *Diagnosis* of the causes of any problems identified by the analysis that will need to be overcome.
3. *Action planning* – the preparation of plans to change or reinforce the culture and deal with the requirements and problems. Plans may deal with specifically cultural matters such as creating and disseminating mission and value statements and ensuring that they are acted upon. Or they may be concerned with human capital factors such as the skills, behaviour, motivation and commitment of people. Alternatively, action plans may address issues concerning organizational processes such as the development of continuous improvement and total quality programmes, provisions for achieving higher standards of customer service, or performance management.
4. *Implementation* – delivering the results required by the action plan.

Behavioural change

Behavioural change involves taking steps to encourage people to be more effective by shaping or modifying the ways in which they carry out their work. Organizations depend on people behaving in ways which will contribute to high performance and support core values. They must recognize that people at work often have discretion on the way they do their work and the amount of effort, care, innovation and productive behaviour they display. Expectations of what sort of discretionary behaviour is considered desirable need to be defined and encouraged to attain behavioural commitment – people directing their efforts to achieving organizational and role objectives.

Behavioural expectations can be defined in the form of a set of values such as the core values of the Scottish Parliament:

Integrity	We demonstrate high standards of honesty and reliability.
Impartiality	We are fair and even-handed in dealing with members of the public and each other.
Professionalism	We provide high quality professional advice and support services.
Client focus	We are responsive to the needs of members, the public and one another.
Efficiency	We use resources responsibly and cost-effectively.
Mutual respect	We treat everyone with respect and courtesy and take full account of equal opportunities issues at all times.

Competency frameworks can also be developed which define behavioural requirements under such headings as:

- team working;
- leadership;
- developing others;
- quality focus;
- customer focus;
- results orientation;
- initiative;
- business awareness.

Behavioural change can be achieved by getting people involved in setting objectives, giving them more responsibility to manage their own jobs as individuals or as teams (empowerment) and providing for rewards to be clearly related to success in achieving agreed goals. The following sequence of behavioural modification steps as defined by Luthans and Kreitner (9) can be adopted:

1. Identify the critical behaviour – what people do or do not do which needs to be changed.
2. Measure the frequency – obtain hard evidence that a real problem exists.
3. Carry out a functional analysis – identify the stimuli that precede the behaviour and the consequences in the shape of reward or punishment which influence the behaviour.

4. Develop and implement an intervention strategy – this may involve the use of positive or negative reinforcement to influence behaviour (ie providing or withholding financial or non-financial rewards).
5. Evaluate the effects of the intervention – what improvements, if any, happened and if the interventions were unsuccessful, what needs to be done next?

Organizational development (OD) processes can also be used. These involve the planning and implementation of programmes designed to improve the effectiveness with which an organization functions and responds to change. Organizational development is concerned with process, not structure or systems – with the way things are done rather than what is done. Process refers to the ways in which people act and interact. It is about the roles they play on a continuing basis to deal with events and situations involving other people and to adapt to changing circumstances.

HOW CHANGE HAPPENS

Change, as Rosabeth Moss Kanter (10) puts it, is the process of analysing 'the past to elicit the present actions required for the future'. It involves moving from a present state through a transitional state to a future state.

The starting point is an analysis of the here and now. This can take the form of an assessment of strengths and weaknesses which will be based on an understanding of what is happening, how it is happening and what effect it has. A diagnosis of the causes of any problems follows the analysis. The desirable outcome of any change – the future state – can then be specified. This forms the basis for defining of the objectives of the change programme. Options – alternative courses of action – can then be considered and a choice made of the action which usually, on balance, seems to provide the best chance of achieving the objectives of change.

It is then necessary to consider how to get from here to there. This is the transitional state and managing the transition is the most challenging stage in introducing change. It is here that the problems emerge and have to be managed. These problems can include resistance to change, low stability, high levels of stress, misdirected energy, conflict and loss of momentum. The transitional stage leads to implementation which, as described by Pettigrew and Whipp (11), is an 'iterative, cumulative and reformulation-in-use process'.

ORGANIZATION DYNAMICS – HOW ORGANIZATIONS GROW AND CHANGE

Equilibrium and stability are desirable qualities in organizations. But they are difficult to achieve and maintain. Organizations are in a constant stage of motion. They do not stand still. Disequilibrium and instability are frequently present in rapidly growing and changing organizations and have to be managed.

Equilibrium, stability and disequilibrium

Equilibrium exists in organizations when a balance is achieved between the competing claims of growth and stability. There is a constant battle to promote growth while at the same time consolidating advances so that they can be 'operationalized', that is, become a stable part of the normal operating processes of the organization so that continuity is attained and people become familiar with the requirements of the changed situation having acquired the necessary expertise in coping with them. Disequilibrium sets in when operational processes are no longer in balance, when new situations arise which cannot be managed effectively through the use of tried and tested techniques. To achieve stability while still maintaining growth requires the successful use of the change management approaches described in Chapter 12.

Stages of development

The pursuit of equilibrium and stability has to be carried out in dynamic organizations which inevitably go through successive stages of development. It is necessary to understand the stage which has been reached by an organization to determine how the changes can be managed without causing disruption in the shape of instability or disequilibrium. There are typically four stages of development:

1. *Start-up* – this is the stage at which a new organization is born. It may be a new venture launched by someone with a bright idea, a 'stand-alone' business resulting from diversification, or a business formed by a group of executives from one or more larger employers fired with the desire to create something new and leave behind the strictures of their old organization. The stage may last for several years and can involve rapid growth until the curve begins to flatten.
2. *Maturity* – a mature organization is one that has reached a fairly stable stage. Management, however, may still be responsive and flexible, reacting effectively to competitive pressure, proactively seeking new markets and products and developing its management processes and systems to grow and improve performance.
3. *Stagnation* – this is the stage organizations reach if they have grown too large and set in their ways to do anything other than maintain their market share and influence. Hierarchy and bureaucracy may have become a way of life and the organization becomes progressively more traditionalist in its management style and culture. Such organizations are often characterized by management teams that have grown up and matured together and have not sought actively to bring in new blood or to challenge their established assumptions and practices. In the UK,

many older, larger organizations and much of the public sector have been through this stage and are emerging from it in varying ways.

4. *Regeneration* – this stage follows the collapse of the 'old age' organization. It may start with a merger or a management buyout or the replacement of most of the top management. This enables it to pull together what is left, reorganize and head off in a new direction with renewed vigour. Organizations in this phase often have to operate in a constrained economic environment in the first years. The phase has much in common with the start-up stage except that the organization is not operating in a greenfield situation and may still have to tackle the remains of the past as well as the future. If regeneration fails, the organization will not survive – it will be taken over or wound up.

SUMMARY

- There are seven types of change: incremental, transformational, strategic, organizational, systems and processes, cultural, and behavioural.
- Incremental change is gradual change. It takes place in small steps at the operational as distinct from the strategic level.
- Transformational change is the process of ensuring that an organization can develop and implement major change programmes so that it responds strategically to new demands and continues to function effectively in the dynamic environment in which it operates. Organizational transformation activities may involve radical changes to the structure, culture and processes of the organization.
- Strategic change is concerned with broad, long-term and organization-wide issues. It is about moving to a future state which has been defined generally in terms of strategic vision and scope.
- Organizational change deals with how organizations are structured and, in broad terms, how they function.
- Changes to systems and processes affect operations and impact on working arrangements and practices in the whole or part of an organization. They take place when operating methods are revised, new technology is introduced or existing technology is modified. Changes to systems and processes affect the daily lives of people in the organization – the jobs they do, how they are required to do them and how they are treated. Their immediate impact may therefore be as high as, if not higher than, strategic or organizational change and they have to be handled just as carefully.
- Cultural change aims to change the existing culture of an organization. It involves developing a more appropriate set of the values which influence behaviour.
- Behavioural change involves taking steps to encourage improved performance from people by shaping or modifying the ways in which they behave.

- Change is the process of moving from a present state through a transitional state to a future state.
- Equilibrium and stability are desirable qualities in organizations. But they are difficult to achieve and maintain.
- Equilibrium exists in organizations when a balance is achieved between the competing claims of growth and stability.
- The pursuit of equilibrium and stability has to be carried out in dynamic organizations which inevitably go through successive stages of development.
- The four stages of development are start-up, maturity, stagnation and regeneration.

REFERENCES

1 Sloan, A P (1967) *My Years with General Motors*, Pan Books, London
2 Quinn, J B (1980) Managing strategic change, *Sloane Management Review*, **11** (4/5), pp 3–30
3 Pascale, R (1990) *Managing on the Edge*, Viking, London
4 Child, J (1977) *Organization: A guide to problems and practice*, Harper & Row, London
5 Ghoshal, S and Bartlett, C A (1995) Changing the role of top management: beyond structure to process, *Harvard Business Review*, Jan–Feb, pp 86–96
6 Deal, T and Kennedy, A (1982) *Corporate Cultures*, Addison-Wesley, Reading, MA
7 Purcell, J, Kinnie, K, Hutchinson, S, Rayton, B and Swart, J (2003) *Understanding the People and Performance Link: Unlocking the black box*, CIPD, London
8 Gratton, L A and Hailey, V H (1999) The rhetoric and reality of new careers, in *Strategic Human Resource Management*, ed L Gratton, V H Hailey, P Stiles and C Truss, Oxford University Press, Oxford
9 Luthans, F and Kreitner, R (1975) *Organizational Behaviour Modification*, Scott-Foresman, Glenview, IL
10 Kanter, R M (1984) *The Change Masters*, Allen & Unwin, London
11 Pettigrew, A and Whipp, R (1991) *Managing Change for Competitive Success*, Blackwell, Oxford

11

The context of change

To manage change effectively it is necessary not only to understand the process of change as described in the last chapter but also to analyse the context within which change takes place. This context, as examined in this chapter, consists of organizations in which change takes place and which have to be designed, modified and maintained, the different types of organizations, the process of developing and maintaining structures and systems, the various organization functions (the activities and processes carried out within organizations), the organizational culture, which strongly influences 'the way things are done around here' and therefore how change is managed, and the processes of exercising power and authority as they influence the delivery of change.

THE BASIS OF ORGANIZATION

Organizations exist to get things done. They are entities which are there for a purpose. They consist of people whose activities, if they are carried out properly, ensure that the organization achieves that purpose. Responsibility for activities and decision making is allocated to individuals and groups and arrangements are made to plan, direct, coordinate and control them.

Organizations can be regarded as open systems which transform inputs into outcomes and are continually dependent on and influenced by their environments. The issues they face relate to structure, relationships and interdependence. The socio-technical model of organizations developed by the Tavistock Institute researchers (1) develops basic open systems theory by expressing the principle that in any system of organization, technical or task aspects are interrelated with the human or social aspects. The emphasis is on relationships between, on the one hand, the technical processes of transformation carried out within the organization and, on the other hand, the organization of work groups and the management structures of the enterprise.

The relationships in an organization may be described in an organization chart which sets out lines of command and control – this is the formal organization. But organizations also function informally through networks of relationships involving cooperation, communication and the exercise of authority and power.

Organization structures

Organization structures provide the framework for the activities required to achieve these goals. They have been defined by Child (2) as comprising 'all the tangible and regularly occurring features which help to shape its members' behaviour'. They define and clarify how the activities required are grouped together into units, functions and departments, who is responsible for what, who reports to whom and the lines of authority emanating from the top of the organization.

Organizing

Organizing can be described as the design, development and maintenance of a system of coordinated activities in which individuals and groups of people work cooperatively together under leadership towards commonly understood and accepted goals. The management of people in organizations constantly raises questions such as 'Who does what?', 'How should activities be grouped together?', 'What lines and means of communication need to be established?'

The process of organizing may involve the grand design or redesign of the total structure, but most frequently it is concerned with the organization of particular functions and activities and the basis upon which the relationships between them are managed. The aim is to optimize the arrangements for conducting the affairs of the business.

Organizations are not static things. Changes are constantly taking place in the business itself, in the environment in which the business operates, and in the people who work in the business, and these changes have to be managed. There is no such thing as an 'ideal' organization. The most that can be done is to optimize the processes involved, remembering that whatever structure evolves it will be contingent on the environmental circumstances of the organization, and one of the aims of organization is to achieve the 'best fit' between the structure and these circumstances.

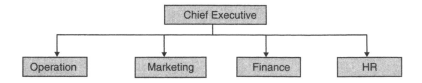

Figure 11.1 A unitary organization structure

An important point to bear in mind is that organizations consist of people working more or less cooperatively together. Inevitably, and especially at managerial levels, the organization may have to be adjusted to fit the particular strengths and attributes of the people available. The result may not conform to the ideal, but it is more likely to work than a structure that ignores the human element. It is always desirable to have an ideal structure in mind, but it is equally desirable to modify it to meet particular circumstances, as long as there is awareness of the potential problems that may arise.

TYPES OF ORGANIZATIONS

The basic types of organization structures can be classified as unitary, divisionalized, centralized, decentralized, matrix and process.

Unitary structures

Unitary structures are those that exist as single and separate units which have not been subdivided into divisions. In such structures the heads of each major function usually report directly to the top, although organizations may differ in defining what these key functions are. A unitary structure is illustrated in Figure 11.1.

This is the most common structure. It is simple and relationships are clearly defined. However, there is an ever-present risk of lack of cooperation between functions or departments and, to avoid this, the chief executive has a key role in coordinating as well as directing activities.

Centralized structures

A centralized structure is one where authority is located at the centre which exercises total control over the activities and decisions of any divisions, subsidiaries or regionalized units. This control is exercised by authority emanating from headquarters. This

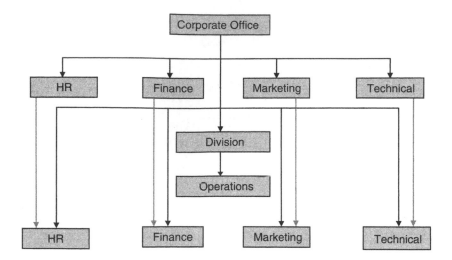

Figure 11.2 A centralized organization structure

defines policies, procedures, targets and budgets which have to be followed and achieved. A centralized structure is illustrated in Figure 11.2.

In a centralized structure close control can be maintained over divisional activities, standardized procedures and systems can be used and guidance is provided by functional specialists at headquarters. The disadvantage is that centralization restricts the scope of divisional management to handle their own affairs in the light of local knowledge, and the lack of autonomy in divisions can constrain initiative and entrepreneurship.

Decentralized organizations

In a decentralized or divisionalized organization, divisions, subsidiaries or strategic business units (SBUs) are given operational autonomy under the overall direction of the centre in order to achieve required results. The amount of autonomy might be constrained to a degree by group financial, marketing, operational or HR policies and there could be restrictions on the activities carried out or the markets served. Headquarters functions might be staffed by only a few specialists in such activities as finance, taxation, legal and HR who deal with matters concerning the organization as a whole, for example preparing consolidated accounts and monitoring financial performance. In some organizations there may also be central technical or research and development facilities providing services to operational divisions. A decentralized organization is illustrated in Figure 11.3.

Conglomerates are in a sense decentralized organizations, the difference being that the businesses grouped together in a conglomerate operate entirely independently

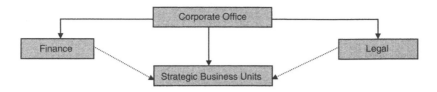

Figure 11.3 A decentralized organization structure

and their only obligation to the holding company is to achieve financial targets and increase shareholder value.

The advantage of decentralization is that divisions or strategic business units can manage their own affairs on the basis of particular knowledge of their products, services or markets without undue interference from the centre. They can respond quickly and appropriately to specialized or local demands. The disadvantages are that the centre might not be able to exercise enough control and activities which could be carried out more effectively or economically in the centre might be duplicated in divisions.

Matrix organizations

Matrix organizations carry out projects in such fields as contracting, research and development, and consultancy. Staff from various disciplines, for example electrical and mechanical engineering in a contracting firm or finance and IT in a consultancy one, are assigned to projects. When a project is set up a project leader is appointed and draws staff from the appropriate disciplines. Project leading may be a full-time occupation or leaders may be senior specialists from the key project disciplines. While working on the project team, members are responsible to the project leader for the project work they do, but the functional head of the discipline has a general responsibility for ensuring that proper standards are maintained by discipline members. The latter continue to be functionally responsible to the head of the discipline and when a project ends they return to the discipline until they are assigned to a new project. The head of the discipline is responsible for the recruitment and career development of specialist staff and for making decisions about their promotion and pay. Thus, while on a project, individuals are placed in the matrix intersection, being responsible on a day-to-day basis to the project leader but continuing to be functionally responsible to the head of their discipline. A matrix organization is illustrated in Figure 11.4.

Matrix organizations are appropriate in project-based organizations which need to assemble teams drawn from different disciplines so that they respond quickly and flexibly to new demands. They can draw on experienced project managers and provide individuals with varied experience. Their downside is that there is no continuity

		Disciplines			
		A	B	C	D
Project teams	1	●		●	
	2		●		●
	3	●	●	●	
	4		●	●	●

Figure 11.4   A matrix organization

in team leadership or membership. They can therefore be fragmented and difficult to manage and control.

Process-based organizations

A process-based organization is one in which the focus is on horizontal processes that cut across organizational boundaries. There will still be designated functions for, say, operations, marketing and distribution. But the emphasis will be on how these areas work together on multi-functional projects or how a smooth flow of work can be maintained between functions. Part of a process-based organization is illustrated in Figure 11.5.

Process-based organizations are the 'boundaryless' organizations favoured by Jack Welch at General Electric. He used to say that boundaryless behaviour evaluates ideas based on their merit, not on the rank of the person who came up with them. They abolish the vertical 'chimneys' in traditional organizations which inhibit the free flow of ideas and prejudice teamwork, provide for the smooth flow of work between and across functions to meet customer demands and enhance the thrust for quality and cost-effectiveness. They can, however, obscure and diffuse responsibility.

DEVELOPMENT AND MAINTENANCE OF ORGANIZATION STRUCTURES AND SYSTEMS

Organization reviews

Organization reviews provide the basis for developing and maintaining structures in the light of the constantly changing internal and external environment in which organizations operate. They may involve decentralization or centralization, delayering, the regrouping of activities, the reallocation of responsibilities, or the creation of new functions. Internally, changes may be required because of product and market developments, mergers and acquisitions and a belief that the present structure is clearly not working effectively. They often happen because top management is disillusioned with a previous reorganization, for example if they feel that excessive decentralization has

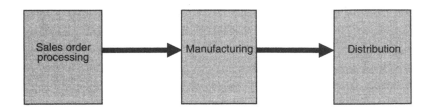

Figure 11.5   A process-based organization

prevented them from exercising sufficient control. Sometimes changes seem to take place for change's sake or because management is adopting a fashionable approach such as developing a process-based organization or delayering. There is a saying amongst management consultants that much of their work in this area arises from the following sequence of events: organization – disorganization – reorganization. Changes also take place when chief executives have a remit to transform or regenerate the organization and want to impose their concept about how the business should be structured.

Externally, the impetus for change arises from competition, financial difficulties, pressure from financial institutions (the City) or the government, and the creation of new markets or changes to existing markets.

Organization reviews are conducted in the following stages:

1. An analysis, as described below, of the existing arrangements and the factors which may affect the organization now and in the future.
2. A diagnosis of what needs to be done to improve the way in which the organization is structured and functions.
3. A plan to implement any revisions to the structure emerging from the diagnosis, possibly in phases. The plan may include longer-term considerations about the structure and the type of managers and employees who will be required to operate within it.
4. Implementation of the plan.

Organization analysis

The starting point for an organization review is an analysis of the existing circumstances, structure and processes of the organization and an assessment of the strategic issues that might affect it in the future. This covers:

● *The external environment* – the economic, market and competitive factors that may affect the organization. Plans for product-market development will be significant.

- *The internal environment* – the mission, values, organization climate, management style, technology and processes of the organization as they affect the way it functions and should be structured to carry out those functions. Technological developments in such areas as cellular manufacturing may be particularly important, as well as the introduction of processes such as the development of an entirely new computer system.
- *Strategic objectives* – as a background to the study it is necessary to identify the strategic objectives of the organization. These may be considered under such headings as growth, competition and market position and standing. Issues concerning the availability of the required human, financial and physical resources would also have to be considered.
- *Activities* – activity analysis covers what is and is not being done, who is doing it and where, and how much is being done. An answer is necessary to the key questions: 'Are all the activities required properly catered for?' 'Are there any unnecessary activities being carried out, ie those which do not need to be done at all or those which could be outsourced – conducted more economically and efficiently by external contractors or providers?'
- *Structure* – the analysis of structure covers how activities are grouped together, the number of levels in the hierarchy, the extent to which authority is decentralized to divisions and strategic business units (SBUs), where functions such as finance, HR and research and development are placed in the structure (eg as central functions or integrated into divisions or SBUs) and the relationships that exist between different units and functions, with particular attention being given to the way in which they communicate and cooperate with one another. Attention would be paid to such issues as the logic of the way in which activities are grouped and decentralized, the span of control of managers (the number of separate functions or people they are directly responsible for), any overlap between functions or gaps leading to the neglect of certain activities, and the existence of unnecessary departments, units, functions or layers of management.

Organization diagnosis

The diagnosis should be based on the analysis and an agreement by those concerned on what the aims of the organization should be. The present arrangements can be considered against these aims and future requirements to assess the extent to which they meet them or fall short.

It is worth repeating that there are no absolute standards against which an organization structure can be judged. There is never one right way of organizing anything and there are no absolute principles which govern organizational choice. The fashion for delayering organizations had much to commend it but it often went too far, leaving units and individuals adrift without any clear guidance on where they fit into the structure and how they should work with one another.

Organization guidelines

There are no absolute principles of organization but there are certain guidelines which are worth bearing in mind at all stages in an organization study. These are set out in Chapter 4 (pages 34–35).

Organization planning

Organization design leads into organization planning, the process of converting the analysis into the design. It determines structure, relationships, roles, human resource requirements and the lines along which changes should be implemented. There is no one best design. There is always a choice between alternatives. Logical analysis will help in the evaluation of the alternatives but the law of the situation will have to prevail. The final choice will depend upon the present and future circumstances of the organization. It will be strongly influenced by personal and human considerations, including the inclinations of top management, the strengths and weaknesses of management generally, the availability of people to staff the new organization and, importantly, the need to ensure that change management approaches are used to ensure that change takes place reasonably smoothly and to take account of the feelings of those who will be exposed to change. Cold logic may sometimes have to override these considerations. If it does, then it must be deliberate and the consequences must be appreciated and allowed for when planning the implementation of the new organization.

It may have to be accepted that a logical regrouping of activities cannot be introduced in the short term because no one with the experience is available to manage the new activities, or because capable individuals are so firmly entrenched in one area that to uproot them would cause serious damage to their morale and would reduce the overall effectiveness of the new organization.

The worst sin that organization designers can commit is that of imposing their own ideology on the organization. Their job is to be eclectic in their knowledge, sensitive in their analysis of the situation and deliberate in their approach to the evaluation of alternatives.

Having planned the organization and defined structures, relationships and roles, it is necessary to consider how the new organization should be implemented. It may be advisable to stage an implementation over a number of phases, especially if new people have to be found and trained.

Developing and maintaining systems

Organizations are run by people with the help of systems. A system is an interlinked set of related processes or methodologies designed and operated to achieve defined results. Systems may be operational or administrative systems which define how a sequence of operations or administrative activities should be carried out and provide the supporting processes required. These include the processes required to deliver a product or service to an internal or external customer. Typical processes are fulfilling a customer order, issuing a new insurance policy, developing a new product or setting up a new retail outlet. Other examples of systems are IT systems using computers to process and provide data, financial systems such as budgetary control, and reward systems which group together a number of related reward activities to achieve the aims of an organization's reward strategy.

The development of systems is carried out by identifying needs, defining the objectives, developing a specification of what the system must be able to do, reviewing and evaluating options for the design and features of the system, setting up a project with the resources required and a staged programme of work, managing the project and implementing the system. Systems are maintained by monitoring how well they meet the original demands and establishing their capacity to respond to new demands.

Because systems impact strongly on the way people work, changes to existing arrangements may be resisted or at least accepted unwillingly. Change management techniques as described in the next chapter are therefore necessary to gain understanding and agreement.

The technique of Business Process Re-engineering (BPR) emerged in the 1990s as an approach to systems design. As originally conceived it was concerned with the systematic analysis and redesign of business processes in order to achieve significant improvement in performance in terms of quality, service, speed and cost. It focused on processes rather than function or tasks as the basis for the design and management of business activities. It could involve fundamental rethinking, radical streamlining or the total redesign of a process from its beginning within the organization to its end with the customer.

BPR became very popular, but like other management fashions such as management-by-objectives and output budgeting it promised more than it achieved. Large BPR projects often failed to deliver. However, the problem was not the BPR concept, which is valid to the extent to which it involves systematic analysis and focuses on work flows rather than isolated activities. What often went wrong was that insufficient attention was paid to the human factor. Many practitioners seemed to be unaware of the fact that change needed careful management and that it could only be achieved through people who had to believe that the change was necessary and would not disadvantage them.

ORGANIZATION FUNCTIONS

Change affects the ways in which functions operate in organizations within the structural framework and it is therefore necessary to understand the basic features of the main functions, namely: operations, administration, manufacturing, marketing, sales, research and development, finance, IT, HR (human resources) and supplies.

Operations management

Operations management is concerned with the planning, direction and control of the fundamental activities which the organization exists to carry out. These activities will be to make, provide or sell products or services to customers, clients or the public at large.

Administration

Administration is the process of delivering the services required by internal and external customers and clients and, in the case of public sector organizations, the public generally. It is concerned with the day-to-day management and operation of processes and systems and with ensuring that the activities required to deliver services are carried out effectively. Administration may involve processing and using the data provided by computers and dealing with the paperwork which, in spite of IT, still exists in huge quantities in many organizations.

Production management

Production management involves the procurement, deployment and use of resources to manufacture products for distribution and sale to customers. It transforms inputs in the shape of raw materials and bought-in or subcontracted parts into outputs in the form of finished goods. Production management activities include production engineering, process planning, production planning, production control, quality management, inventory control and planned maintenance.

Marketing

Marketing identifies, anticipates, influences and satisfies the wants and needs of customers profitably. It involves activities such as marketing planning, product development, advertising, marketing research and product market analysis.

Selling

Selling is the process of persuading customers to buy and continue to buy the products or services of the business.

Research and development

Research and development (R&D) designs and develops new products or services and modifies existing ones to create or satisfy customer needs and wants now and in the future. It involves basic and applied research, development, testing and design.

Financial management

Financial management deals with the financial affairs of an organization, namely: financial planning, financial accounting (keeping the books and preparing financial reports and statements), management accounting (measuring and analysing financial performance) and managing cash flows.

Information technology (IT)

IT develops and operates systems for collecting, storing, processing and communicating data. This will include the specification and selection of hardware, the development of networks and the specification or development of software applications.

HR

HR is concerned with the management and development of people in ways that contribute to the achievement of organizational effectiveness and meet their needs for a satisfactory quality of working life, to be rewarded fairly, for security, and for the opportunity to use their abilities and develop their experience and skills. HR activities include resourcing, employee development, employee reward, employee relations and the administration of health and safety and other procedures.

Supplies management

Supplies management, also known as purchasing, procurement or buying, obtains the materials, plant, equipment and bought-in parts or assemblies required by the organization.

ORGANIZATIONAL CULTURE

Organizational or corporate culture as defined by Charles Handy (3) is the 'pervasive way of life or set of norms and values that evolve in an organization over a period of time'. Norms are unwritten but accepted rules which tell people in organizations how they are expected to behave. They may be concerned with such things as how managers deal with their staff (management style), how people work together, how hard people should work or the extent to which relationships should be formal or informal. Values are beliefs on how people should behave with regard to such matters as care and consideration for colleagues, customer service, the achievement of high performance and quality, and innovation.

Culture manifests in shared beliefs and in particular behaviours and is in turn influenced and modified by behaviour. T S Eliot made this point in *Notes Towards the Definition of Culture* when he wrote that 'What we believe in is not merely what we formulate and subscribe to... behaviour is also belief' (4).

Charles Handy (3) identified four types of culture:

1. *The power culture* in which there is a central power source which exercises control. There are few rules or procedures and the atmosphere is competitive, power orientated and political.
2. *The role culture* in which work is controlled by procedures and rules and the role, or job description, is more important than the person who fills it. Power is associated with positions, not people.
3. *The task culture* in which the aim is to bring together the right people and let them get on with it. Influence is based more on expert power than on position or personal power. The culture is adaptable and teamwork is important.
4. *The person culture* in which the individual is the central point. The organization exists only to serve and assist the individuals in it.

People's attitude to change will be influenced by the culture of their organization. It may provide an environment in which change is welcomed or it may inhibit change. Any attempt to change structures, systems or processes has to take account of the extent to which the new arrangements fit the culture and, if they don't, what needs to be done to ensure a closer fit or to change the culture.

POWER

Organizations exist to get things done and in the process of doing this people or groups exercise power. Directly or indirectly, the use of power in influencing behaviour is a pervading feature of organizations, whether it is exerted by managers, specialists, informal groups or trade union officials. The concept and use of power was discussed in Chapter 5 (pages 57–58).

From a change management viewpoint, power is important because the way it is exercised, possibly along the lines suggested by John Kotter, will make a significant impact on the effectiveness with which change is delivered.

AUTHORITY

Authority is the process of exerting influence on others in order to get things done. This is sometimes referred to as the 'authority to command'. The influence could be achieved by the exercise of power or by more subtle means. Charles Handy (5) advocates the development of a 'culture of consent' and the emphasis is on the virtues of decentralization, empowerment and self-managed teams.

Authority can be structured – vested in the role of manager – or it may be based on expertise or personal 'charisma'. There is also moral authority exercised on the basis of the 'rightness' of the action because it is ethical, fair or equitable. The term authority also refers to the right to make decisions or take action (authority to act).

Change management may require the exercise of authority to ensure that things get done. But developing and applying Handy's culture of consent is likely to be more effective in the long run.

SUMMARY

- Organizations exist to achieve results and in the process of doing this people or groups exercise power. Directly or indirectly, the use of power in influencing behaviour is a pervading feature of organizations, whether it is exerted by managers, specialists, informal groups or trade union officials.
- The relationships in an organization may be described in an organization chart which sets out lines of command and control – this is the formal organization. But organizations also function informally through networks of relationships involving cooperation, communication and the exercise of authority and power.
- Organization structures provide the framework for the activities required to achieve organizational goals.
- The process of organizing can be described as the design, development and maintenance of a system of coordinated activities in which individuals and groups of people work cooperatively together under leadership towards commonly understood and accepted goals.

- Organizations are not static things. Changes are constantly taking place in the business itself, in the environment in which the business operates, and in the people who work in the business, and these changes have to be managed.
- The basic types of organization structures can be classified as unitary, divisionalized, centralized, decentralized, matrix and process.
- Organization reviews provide the basis for developing and maintaining structures in the light of the constantly changing internal and external environment in which organizations operate. They may involve decentralization or centralization, delayering, the regrouping of activities, the reallocation of responsibilities, or the creation of new functions.
- The starting point for an organization review is an analysis of the existing circumstances, structure and processes of the organization and an assessment of the strategic issues that might affect it in the future.
- Organizational culture is defined by Charles Handy (3) as the 'pervasive way of life or set of norms and values that evolve in an organization over a period of time'.
- Norms are unwritten but accepted rules which tell people in organizations how they are expected to behave.
- Values are beliefs on how people should behave with regard to such matters as care and consideration for colleagues, customer service, the achievement of high performance and quality, and innovation.
- Organizations exist to achieve results and in the process of doing this people or groups exercise power. Directly or indirectly, the use of power in influencing behaviour is a pervading feature of organizations, whether it is exerted by managers, specialists, informal groups or trade union officials.
- Authority is the process of exerting influence on others in order to get things done. This is sometimes referred to as the 'authority to command'.

REFERENCES

1   Trist, E L *et al* (1963) *Organizational Choice*, Tavistock Publications, London
2   Child, J (1977) *Organization: A guide to problems and practice*, Harper & Row, London
3   Handy, C (1981) *Understanding Organizations*, Penguin Books, Harmondsworth
4   Eliot, T S (1985) *Notes Towards the Definition of Culture*, Faber & Faber, London
5   Handy, C (1989) *The Age of Unreason*, Business Books, London

12

Change management

Change management is the process of ensuring that an organization is ready for change and takes action to ensure that change is accepted and implemented smoothly. This chapter starts by examining the various models for change that have been developed to explain and assist in the process of managing it. It continues with a description of the ways in which people change, the steps to effective change, an analysis of the reasons why change is often resisted and an assessment of approaches to overcome resistance to change, especially involvement and communications. The central section of the chapter describes change management programmes and the chapter concludes with an analysis of the elements leading to the successful implementation of change.

CHANGE MODELS

A number of models have been developed to explain the process of change management and these are described and evaluated below.

Kurt Lewin

The basic mechanisms for managing change, as described by Kurt Lewin (1), are as follows:

- *Unfreezing* – altering the present stable equilibrium which supports existing behaviours and attitudes. This process must take account of the inherent threats change presents to people and the need to motivate those affected to attain the natural state of equilibrium by accepting change.
- *Changing* – developing new responses based on new information.
- *Re-freezing* – stabilizing the change by introducing the new responses into the personalities of those concerned.

Richard Beckhard

Richard Beckhard (2) explained that a change programme should incorporate the following processes:

- setting goals and defining the future state or organizational conditions desired after the change;
- diagnosing the present condition in relation to these goals;
- defining the transition state activities and commitments required to meet the future state;
- developing strategies and action plans for managing this transition in the light of an analysis of the factors likely to affect the introduction of change.

Keith Thurley

Keith Thurley (3) described the following five approaches to managing change:

1. *Directive* – the imposition of change in crisis situations or when other methods have failed. This is done by the exercise of managerial power without consultation.
2. *Bargained* – this approach recognizes that power is shared between the employer and the employed and change requires negotiation, compromise and agreement before being implemented.
3. *'Hearts and minds'* – an all-embracing thrust to change the attitudes, values and beliefs of the whole workforce. This 'normative' approach (ie one which starts from a definition of what management thinks is right or 'normal') seeks 'commitment' and 'shared vision' but does not necessarily include involvement or participation.
4. *Analytical* – a theoretical approach to the change process using models of change such as those described above. It proceeds sequentially from the analysis and diagnosis of the situation, through the setting of objectives, the design of the change process, the evaluation of the results and, finally, the determination of the objectives for the next stage in the change process. This is the rational and logical

approach much favoured by consultants – external and internal. But change seldom proceeds as smoothly as this model would suggest. Emotions, power politics and external pressures mean that the rational approach, although it might be the right way to start, is difficult to sustain.

5. *Action-based* – this recognizes that the way managers behave in practice bears little resemblance to the analytical, theoretical model. The distinction between managerial thought and managerial action blurs in practice to the point of invisibility. What managers think is what they do. Real life therefore often results in a 'ready, aim, fire' approach to change management. This typical approach to change starts with a broad belief that some sort of problem exists, although it may not be well defined. The identification of possible solutions, often on a trial and error basis, leads to a clarification of the nature of the problem and a shared understanding of a possible optimal solution, or at least a framework within which solutions can be discovered.

Commentary

The least known of the above models – that produced by Professor Keith Thurley of the London School of Economics – provides the best practical and realistic guidance on what change management is about. It is descriptive rather than analytical as is the case with the Lewin and Beckhard models.

HOW PEOPLE CHANGE

A helpful analysis of the ways in which people change was made by Bandura (4). He stated that:

1. People make conscious choices about their behaviours.
2. The information people use to make their choices comes from their environment.
3. Their choices are based upon the things that are important to them, the views they have about their own abilities to behave in certain ways and the consequences they think will accrue to whatever behaviour they decide to engage in.

In essence, this explanation of how people change suggests that change management approaches should spend time explaining the benefits of change to individuals on the grounds that people are more likely to behave in certain ways if they believe that they can alter their behaviour and that the outcome of that behaviour will produce a desirable outcome for them.

THE STEPS TO EFFECTIVE CHANGE

Michael Beer (5) and colleagues suggested that most change programmes are guided by a theory of change which is fundamentally flawed. This theory states that changes in attitudes lead to changes in behaviour. 'According to this model, change is like a conversion experience. Once people "get religion", changes in their behaviour will surely follow.' They believe that this theory gets the change process exactly backwards:

> In fact, individual behaviour is powerfully shaped by the organizational roles people play. The most effective way to change behaviour, therefore, is to put people into a new organizational context, which imposes new roles, responsibilities and relationships on them. This creates a situation that in a sense 'forces' new attitudes and behaviour on people.

They prescribe six steps to effective change which concentrate on what they call 'task alignment' – reorganizing employees' roles, responsibilities and relationships to solve specific business problems in small units where goals and tasks can be clearly defined. The aim of following the overlapping steps is to build a self-reinforcing cycle of commitment, coordination and competence. The steps are:

1. Mobilize commitment to change through the joint analysis of problems.
2. Develop a shared vision of how to organize and manage to achieve goals such as competitiveness.
3. Foster consensus for the new vision, competence to enact it, and cohesion to move it along.
4. Spread revitalization to all departments without pushing it from the top – don't force the issue, let each department find its own way to the new organization.
5. Institutionalize revitalization through formal policies, systems and structures.
6. Monitor and adjust strategies in response to problems in the revitalization process.

According to Beer and colleagues, this approach is fundamental to the effective management of change. But account should be taken of the likelihood of resistance to change and what can be done about it.

RESISTANCE TO CHANGE

Change management programmes have to take account of the fact that many people resist change. There are those who are stimulated by change and see it as a challenge and an opportunity. But they are in the minority. It is always easy for people to select any of the following 10 reasons for doing nothing:

1. It won't work.
2. We're already doing it.
3. It's been tried before without success.
4. It's not practical.
5. It won't solve the problem.
6. It's too risky.
7. It's based on pure theory.
8. It will cost too much.
9. It will antagonize the customers/management/the union/the workers/the shareholders.
10. It will create more problems than it solves.

Reasons for resistance to change

People resist change when they see it as a threat to their established and familiar life at work. They are used to their routines and patterns of behaviour and may be concerned about their ability to cope with new demands. They see change as a threat to familiar patterns of behaviour. They may believe that it will affect their status, security or earnings. They may not believe statements by management that the change is for their benefit as well as that of the organization; sometimes with good reason. They may feel that management has ulterior motives and sometimes, the louder the protestations of managements, the less they will be believed.

Joan Woodward (6) looked at change from the viewpoint of employees and wrote:

> When we talk about resistance to change we tend to imply that management is always rational in changing its direction, and that employees are stupid, emotional or irrational in not responding in the way they should. But if an individual is going to be worse off, explicitly or implicitly, when the proposed changes have been made, any resistance is entirely rational in terms of his best interest. The interests of the organization and the individual do not always coincide.

Overcoming resistance to change

Because resistance to change is natural and even inevitable it is difficult to overcome. But the attempt must be made. This starts with an analysis of the likely effect on change and the extent to which it might be resisted, by whom and why. Derek Pugh (7) points out that: 'It is not enough to think out what the change will be and calculate the benefits and costs from the proposer's point of view. The others involved will almost inevitably see the benefits as less and the costs as greater.' He recommends 'thinking through' the change and systematically obtaining answers to the following questions:

- Will the change alter job content?
- Will it introduce new and unknown tasks?
- Will it disrupt established methods of working?
- Will it rearrange group relationships?
- Will it reduce autonomy or authority?
- Will it be perceived to lower status?
- Will it be established without full explanation and discussion?

On the other side, it is necessary to answer the question: 'What are the benefits in pay, status, job satisfaction and career prospects which are generated by the change as well as the increase in performance?'

Resistance to change may never be overcome completely but it can be reduced through involvement and communications.

Involvement

Involvement in the change process gives people the chance to raise and resolve their concerns and make suggestions about the form of the change and how it should be introduced. The aim is to get 'ownership' – a feeling amongst people that the change is something that they are happy to live with because they have been involved in its planning and introduction – it has become *their* change. Involvement is important because people are more likely to own something they helped to create.

Communicating plans for change

Nadler (8) suggests that the first and most critical step for managing change is 'to develop and communicate a clear image of the future'. He believes that: 'Resistance and confusion frequently develop in an organizational change because people are unclear about what the future state will be like. Thus the goals and purposes of the change become blurred, and individual expectancies get formed on the basis of information that is frequently erroneous.'

Communications should describe why change is necessary, what the changes will look like, how they will be achieved and how people will be affected by them. The aim is to ensure that unnecessary fears are allayed by keeping people informed using a variety of methods – written communications, the intranet, videos and, best of all, face-to-face briefings and discussions.

DEVELOPING AND EMBRACING A CHANGE CULTURE

A positive change culture is one in which the values of the organization emphasize the importance of innovation and change and the norms of behaviour support the implementation of change. The existence of such a culture will assist in overcoming the problems associated with change, but the culture cannot be taken for granted. It will have been developed over time but can easily be damaged by an inept change management programme.

Change cultures result from the experiences of people who have undergone change. If they felt good about what happened they are more likely to embrace change in the future. And the opposite applies if change has consistently been mishandled. People embrace change when they are prepared to welcome it or at least judge it on its merits rather than resisting it automatically. Some people are more likely to embrace change than others because of their dispositions or their experiences. Others may be inherently suspicious of change but can be persuaded to accept it if the culture is right and they are dealt with properly.

For anyone to feel good about change, they must feel that they own the change – it hasn't been imposed upon them – and that they have benefited or at least not been harmed by it. They must be able to trust the organization because management has 'delivered the deal' – promises of what change would involve and how people would benefit have been kept. They must understand that organizations cannot stay still – change is inevitable – but at the same time appreciate that management is aware of the needs of the members of the organization as well as those of the organization itself.

IDENTIFYING THE NEED FOR CHANGE

A positive change culture provides the environment in which change can take place. But there is much to be done to manage change successfully. The first step in a change programme is to identify the need for change and to define why it is necessary. Effective reasons for change are those that are likely to be accepted by stakeholders – top management, middle management, employees generally and their trade union representatives. They must be persuaded that the change is necessary.

Strategic planning activities provide the most comprehensive basis for identifying the need for change. They can develop an integrated, coordinated and consistent view of the route the organization wishes to take and the changes needed to follow that route. Strategic planning also facilitates the adaptation of the organization to environmental change which can be manifested in such aspects as the company's position in the market (leading the market, maintaining or losing market share), competitors' tactics, customer behaviour and government policies. Identifying this need means environmental tracking – noting what is happening and is likely to happen, exploring the implications and deciding how the issues should be addressed. Proposals for changes because of environmental factors are more likely to be accepted if it can be demonstrated that the changes must take place and are appropriate and relevant.

The need for change may also emerge because of internal imperatives. This may be a proactive step arising from a review of areas for improvement. Or it may be a result of a systematic process of 'benchmarking' – finding out how other organizations are performing in certain areas – when as a result it becomes evident that the organization is falling behind in such areas as profitability, productivity, cost management, quality or levels of customer service.

Reactive or remedial change may be required to respond to internal problems, even crises. The need for change can be determined by events. A proactive approach to anticipating the need for change has not happened and something has to be done in a hurry (often a recipe for disaster).

The identification process should generate hard evidence and data on the need for change. These are the most powerful tools for its achievement, although establishing the need for change is easier than deciding how to satisfy it.

The drivers of change

Change, as mentioned above, can be driven by events – the need to change is forced upon the organization. More proactively, the driver for change may be an innovatory strategic plan or a positive response to environmental trends. Change may be inspired by an energetic and determined individual who wants to get things done. Continuous improvement programmes as described in Chapter 16 may drive incremental change.

THE BENEFITS AND RISKS OF CHANGE

Benefits of change

Clearly, the main benefit of effective change is an improvement in organizational performance. Organizations can stagnate or decay. They may only revive or survive if radical changes take place to their ways of doing things. Change can be stimulating. Resistance to change may be a matter of a reaction to the 'shock of the new', but there is also such a thing as 'the challenge of the new'. Fortunately, most organizations will have people who, if they wanted a motto, would quote Horace – *carpe diem* (seize the day). They will be stimulated by the opportunity presented by change to the benefit of the organization and their own career. As Peter Drucker (9) wrote: 'Opportunity is the source of innovation.'

Risks of change

There is a downside to change. It can go wrong because it is inappropriate or badly managed. Change can upset well-established and effective practices. The premise for change may be that if something is new it must be better, and this is by no means inevitable. There is such a thing as change for change's sake. Organizations can adopt the latest fashions or fads without thinking through their value or relevance to them. Failed changes can create a climate in which people become suspicious of any new ideas and unwilling to adopt them.

MAKING THE BUSINESS CASE FOR CHANGE

A business case sets out the reasons for doing something and the resulting benefits. The latter are expressed wherever possible in quantitative terms such as improvements in profitability, productivity, customer satisfaction or sales turnover. Proposals for change should always be based on a convincing business case supported by a practical programme for implementing the change and reaping the benefits. This again underlines the importance of thinking through a proposition. Thinking through means considering not only what needs to be done but also why it needs to be done, the quantified benefits it will produce, the likely reactions of people and how they should be dealt with, the objections that may be made and how they should be overcome, the resources required and the cost of implementation (a cost/benefit analysis).

PLANNING THE CHANGE PROGRAMME

The basis for a change programme will be the business case. This defines the broad aims of the change and how it is to be achieved. In more detail the programme needs to cover the following points.

Objectives

The goals to be achieved by the change should be discussed and agreed, wherever possible in quantified terms in the form of targets. If precise targets cannot be defined, then more generalized statements of the expected outcomes may have to be made, but these should be as specific as possible. It is often helpful to draw up success criteria so that everyone knows what they are striving to achieve and the extent to which the results have been achieved can be monitored and evaluated. A success criterion can be expressed in the form: 'This project (or aspect of the project) will be deemed to be successful if it delivers the following outcome...' It is important to involve as many people as possible in setting the objectives. This will increase their identification with the project and enhance their commitment.

Assessment of barriers to change and the development of solutions

The main barrier to change may be the sheer difficulty of planning and implementing a radical departure from the present ways of doing things. The difficulties have to be anticipated – no surprises later on – and approaches to dealing with them decided in advance. A major barrier to change may well be the objections of those exposed to it.

Kurt Lewin (1) produced a methodology for analysing change which he called 'field force analysis'. This involves:

- analysing the restraining and driving forces which will affect the transition to the future state – the restraining forces will include the reactions of those who see change as unnecessary or as constituting a threat;
- assessing which of the driving or restraining forces are critical;
- taking steps both to increase the critical driving forces and to decrease the critical restraining forces.

Defining responsibilities for managing change

The responsibility for managing change may be given to individual managers. This could be regarded as an important part of any manager's job and there is much to be said for making individuals accountable for results. In this role as defined by Pugh (7):

> An effective manager *anticipates* the need for change as opposed to reacting after the event to the emergency; *diagnoses* the nature of the change required and carefully considers a number of changes that might improve organizational functioning; and *manages* the change process over time so that it is effective and accepted as opposed to lurching from crisis to crisis.

Project teams or task forces can be set up to plan and implement change, the members of which would probably include managers and other people affected by the proposed change as well as specialists. Ultimately, however, someone has to be made accountable for the whole project. The task force can contribute to planning and decision making but cannot assume the final responsibility for making change happen.

It is often useful to identify people in the organization who welcome the challenges and opportunities that change can provide and can become 'champions for change'. They can act as 'change agents' with the role of facilitating change by providing advice to project teams or individuals. This role can also be fulfilled by management consultants who have expertise in the area in which change is to take place.

Organizations have sometimes used process consultants as change agents. The role of the process consultant as defined by Schein (10) is to 'help the organization to solve its own problems by making it aware of organizational processes, or the consequences of those processes and of the mechanisms by which they can be changed'. Processes such as inter-group or interpersonal relations and communications might be covered. Process consulting is one of the approaches which may be used in organization development (OD) programmes in which 'interventions' are made to increase the effectiveness of organizational processes. However, the massive and all-embracing OD programmes of the 1970s and 1980s have now been replaced by interventions which focus on more specific processes such as total quality management, performance management or customer relations management.

Project planning

Project planning:

- identifies all the activities in the project and the order in which they have to be done – the aim is to break the change programme down into actionable segments for which people can be held accountable;
- estimates the time for each activity, the total length of the project and the time when each activity must be finished;
- finds out how much flexibility there is in the timing of activities and which activities are critical to the completion time;
- estimates costs and schedules activities so that overall cost is minimized;
- allocates and schedules resources;
- anticipates problems and takes the actions required to avoid them.

Monitoring and evaluating progress

Reporting systems should be set up so that progress can be measured against the plan. Milestones that can be used to monitor the project should be identified. Progress should be evaluated against the agreed objectives. Checks should be made after the change has been implemented to ensure that it is providing the expected benefits. These may indicate the need to reinforce the change or to make minor modifications.

REQUIREMENTS FOR SUCCESS IN MANAGING CHANGE

Success in managing change depends largely on thinking through the reasons for change, project planning, allocating the right resources, finding the right people to act as change agents and anticipating and dealing with problems, especially resistance to change. It is a good idea positively to encourage those concerned to articulate their reservations. It is better for these to come out into the open so that they can be dealt with than to allow them to fester. It is advisable to bear in mind the comments of Pettigrew and Whipp (11) that change implies streams of activity across time and 'may require the enduring of abortive efforts or the build up of slow incremental phases of adjustment'. It is necessary to focus on short-term goals as well as longer-term deliverables. An incremental approach may well get better results in the long run than a 'big bang' approach. However, although flexible responses to new situations are important, it is necessary to avoid losing sight of long-term goals.

Success in change management often depends on a climate in which innovation is fostered. As Drucker (9) points out: 'change always provides the opportunity for the new and the different'. He went on to comment that: 'Systematic innovation therefore consists in the purposeful and organized search for changes, and in the systematic analysis of the opportunities such changes make for economic or social innovation' and that 'successful innovations *exploit* change'. However, innovation necessarily involves risk and successful innovators define risks and confine them.

Ultimately, however, successful change depends upon successful people management. It is necessary to understand and show empathy with their needs, feelings and motivation. Unless this is done, the risk of creating a negative climate which inhibits change is considerable.

ELEMENTS LEADING TO THE SUCCESSFUL IMPLEMENTATION OF CHANGE

The following guidelines on change management have been produced by General Electric. These are to ensure that:

- employees see the reason for change;
- employees understand why change is important and see how it will help them and the business in the long and short term;
- the people who need to be committed to the change to make it happen are recognized;
- a coalition of support is built for the change;
- the support of key individuals in the organization is enlisted;
- the link between the change and other HR systems such as staffing, training, appraisal, rewards, structure and communication is understood;
- the systems implications of the change are recognized;
- a means of measuring the success of the change is identified;
- plans are made to monitor progress in the implementation of change;

- the first steps in getting change started are recognized;
- plans are made to keep attention focused on the change;
- the likely need to adapt the change over time is recognized and plans can readily be made and implemented for such adaptations.

SUMMARY

- Change management is the process of ensuring that an organization is ready for change and takes action to ensure that change is accepted and implemented smoothly.
- The change model developed by Kurt Lewin (1) describes change management as the process of unfreezing, changing and re-freezing.
- The change model of Richard Beckhard (2) explained that a change programme should incorporate setting goals and defining the future state, diagnosing the present condition in relation to these goals, defining the transition state activities and developing strategies and action plans for managing this transition.
- Keith Thurley (3) described the following approaches to managing change: directive, bargained, 'hearts and minds', analytical and action based.
- Bandura (4) stated that people make conscious choices about their behaviours based upon the things that are important to them, their views about their abilities to behave in certain ways and what they think will be the consequences of their behaviour. This suggests that change management approaches should spend time explaining the benefits of change to individuals on the grounds that people are more likely to behave in certain ways if they believe that they can alter their behaviour and that the outcome of that behaviour will produce a desirable outcome for them.
- Michael Beer (5) and colleagues state that to be effective change should concentrate on 'task alignment' – reorganizing employees' roles, responsibilities and relationships to solve specific business problems in small units where goals and tasks can be clearly defined.
- Change management programmes have to take account of the fact that many people resist change.
- People resist change when they see it as a threat to their established and familiar life at work.
- To overcome resistance to change it is necessary to assess the likely effect on change and the extent to which it might be resisted, by whom and why. Involvement in the change process gives people the chance to raise and resolve their concerns and make suggestions about the form of the change and how it should be introduced. The aim is to get 'ownership'. Communicating plans for change should aim to allay unnecessary fears.

- A positive change culture is one in which the values of the organization emphasize the importance of innovation and change and the norms of behaviour support the implementation of change. The existence of such a culture will assist in overcoming the problems associated with change.
- Change cultures result from the experiences of people who have undergone change. If they felt good about what happened they are more likely to embrace change in the future. And the opposite applies if change has consistently been mishandled.
- The first step in a change programme is to identify the need for change and to define why it is necessary. Effective reasons for change are those that are likely to be accepted by stakeholders.
- Change may be inspired by an energetic and determined individual who wants to get things done. Continuous improvement programmes may drive incremental change.
- The main benefit of effective change is an improvement in organizational performance.
- Change can go wrong because it is inappropriate or badly managed.
- Proposals for change should be based on a convincing business case supported by a practical programme for implementing the change and reaping the benefits.
- The basis for a change programme will be the business case.
- The goals to be achieved by the change should be discussed and agreed, wherever possible, in quantified terms in the form of targets.
- Success criteria should be determined so that everyone knows what they are striving to achieve and the extent to which the results have been achieved can be monitored and evaluated.
- The main barrier to change may be the sheer difficulty of planning and implementing a radical departure from the present ways of doing things.
- A methodology for analysing change called 'field force analysis' as developed by Kurt Lewin (1) involves analysing the restraining and driving forces which will affect the transition to the future state, assessing which of the driving or restraining forces are critical and taking steps both to increase the critical driving forces and to decrease the critical restraining forces.
- The responsibility for managing change may be given to individual managers.
- Project teams or task forces can be set up to plan and implement change.
- 'Change agents' with the role of facilitating change by providing advice to project teams or individuals should be identified.
- Project planning identifies the activities in the project and the order in which they have to be done, estimates the time for each activity, finds out how much flexibility there is in the timing of activities and which activities are critical to the completion time, estimates costs, schedules activities and resources and anticipates problems.

- Reporting systems should be set up so that progress can be measured against the plan.
- Success in managing change depends largely on thinking through the reasons for change, project planning, allocating the right resources, finding the right people to act as change agents, and anticipating and dealing with problems, including resistance to change.

REFERENCES

1 Lewin, K (1951) *Field Theory in Social Science*, Harper & Row, New York

2 Beckhard, R (1969) *Organization Development: Strategy and models*, Addison-Wesley, Reading, MA

3 Thurley, K (1979) *Supervision: A reappraisal*, Heinemann, London

4 Bandura, A (1977) *Social Learning Theory*, Prentice-Hall, Englewood Cliffs, NJ

5 Beer, M, Eisenstat, R and Spector, B (1990) Why change programs don't produce change, *Harvard Business Review*, November–December, pp 158–66

6 Woodward, J (1968) Resistance to change, *Management International Review*, 8, pp 78–93

7 Pugh, D (1993) Understanding and managing organizational change, in *Managing Change*, 2nd edn, ed C Mabey and W Mayon-White, Chapman/Open University, London

8 Nadler, D A (1993) Concepts for the management of organizational change, in *Managing Change*, 2nd edn, ed C Mabey and W Mayon-White, Chapman/Open University, London

9 Drucker, P (1985) *Innovation and Entrepreneurship*, Heinemann, London

10 Schein, E H (1969) *Process Consultation: Its role in organizational development*, Addison-Wesley, Reading, MA

11 Pettigrew, A and Whipp, R (1991) *Managing Change for Competitive Success*, Blackwell, Oxford

Part III

Enhancing customer relations

13

Basis of customer service

THE NATURE OF CUSTOMER SERVICE

What is customer service?

A customer is anyone who purchases a product or service. By making that purchase, customers enter into a relationship with the supplier or provider who, if he or she wants to create a satisfied customer, is obliged to meet the customer's expectations. Customers can be distinguished from users, who simply take advantage of a service which is available to them, eg the National Health Service, clients with whom suppliers, eg management consultants, enter into a fiduciary relationship for the provision of paid advice or other services, and payers who, for example, are members of an accounts payable department and arrange the payment, eventually, for something another person has purchased. Users and clients expect good service and should be provided with the same level of service as other customers. Payers need to be treated with courtesy even if an invoice from a supplier has not been paid for three months or more (it may not be their fault).

Customer service is about all the activities carried out by organizations which meet customer needs and expectations. Needs will be expressed in terms of the types of products or services they want. Expectations will consist of what customers believe to be a satisfactory level of quality and reliable service in terms of providing what they want (service delivery), attention to their needs, value for money, speed in dealing satisfactorily with orders, enquiries and requests, level of support and after-sales service and willingness to listen to complaints and respond to them.

External and internal customers

It is often assumed that customer service programmes deal only with external customers. But internal customers are also important. Internal customers are the teams and individuals within an organization who rely on the services provided by others to carry out their work. The services may be provided by what are primarily service functions such as IT and HR, but operating departments also depend on each other.

Aims of customer service

The overall aim of customer service for external customers is to meet and exceed customer expectations in order to increase the profitability of a business or the effectiveness of a service provider organization. Specifically, the aim is to provide a reliable product to fit customer needs complemented by helpful and efficient service and support. This involves improving customer service by managing all customer contacts to mutual benefit and persuading customers to purchase again – not to switch brands or change to another supplier.

The aim for internal customers is to ensure that efficient services are provided for colleagues, bearing in mind that it is the customer who buys the products or services that matters and everyone's efforts within the organization should be channelled towards helping those at the 'sharp end' deliver the best possible service to the customer.

Product and process

Customer service is concerned with both product – what the customer actually gets, and process – the way in which the service is delivered. These two facets of customer service are closely interlinked. Customer satisfaction is only attained if they are both attended to.

Importance of customer service for external customers

It is not enough simply to offer what the organization believes to be good products or services to external customers. An organization will only succeed if its products or services meet consumer or user requirements. These may be expressed as service standards or targets in public sector or not-for-profit organizations, or quality, value for money and service-level expectations in private sector companies. If these are not met, a public or not-for-profit sector organization will be deemed to have failed in achieving its purposes, with adverse consequences for its future. In the private sector, poor levels of customer service will result in inability to attract and, importantly, retain customers and falling sales and therefore profitability, again with undesirable consequences for management and staff of such organizations.

The following ways in which customer care can increase profitability have been listed by Stone (1):

- less lost business;
- fewer lost customers;
- repeat sales through increased customer loyalty;
- better opportunities for communicating effectively with customers to increase sales;
- more scope to identify the potential for increasing revenue from existing customers;
- increased revenue and profit by targeting sales to customer needs;
- more revenue due to the ability of sales staff to concentrate on calling on higher revenue prospects;
- better and more efficient arrangements for service delivery and therefore lower staff and administration costs.

Importance of customer service for internal customers

Organizations cannot thrive, even survive, if levels of service for internal customers are poor. Organizations succeed and prosper by ensuring that cooperative effort is directed to achieving their goals. Departments and individuals depend on one another. Poor service between them can have a dire effect on performance and productivity and therefore on satisfying external customers.

Customer service priorities

The customer service ethos in an organization should be founded on the principle that everything that anyone does will ultimately impact on customers and that meeting their needs should be given priority. As the slogan in one retail organization put it: 'If you're not serving a customer, you should be serving someone who is.' This is a good reason for developing improved standards of service for internal customers as well as focusing on the needs and expectations of external customers. Customer service priorities should be reflected in statements of core values, training, performance management and reward policies and practices which influence the behaviour of employees to customers as well as developing better customer service processes.

CUSTOMER SERVICE ACTIVITIES

The following are the main customer service activities:

- ascertaining customer needs and expectations;
- using customer relationship management (CRM) processes to identify those needs and target sales;
- developing products and services that meet those needs and expectations;
- seeking and taking orders for products or services by advertising, promotions, direct selling, and the use of call centres or telesales;
- delivering the product or service effectively and efficiently;
- conducting interpersonal working relationships between employees and external customers and between individuals within the organization and their internal customers;
- setting standards and targets for customer service;
- developing customer service skills and influencing the behaviour of staff to customers;
- setting up customer service centres and websites;
- providing after-sales service – help, advice, repair and maintenance;
- dealing with customer queries and complaints;
- measuring the effectiveness of customer service and taking remedial action when necessary.

ELEMENTS OF CUSTOMER SATISFACTION

The aim of an organization's customer service policies and practices is to create and maintain customer satisfaction and retention. Loyal customers are worth nurturing. They buy more and buy more regularly. And the cost of selling to them is low whereas finding new customers can be expensive. Satisfied customers will recommend products and services to others. Dissatisfied customers will complain to as many as 10 other customers and potential customers.

To achieve and sustain customer satisfaction the following requirements must be met:

- *Quality* – the product or service meets customer expectations on the degree of quality they require by delivering what was promised. For products this will refer to such criteria as fitness for purpose, reliability, durability and low maintenance. For services it will be concerned with the achievement of an acceptable level of provision, reliability and accessibility.

- *Value for money* – the product or service meets customer requirements on value for money in the sense of giving them at least what they paid for and preferably more. Belief on whether value for money is provided will often be on a comparative basis, setting off one manufacturer or supplier against others.
- *Reliability* – customers are most likely to be satisfied when the manufacturer or supplier 'delivers the deal' by achieving a consistent level of performance and dependability.
- *Responsiveness* – increasingly, customers expect their supplier to be willing and ready to provide prompt service and help at the point of sale and afterwards. Individual attention, speed and flexibility are required.
- *Competence* – the supplier must have the required skills and knowledge to produce value for money and to provide a satisfactory level of service.
- *Access* – customers must be able to gain access to the supplier or provider with the minimum of trouble. They have learnt to put up with mechanized answering services but hate endless delays in getting through, listening to the *Four Seasons* and to seemingly insincere assurances that their custom is valued. They like to talk to human beings who will respond to their query or complaint.
- *Courtesy* – customers require politeness, respect, consideration and friendliness from the people they contact over the counter, in a call centre or when faced with a service problem.
- *Communication* – it is essential to keep customers informed, in language they can understand, about the product or service and how they can make quick and easy contact if they have a problem. It should be obvious that when they make contact they are listened to so that their specific query is dealt with quickly.
- *Credibility* – customers are more likely to be satisfied if they find as a result of their experiences that the supplier or provider is trustworthy, believable and honest. This is based on the knowledge and courtesy displayed by staff and their ability to inspire trust and confidence.
- *Security* – customers want to be confident that the product or service will be safe.
- *Tangibles* – physical facilities, equipment and staff appearance.

Changing customer dynamics and satisfaction

When considering how to satisfy customers it should be remembered that customer expectations tend to rise. They expect continually rising levels of service and more choice and will be dissatisfied if standards are only maintained at a level which they once found acceptable. Customers are changing the way in which they purchase, especially through the internet which gives them more choice and enables them to compare product prices and attributes. It should also be noted that other organizations improve the services they offer and competitive edge will be lost if these are not matched or preferably exceeded.

Simply to seek satisfaction is not enough. It is necessary to go beyond satisfaction by exceeding expectations in anticipation of what customers will want in the future and what competitors will be doing. It is for this reason that careful attention has to be given to how customer relations are managed and to assessing customer needs as discussed in the next chapter.

SUMMARY

- A customer is anyone who purchases a product or service. By making that purchase, customers enter into a relationship with the supplier or provider who, if he or she wants to create a satisfied customer, is obliged to meet the customer's expectations.
- Customer service is about all the activities carried out by organizations which meet customer needs and expectations.
- As well as external customers, internal customers are important. Internal customers are the teams and individuals within an organization who rely on the services provided by others to carry out their work.
- The aim of customer service for external customers is to meet and exceed customer expectations in order to increase the profitability of a business or the effectiveness of a service provider organization.
- The aim for internal customers is to ensure that efficient services are provided for colleagues.
- Customer service is concerned with both product – what the customer actually gets, and process – the way in which the service is delivered.
- An organization will only succeed if its products or services meet consumer or user requirements.
- Organizations cannot succeed if levels of service for internal customers are poor. Departments and individuals depend on one another. Poor service between them can have a dire effect on performance and productivity and therefore on satisfying external customers.
- The customer service ethos in an organization should be founded on the principle that everything that anyone does will ultimately impact on customers and that meeting their needs should be given priority.
- The main customer service activities are ascertaining customer needs and expectations, using customer relationship management (CRM) processes to identify those needs and target sales, developing products and services that meet those needs and expectations, seeking and taking orders for products or services by advertising, promotions, direct selling, and the use of call centres or telesales, delivering the product or service effectively and efficiently, conducting interpersonal working relationships between employees and external customers and

between individuals within the organization and their internal customers, setting standards and targets for customer service, developing customer service skills and influencing the behaviour of staff to customers, setting up customer service centres and websites, providing after-sales service – help, advice, repair and maintenance, dealing with customer queries and complaints, measuring the effectiveness of customer service and taking remedial action when necessary.

● To achieve and sustain customer satisfaction it is necessary to ensure that the product or service: (1) meets customer expectations on the degree of quality they require, (2) provides value for money, and (3) achieves a consistent level of performance and dependability. It is also necessary to be willing and ready to provide prompt service and help at the point of sale and afterwards. Courteous and competent attention, speed and flexibility are also required.

● It is necessary to go beyond satisfaction by exceeding expectations in anticipation of what customers will want in the future and what competitors will be doing.

REFERENCE

1   Stone, M (1997) Evaluating the profitability of customer service, in *The Gower Handbook of Customer Service*, ed P Marley, Gower, Aldershot

14

Approaches to customer service

A systematic approach is required to ensure the delivery of high standards of customer service for external customers. Fundamentally, as described below, this means that the organization has to create and maintain good relationships with customers in order to ensure that they will continue to want the goods or services provided by the organization because their expectations have been met. It is not enough for a commercial company to obtain customers; they must be retained as well by establishing a continuing relationship which satisfies their needs and thus contributes to business success. This attitude to customer service is just as important in organizations in the public sector such as local authorities and NHS Trusts where they are expected to achieve defined customer service standards. Not-for-profit organizations such as housing associations and charities are equally concerned in meeting the needs of their customers or clients, for example when they contract with an international or public sector organization to provide certain services.

The approach outlined above is the basis for the customer service activities discussed in this chapter, namely:

- manage customer relationships;
- assess customer needs and expectations;
- identify target customers;

- communicate the availability and benefits of goods and services;
- measure customer satisfaction and enter into dialogues with customers;
- develop products or services that will meet customer needs and increase or at least maintain customer satisfaction;
- provide the required infrastructure for customer service;
- evaluate models of customer service;
- set standards for customer service;
- monitor the delivery of those standards;
- take whatever steps are required to build customer satisfaction and therefore to keep customers.

The actions necessary to meet the needs of internal customers are also examined in this chapter.

In the next chapter a more detailed analysis is made of methods of achieving high levels of customer service by developing customer service strategies, creating a customer-centric culture and developing customer service skills and appropriate behaviours.

MANAGING RELATIONSHIPS WITH CUSTOMERS

An effective approach to customer service means that the organization must establish and maintain good relationships with customers – instilling confidence that their requirements will be met, on time, with cost-effective solutions and adequate support availability. To do this, it is first necessary to understand what these requirements are, and then take steps through the development of the products and services required, targeting individual customers as much as possible, developing a customer-centric culture and providing the infrastructure in the shape of the required delivery (order processing and fulfilment) and customer support systems.

Managing relationships with customers is conducted by what is known as relationship marketing. This is an approach to marketing which emphasizes the continuing relationships which should exist between the organization and its customers, with the emphasis on customer service and quality. Relationship marketing is therefore a concept which adds customer service and quality to the traditional marketing mix of product, price, promotion and place.

Description of the concept of relationship management

The term 'relationship management' was first formulated by Theodore Levitt in *The Marketing Imagination* (1). He suggested that the relationship between a seller and a buyer seldom ends when the sale is made. He wrote: 'In a great and increasing proportion of transactions, the relationship actually intensifies after the sale. This becomes the central choice in the buyer's choice of the seller the next time round.' According to Levitt, the relationship between the buyer and the seller is 'inextricable, inescapable and profound'.

Objectives of relationship marketing

The three objectives of customer relationship marketing are:

1. to achieve competitive advantage by creating value for the organization's customers;
2. to ensure that enough value is created in the sale to bring customers back for more;
3. to build and maintain mutually satisfying relationships with customers.

Essence of relationship marketing

The essence of relationship marketing is the concept of the value chain developed by Michael Porter (2) as a tool to identify which of an organization's activities are strategically relevant. The value chain consists of five activities:

1. *inbound logistics* – the reception, storage and internal transport of inputs to the product;
2. *operations* – the transformation of those inputs into the final product;
3. *outbound logistics* – the collection, storage and distribution of the product to buyers;
4. *marketing and sales* – persuading buyers to purchase the product and making it possible for them to do so;
5. *service* – the provision of service to enhance or maintain the value of the product.

Michael Porter believes that service and the value provided to the customer are integral and key parts to the chain, leading to competitive advantage.

Relationship marketing involves the provision of service support activities which will be perceived by the customer as being of unique value, thus extending the offer beyond the customer's expectations and contributing to a shift in the customer's perception of the organization. Service support includes such activities as pre-sale information, objective advice, care and attention during the sales negotiation, financing options, and after-sales support in the form of warranties, accessories, repair centres and help lines.

Developing a relationship marketing approach

The development of a relationship marketing approach requires the alignment of the three activities of marketing, customer service and quality. The starting point is to chart the service delivery system and to identify critical service issues by research and analysis of customer wants, needs and reactions as described below. Service standards are then set for each part of the system, especially the 'encounter points' – the critical events in the system when the customer comes face to face with the service process. Monitoring systems are developed which check how well the service standards are being achieved and programmes are established for maintaining continuing good relationships with customers on the basis of this control information.

Above all, relationship marketing has to focus on the organization's staff in all functions – product development, operations, distribution and support services as well as sales and marketing. Their responsibility for building and maintaining good relationships with customers should be constantly emphasized and supported by training and the performance management and reward systems.

ASSESS CUSTOMER NEEDS

Customer service policies should be based on assessments of what customers want and need. Expectations can be defined as 'deliverables' – what the organization intends to provide for customers and what customers expect organizations to provide for them. Deliverables can be expressed in terms of the type of product or service to be provided, quality, conformity to specifications, price, reliability, delivery and after-sales service. Needs can be established in four ways: (1) buying behaviour analysis, (2) customer relationship management (CRM) techniques, (3) marketing research and (4) competitor analysis.

Buying behaviour analysis

Buying behaviour analysis aims to determine the factors affecting the behaviour of customers with regard to the purchase of existing or proposed products or services. The analysis has to be based on an understanding of what influences buyer behaviour, and uses various models.

Influences on individual buying behaviour

The psychological concepts explaining individual buying behaviour are:

● *Motivation*, ie goal-directed behaviour – the emotional and rational motives that offer buying decisions and involve a reaction to a stimulus.

- *Self concept* – consumers tend to make purchases that confirm their self-image so that they can safeguard and boost it.
- *Personality* – this strongly influences buying behaviour and an aim of buyer behaviour analysis will be to identify what sort of products or services might appeal to different personality types.
- *Perception* – the analysis identifies the meaning buyers attach to stimuli and how they discern between products and services and how these fulfil their need satisfaction.
- *Attitudes* – the set of perceptions an individual has, leading to beliefs a buyer might have regarding a possible purchase. Potential positive or negative attitudes need to be identified so that marketing action such as repositioning can be taken.

Models of consumer buying behaviour

The simplest model simply means responding to immediate needs in the following 'AIDA' sequence: awareness > interest > desire > action.

An alternative model is the buyer/decision sequence:

- problem recognition – establishing a need;
- information search – seeking ways of satisfying the need which can be influenced by marketing;
- evaluation of alternatives – this can be influenced by promoting the product or service;
- purchase decision – to purchase or not to purchase based upon the evaluation;
- post-purchase behaviour – the degree of satisfaction or dissatisfaction will affect future purchasing decisions and customer service tactics will aim to produce a positive reaction.

Customer relationship management (CRM) techniques

As an approach to managing customer relations, CRM is based on the philosophy of relationship management. Its rationale is the concept that besides managing a portfolio of products and services, companies also manage a portfolio of customers and customer relationships. Its objective is to make customers and their needs the most important drivers of organizational behaviour.

The term CRM describes the way in which businesses manage the information they gather on their customers and use that information to enhance the quality of their customer relationships. Its two main purposes are, first, to improve the speed and efficiency with which customer queries are addressed and resolved, and second, to analyse customer data to predict their behaviour, find ways to make them more profitable and ensure that customer loyalty is enhanced. CRM is sometimes described as 'one-to-one marketing' because it enables businesses to focus on meeting the needs of individual customers who can be differentiated according to their buying habits and offered a personalized service. Customers are always a moving target and CRM systems can keep track of them. Much of the thinking behind CRM is based on the 20/80 rule that the top 20 per cent of an organization's customers account for 80 per cent of its revenues.

The database in a CRM system provides the company with the means to target advertising and mail shots because a better understanding has been achieved of the buying habits and wants of individual customers. Telesales can be facilitated by providing the telesales team with immediate access to customer information. Queries and complaints can be handled more easily from the online customer database.

A CRM system is based on a number of software applications. First, there is an integrated 'front-office' system. This is used by the people in immediate contact with customers, ie those in sales, marketing and customer service (help line) teams. Customer information can be viewed on screen and relevant data can be captured for future reference. In addition, the system can provide a 'data warehouse' and 'data mining tools'. Customer information obtained at the front-line level is fed into a data warehouse. There, the information is used to identify customer behaviour, and from that behaviour, product and service configuration, sales and marketing strategies and loyalty schemes can be devised and directed to specific customers.

A complete CRM system contains four distinct sub-processes that feed into each other in a loop:

1. *Data gathering* – customer data is gathered and organized by segment. Data on customer purchasing patterns and complaints is particularly important.
2. *Data analysis and value identification* – the segmented data is analysed to provide information on customer motivations and behaviour.
3. *Value delivery* – the new insights obtained by the analysis are used to indicate where changes to the marketing mix (product, price, promotion and place) are required.
4. *Monitoring, feedback and control* – ensuring that the changes are viable and make overall strategic sense.

Marketing research

Marketing research provides information on consumer tastes, preferences and buying habits. Importantly, it can identify consumer beliefs, opinions and attitudes not only about products and services but also about the level and type of customer service provided.

Competitor analysis

A comparative analysis can be made of competitors' products or services and customer service arrangements from the viewpoint of how and why they attract customers. This leads to decisions on what changes need to be made to maintain competitive edge. The analysis can be conducted by individual interviews, through focus groups or by using the Kelly repertory grid. The latter technique involves obtaining the opinions of respondents on competing products and their brand images. The interviewer presents informants with the names of products in groups of three for them to select the product that is different from the other two and how it is different. A final sifting then takes place through all the products to check out the characteristics attributed to them.

IDENTIFY TARGET CUSTOMERS

Target customers need to be identified to ensure that products or services are developed specifically to meet their needs, and promotion, sales and customer care practices are aligned to their preferences. Field research is used to establish user and non-user profiles, the factors affecting choice and preference, and reactions to new product concepts. The techniques used are described below.

Sampling

Sampling involves the analysis of attitudes, opinions and facts about products or services – planned or on offer – from a representative sample of people in the total population. The typical technique is random sampling, which means picking the people from whom information is to be obtained on the basis that every individual has an equal chance of being selected.

Interviewing

Face-to-face interviews enable direct contact to be made with potential users to find out who is most likely to want to buy the product. Interviews can be structured (ie the interviewer has to cover pre-determined areas) or unstructured (ie in-depth interviews which aim to obtain information on feelings and attitudes).

Panels

Panels measure the consumer behaviour of a representative sample of individuals or households over extended periods. The two basic methods are home audits in which levels of household stocks of specified products are checked, and diaries in which panel members record all purchases made.

COMMUNICATE TO CUSTOMERS

It is necessary to inform customers of what is on offer and how it will satisfy their needs.

Availability of goods or services

The availability of goods or services is communicated by means of promotion activities. These consist of:

- *Selling*, which involves direct contact with customers to explain the product and persuade them to purchase it. This is carried out by sales representatives and assistants in retail outlets, by telephone (telesales), via websites and through call or contact centres.
- *Merchandising*, which ensures that retailers display products prominently.
- *Display*, which displays the products in retail outlets or in exhibitions.
- *Advertising*, which aims to present the product to customers in a way which will persuade them to purchase it. Advertising is sometimes referred to as *above the line* when agencies receive a commission for placing the sponsor's advertisements.
- *Sales promotion*, which refers to short-term activities like competitions and free samples which encourage quick action by buyers. This is referred to as *below the line* because a direct charge is made to the sponsor for the work performed and the advertising agency does not receive a commission.
- *Public relations*, which publicizes information about the company's products or services through the media.
- *Exhibitions*, in which the company's products are displayed and promoted.

Helping customers to select the products and services they need

The communications to customers should indicate how the products or services will meet their needs. This message is referenced to the research which has established what those needs are and the characteristics of the product or service and the benefits it provides.

MEASURE CUSTOMER SATISFACTION

It is essential to measure the extent to which customers are satisfied with the products or services provided by the organization. This means entering into dialogues with customers through responses to enquiries and complaints, questionnaires, surveys, group discussions (focus groups) and employee feedback.

Responses to enquiries and complaints

Every time a customer contacts an organization an opportunity is created to assess the level of satisfaction. Formal procedures can be set up to log enquiries and complaints under appropriate headings. These can be analysed and the outcome distributed to staff with an indication as to what action is required or, better still, a request that they should get together with colleagues and discuss what needs to be done.

Customer questionnaires

Customer questionnaires are a commonly used method of measuring satisfaction. Answers are often obtained just after the service has taken place, for example staying in a hotel or purchasing a car. Customers are asked to assess the service provided on a rating scale covering such aspects as helpfulness, courtesy, meeting needs, delivering as promised and the overall quality of the services provided. The questionnaires are analysed and the analysis is fed back to staff and steps are taken to deal with any problems. Customer questionnaires provide immediate reactions but they may only be completed by an unrepresentative sample of customers; for example, those who were highly satisfied or dissatisfied.

Customer surveys

Customer surveys, often conducted by specialized consumer research firms, cover a much wider and more balanced sample of customers. They can be carried out by means of face-to-face interviews, postal questionnaires or through the internet. Surveys will ask questions or get customers to respond on a scale (eg fully agree, generally agree, disagree) to statements such as:

- Staff are polite.
- Staff are helpful.
- Customer requests are dealt with politely and promptly.
- Staff do not provide individual attention.

- You have to wait ages to get through to someone in the company by telephone.
- Staff return your calls quickly.

Customer surveys are best conducted regularly in order to analyse trends. Results should be fed back to staff so that action can be taken. But surveys, like questionnaires, cover only shoppers who buy and, therefore, they do not identify any aspects of customer service which put off customers.

Group discussions

Group discussions, commonly called focus groups, are frequently used as a means of conducting dialogues with customers. A small group of typical customers is assembled and prepared questions are put to them on products or services and how they have been treated as customers. The person conducting the focus group acts as a facilitator, encouraging but not dominating the discussion. The aim is not only to obtain direct responses from individuals but also to get group members to discuss the questions amongst themselves so that an in-depth response can be achieved. Facilitators have to be careful to pose open questions which prompt discussion but do not reveal what answer is expected.

The effectiveness of a focus group depends on the quality of the facilitation process. Because only small numbers of people are usually involved it is risky to infer too much from them. They indicate what some customers feel about what the organization provides but they are only a sample.

Employee feedback

Employees can be encouraged to feed back to management and each other anything they have learnt about customer concerns and attitudes.

Popularity of measures

A survey conducted by CRL Solutions in 2002 (Measuring Customer Satisfaction: The Views of Customer Service Professionals) established that enquiries and complaints data was the most popular method of measuring customer satisfaction, followed by telephone surveys, employee feedback and mail surveys.

Use of measures

Measures are only useful if they lead to action. That is why any data collected must be distributed to management and all staff concerned with customer service, which might mean every employee. Processes need to be established to learn from the data

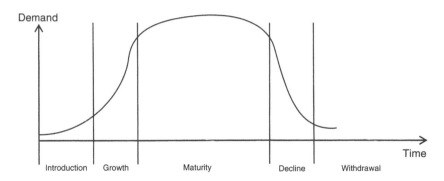

Figure 14.1 Stages in a typical product life cycle

and do something about it. These might consist of regular meetings to review customer service issues or improvement groups (groups set up to deliver continuous improvement programmes, see Chapter 16).

Measures should be used to identify customers at risk. It is also desirable to segment customers according to their value to the organization. An important aim of customer satisfaction surveys should be to maximize the satisfaction and loyalty of those customers making the most significant contribution to profitability. It is advisable to record trends so that improvements or declines in satisfaction can be noted so that improvements can be maintained and declines arrested.

DEVELOP PRODUCTS AND SERVICES TO MEET CUSTOMER NEEDS

The process of developing products and services is usually referred to as product planning. This is defined as the activities required to inform decisions on the introduction of new products or services, changes to existing products or services and the withdrawal and replacement of unwanted products or services. The aim of product planning is to keep customers by ensuring that the organization continues over the long term to supply products that they need and want. Product planning takes place within the 'product life cycle'.

The product life cycle

An obvious problem with making products or providing services that satisfy the demands of customers is that their demands keep on changing. A product or service that is popular may be much less in demand next year. Demand follows a standard life cycle with the following five stages as illustrated in Figure 14.1:

1. *Introduction* – a new product appears on the market and demand is low while people learn about it, try it, and see if they like it.
2. *Growth* – new customers buy the product and demand rises quickly.
3. *Maturity* – demand stabilizes when most potential customers know about the product and buy it in steady numbers.
4. *Decline* – sales fall as customers start buying new, alternative products.
5. *Withdrawal* – demand declines to the point where it is no longer worth making the product.

The significance of the product life cycle from a customer relations viewpoint is that it shows the need to track sales systematically. The purpose is to identify where a product is in the life cycle and to take action to ensure that a favourable trend continues or that any actual or potential decline is arrested by product redesign or replacement, or by improving customer service practices as set out below.

Introduction stage

- Increase advertising and promotional expenditure to accelerate growth.
- Adjust prices to increase penetration.
- Adjust promotional messages and sales approaches in response to analysis of consumer reactions.
- Improve product features in response to initial consumer reaction.
- Improve customer service facilities.

Growth stage

- Improve quality.
- Modify product characteristics.
- Extend market into new segments.
- Develop new distribution channels.
- Reduce prices to attract the next layer of price-sensitive buyers.
- Improve customer service facilities.

Maturity stage

- Find new markets and customers.
- Reposition brand to appeal to a larger or faster-growing segment.
- Encourage increased usage amongst existing customers.
- Modify product characteristics – new features, style improvements.
- Modify marketing mix, eg cut prices, advertise or promote more aggressively, move into higher volume market channels.
- Improve customer service facilities.

Decline stage

- Reinforce measures taken at the maturity stage.
- Maintain brand in the hope that competitors will withdraw their products.
- Harvest brands, ie maximize profits by reducing costs but keeping up sales pressure.
- Withdraw and replace product.
- Take further action to improve customer service facilities if that is the problem.

PROVIDE THE INFRASTRUCTURE FOR CUSTOMER SERVICE

The infrastructure for customer service consists of:

- the counters, showrooms and display units which offer and show goods for purchase;
- the arrangements for order processing or fulfilment;
- the distribution system;
- customer service or contact centres and help lines to answer enquiries and deal with problems;
- call centres to receive and process orders.

In each case, it is necessary to ensure that the arrangements are customer-friendly and provide the basis for achieving high standards of customer service.

EVALUATE MODELS OF CUSTOMER SERVICE

The following models of customer service are available. Each needs to be evaluated in terms of fitness for purpose, operational efficiency and effectiveness and the extent to which defined customer service standards are being met.

Customer service centre

A customer service or contact centre is a facility which provides help and advice to customers and deals with their enquiries, problems and complaints. There are three evolutionary stages to most service centres, ranging from a reactive cost centre to the proactive high-value service centre:

Stage 1 The message centre – this is someone who simply routes enquiries and complaints to someone who can respond to them. Problem resolution is not attempted and the service is entirely reactive. Automated telephone queuing systems may be used and they do help to channel enquiries. However, they can create dissatisfaction on the grounds that it seems to be more difficult to make contact with a human being. This may lead customers to conclude that the company is using the system solely as a means of economizing on staff rather than making life easier for customers.

Stage 2 The reactive/problem service centre – this may be a 'help line' or 'help desk' which is staffed by one or two people and acts as a single point of reference for customers, attempting to resolve problems such as defective products, delivery delays and difficulties in setting up or operating equipment. It is better than a message centre but it is still reactive with typically low levels of problems resolved following the first call.

Stage 3 The full customer service centre – this is staffed by trained people fully supported by software and, where appropriate, including technicians who can resolve technical problems. The aim is to achieve a quick and accurate resolution of customer issues with the help of automated processes.

The operation of customer service or contact centres can be improved significantly by the use of software designed to speed the process of dealing with customer enquiries. An example of the use of such software in Scottish Water is given on page 178.

Call centres

Call centres use specially trained staff to handle sales, enquiries and orders by telephone. They usually focus more on gaining new customers rather than servicing existing customers.

Websites

Websites are used by many companies such as Amazon to enhance customer service. They are also useful sources of data on customers as part of a CRM system.

Service level agreements

A service level agreement is an agreement between the provider of a service and the customers who use that service. The starting point of a service level agreement is a clarification of what the needs of customers are and which are the more important. The aim in setting service targets is that they should be stretching but achievable, although some providers under-promise so that they can appear to over-achieve. A service level agreement defines the nature of the service(s) provided, the volumes and quality to be achieved by each of the services and the response times to be achieved by the providers when their services are requested. Service level agreements are most commonly found in the public sector but they are equally applicable elsewhere. They can operate between providers and either external or internal customers.

Preferred supplier status

Organizations can designate firms as preferred suppliers, which means that the supplier will be given the first opportunity to provide the goods or services and can safely assume that any preferred supplier contract will run over a period of time and will be renewable.

Telesales

Businesses selling products such as double glazing often rely to a large extent on doing so by means of unsolicited telephone calls. The proportion of sales in relation to calls made by this direct approach may appear to be small but as long as well-trained, highly motivated and albeit persistent staff are used, this method pays off.

Accounts management

Businesses with customers who buy heavily and continuously from them may appoint accounts managers whose job is to 'nurse' customers and ensure that their needs are met and any problems are resolved swiftly. Accounts managers monitor sales and levels of service and take action if sales decline or levels of service show signs of slipping.

SET STANDARDS FOR CUSTOMER SERVICE

Customer service standards define the levels of service to be achieved for each of the main aspects of customer service. Levels of service standards can be classified under these three headings:

1. *Desired level of service* – what customers would really like to experience by reference to the best level of relevant experience the customer has received.
2. *Expected level of service* – what customers expect, given their knowledge of circumstances and their experience.
3. *Minimum acceptable level of service* – the minimum level of service customers will expect, which will lead to loss of business if it is not achieved.

The standards form the basis for guidelines to staff on what they should achieve and for monitoring service levels. The areas covered can include:

- *Order processing* – speed of response and delivery of products ordered by customers, including replacement parts and requests for service. Response rates can be measured by recording the proportion of letters or calls answered in a defined number of hours or days, and delivery standards can be expressed as the time taken between taking the order and delivery. Standards can also be set for the backlog of unprocessed orders at the end of a day or week (ideally none, but a small incidence of backlog orders may be allowed in peak periods, eg before Christmas) or when order fulfilment is highly complex.
- *Quality of relationships with customers* – how customers should be approached and be responded to; how complaints should be dealt with; the information that should be provided in response to enquiries; the levels of service to be achieved in terms of reliability, responsiveness, competence, access, courtesy, communication, understanding customers and dealing with difficult customers.
- *Complaints* – assessed by reference to the number of complaints as a proportion of total orders, the backlog of complaints, the proportion of complaints dealt with satisfactorily when first raised and the quality of response to complaints.
- *Service and call centres* – call pick-up rates (proportion of calls answered in so many seconds or within a certain number of rings), lost call rates (proportion of inbound calls lost), proportion of problems resolved at first contact, backlogs (number of orders, enquiries or complaints outstanding at the end of a day or week), quality of response to enquiries or complaints.

For example, British Gas Trading has agreed with the industry regulator, OFGEM, 24 standards of service. Below are the standards for customer contact with the level of performance:

- Customer telephone calls will be answered within 30 seconds of the call being connected (90 per cent of calls).
- Other than where immediate action is required, all customer correspondence will receive a reply within five working days of receipt of that correspondence (90 per cent of replies).
- A record will be kept of all written complaints (99 per cent of all written complaints).
- For all customer correspondence which requires a visit, contact will be made within two working days of receipt of the correspondence and the subsequent visit will be made within five days of that contact, or later as agreed with the customer (93 per cent of all visits).

MONITOR THE DELIVERY OF SERVICE STANDARDS

To monitor the achievement of service standards it is necessary to set up systems for recording the number of enquiries and complaints, analysing the reasons for complaints, response rates (time taken to deal with complaints and enquiries), lost calls, backlogs and delivery times. The quality of relationships with customers can be assessed by observation, by recording telephone conversations and by collecting and reviewing documented evidence of how complaints were dealt with and how customers reacted. The outcome of customer satisfaction surveys should also be analysed to determine areas for improvement against the standards set.

Mystery shopping

Mystery shopping is often used to enable the quality of customer service to be assessed at the critical point at which customers come into contact with sales staff – in a retail or service outlet or over the telephone. People (usually from market research firms) are sent into a retail outlet to observe how they are treated. Or they may make a telephone enquiry. They then record their observations of how well or badly they were handled against a set of basic standards covering such aspects of service as friendly reception, paying attention to the shopper's wants, helpfulness, knowledge of the product, willingness to listen to and respond to the customer's requests and queries, and avoiding pressurized sales techniques.

BUILD SATISFACTION AND KEEP CUSTOMERS

Loyalty cards are used by stores, and airlines have air miles to keep customers, but customer loyalty is best achieved by building and maintaining high levels of satisfaction and developing a customer-centric culture as discussed in the next chapter. This culture should be based on a well-defined customer relations strategy supported by the processes described in this chapter of managing customer relationships, assessing needs and expectations, measuring customer satisfaction, developing products and services that meet customer needs, providing the infrastructure for customer service, setting and monitoring service delivery standards and taking action to overcome shortfalls in the achievement of those standards.

INTERNAL CUSTOMERS

An internal customer is anyone who makes use of the outputs or services provided by other departments or individuals in the organization. This means everyone – all employees are customers of other employees and they all provide services to other employees. Some departments such as IT, HR and facilities management exist primarily to provide professional or technical services directly to other departments. Some departments exist to produce outputs upon which other departments rely to achieve their objectives. Research and development has to deliver products which can be promoted and sold by marketing and sales departments. Production or operating departments exist to deliver the products or services that are required by sales to meet customer demands. Marketing and sales departments produce the information on forecast demand which enables production and operating departments to plan their activities. At British Gas Trading the concept of internal customer satisfaction is used so that the whole of the business has a customer focus. For example, the customers of the HR, finance and IT staff are the business managers. To determine their level of satisfaction, these departments conduct their own customer surveys.

J M Juran, the quality guru, has stated that: 'meeting the needs of internal customers is a prerequisite for meeting the needs of external customers' (3). If, for example, marketing gets its sales forecasts wrong or manufacturing fails to meet the requirements specified by sales, then it is the level of service to external customers that suffers and this has a negative impact on satisfaction and loyalty.

The basic approach to creating high standards of service for internal customers is to define how the different parts of the organization interrelate and spell out who serves whom and who receives service from whom. It is then necessary to ensure that all the parties concerned know how important service to internal customers is and what is expected of them from their internal customers. This can be defined formally as a service level agreement. For example, an agreement for an HR department could set out standards under the following headings:

- level of response to requests for help or guidance in areas such as recruitment, training, handling disciplinary cases and grievances, and health and safety;
- the time taken to prepare and agree role profiles, fill vacancies or conduct a job evaluation exercise;
- the quality of candidates submitted for appointments;
- the proportion of discipline or grievance issues settled at the first time HR is involved;
- the number of appeals (successful and unsuccessful) against job grading decisions;
- the results of evaluations of training carried out by participants in training programmes;
- the outcome of employee attitude surveys.

SUMMARY

- The organization must establish and maintain good relationships with customers – instilling confidence that their requirements will be met, on time, with cost-effective solutions and adequate support availability.
- Managing relationships with customers is conducted by what is known as relationship marketing, which emphasizes the continuing relationships which should exist between the organization and its customers with the emphasis on customer service and quality.
- Customer service policies should be based on assessments of what customers want and need. Expectations can be defined as 'deliverables' – what the organization intends to provide for customers and what customers expect organizations to provide for them.
- Buying behaviour analysis aims to determine the factors affecting the behaviour of customers with regard to the purchase of existing or proposed products or services.
- The term customer relationship management (CRM) describes the way in which businesses manage the information they gather on their customers and use that information to enhance the quality of their customer relationships. A CRM system is based on a number of integrated software applications.
- The database in a CRM system provides the company with the means to target advertising and mail shots because a better understanding has been achieved of the buying habits and wants of individual customers. Telesales can be facilitated by providing the telesales team with immediate access to customer information. Queries and complaints can be handled more easily from the online customer database.
- Marketing research provides information on consumer tastes, preferences and buying habits. Importantly, it can identify consumer beliefs, opinions and attitudes not only about products and services but also about the level and type of customer service provided.
- A comparative analysis can be made of competitors' products or services and customer service arrangements from the viewpoint of how and why they attract customers.
- Target customers need to be identified to ensure that products or services are developed specifically to meet their needs, and promotion, sales and customer care practices are aligned to their preferences.
- It is necessary to inform customers of what is on offer and how it will satisfy their needs.
- The communications to customers should indicate how the products or services will meet their needs.

- It is essential to measure the extent to which customers are satisfied with the products or services provided by the organization. This means entering into dialogues with customers through responses to enquiries and complaints, questionnaires, surveys, group discussions (focus groups) and employee feedback.
- Product planning aims to keep customers by ensuring that the organization continues over the long term to supply products that customers need and want.
- The infrastructure for customer service consists of the counters, showrooms and display units which offer and show goods for purchase, the arrangements for order processing, the distribution system, customer service or contact centres to answer enquiries and deal with problems and call centres to receive and process orders.
- Customer service standards define the levels of service to be achieved for each of the main aspects of customer service. Levels of service standards can be classified under these three headings: desired level of service, expected level of service and minimum acceptable level of service. Standards form the basis for guidelines to staff on what they should achieve and for monitoring service levels.
- To monitor the achievement of service standards it is necessary to set up systems for recording the number of enquiries and complaints, analysing the reasons for complaints, response rates (time taken to deal with complaints and enquiries), lost calls, backlogs and delivery times.
- Meeting the needs of internal customers is a prerequisite for meeting the needs of external customers.
- To create high standards of service for internal customers it is necessary to define how the different parts of the organization interrelate and spell out who serves whom and who receives service from whom. It is then necessary to ensure that all the parties concerned know how important service to internal customers is and what is expected of them from their internal customers.

REFERENCES

1   Levitt, T (1983) *The Marketing Imagination*, The Free Press, New York
2   Porter, M (1980) *Competitive Strategy*, The Free Press, New York
3   Juran, J M (1989) *Juran on Leadership for Quality*, The Free Press, New York

15

Achieving high levels of customer service

High levels of customer service are achieved and maintained by developing and implementing a customer service strategy, building a customer-centric culture, defining the attitudes, skills and behaviours in relation to customers required by staff and ensuring that employees adopt those attitudes, possess the skills and behave appropriately when in contact with customers. These requirements are discussed in this chapter which begins with a summary of what is needed (The Twelve Pillars of World-Class Service Excellence) produced by the Institute of Public Service and ends with examples of how world-class organizations approach customer service.

THE TWELVE PILLARS OF WORLD-CLASS SERVICE EXCELLENCE

The twelve pillars of world-class service excellence devised by Dr Ted Johns for the Institute of Customer Service (ICS) provide a comprehensive basis for the development and implementation of customer service strategies and processes.

Your strategy

1. *Commitment*: The organization sees customer service as a key corporate scorecard indicator, with both transformational and incremental improvement goals, action programmes, top-level accountabilities, and regular high-level discussions about service performance.
2. *Credibility*: The organization works hard to make sure that customers have good grounds for believing its promises.
3. *Classification*: The organization segments its customers, periodically reviews its segmentation profiles, and varies its product/service offer between segment boundaries.
4. *Concentration*: The organization focuses its efforts on its most profitable (and its potentially most profitable) customers, or, in a not-for-profit environment, those customers in greatest need.

Your people

5. *Capability*: All the organization's people, in direct contact with people or not, are recruited and trained against a company blueprint that gives high priority to customer-friendly attitudes.
6. *Continuity*: The organization's retention, reward and recognition strategies encourage those people who deliver excellent service to stay.
7. *Courtesy*: The organization's people are polite, considerate, tolerant and friendly when dealing with their customers, whether internal or external, and are always willing to go 'the extra mile'.
8. *Creativity*: The organization systematically encourages its people to take part in continuous improvement programmes and to produce ideas for service innovations.

Your customer relationships

9. *Consistency*: One of the principal reasons why your customers keep on coming back is that they know what to expect from you.
10. *Communication*: Your customers understand what you say to them, you listen to them, and you actively promote opportunities for two-way dialogue (with both internal and external customers).
11. *Comfort*: Your customers feel comfortable about your products, your services, your user instructions, your help line, your complaints procedures and your service recovery/restitution systems – indeed, everything that collectively comprises your reputational asset value.
12. *Contact*: You offer customer service at times to suit your customers, not at times to suit you.

CUSTOMER SERVICE STRATEGY

A strategic approach to customer service is necessary to ensure that a longer-term view is developed on what needs to be done to develop effective, coherent and integrated policies, processes and practices. A customer service strategy provides the framework for continuous improvement. It will indicate what the organization intends to do about customer service in the future and how it proposes to do it.

The aim of the strategy will be to achieve service excellence. As defined by Robert Johnston (1): 'Service excellence is simply about being easy to do business with, which involves delivering the promise, providing a personal touch, going the extra mile and resolving problems well.' He suggests that a reputation for service excellence can be developed and sustained by: 'having a strong service culture, a distinct service personality, committed staff and customer-focused systems'.

The strategy will cover what action will be taken to create a customer-centric culture, how the customer service infrastructure will be developed, the processes required to identify and meet customer needs and expectations and measure satisfaction, how the right attitudes, skills and behaviours will be fostered, and how the various internal systems and processes – the infrastructure that supports customer service – can be improved. The strategy will deal with both external and internal customers. It will be concerned with integrating the programmes for continuous improvement and quality management which ensure that a quality product or service is delivered to customers. It will also address issuers relating to the recruitment, training and reward of customer-focused staff.

DEVELOPING A CUSTOMER-CENTRIC CULTURE

A customer-centric culture is one in which everyone in the organization is aware of the importance of customer service and works cooperatively with colleagues to achieve and exceed customer service standards. Everything done in the organization is focused on delivering service excellence for both external and internal customers. Singapore Airlines, as reported by Johns, Wirtz and Johnston (2), has 'created a culture which expects all staff to add value – to think about their processes, systems and routines all the time, to search for incremental improvements, even to think of radically different ways of delivering service enhancements to the customer'.

Creating a customer-orientated culture

As reported by Sarah Cook and Colin Bates (3), organizations such as Virgin and US retailer Nordstorm have created a customer-orientated culture by developing strong brands with powerful brand promises:

Through listening to customer needs and via consultation with employees, they have been able to identify brand values which form the backbone of how they do business with the customer and how employees are managed... The 'inside out' concept starts at the top of the organization. Employees look to the top team to model the desired behaviours... Organizations such as Barclays and AT&T have developed leadership behaviours and core competencies which directly reflect brand values. These in turn are linked to customer needs. How you lead is how you serve.

The Sewell Cadillac approach

It is important to convey values for customer service to all staff and for everyone, including top management, 'to live the values'. At a major car dealer in the United States, Sewell Cadillac in Texas, as reported by *Customer Service Management Journal* (4), the mission statement states that: 'We will provide the best vehicle sales and service experience for our customers. We will do this in a way that will foster the continuous improvement of our people and our company. We will be a top performing, thoroughly professional and genuinely caring organization in all we do.' The essential characteristics of their approach to customer service are:

- Listen to the customer – and keep listening.
- Listen to your staff – they will respond with ideas and loyalty.
- Keep your staff – customers trust people they know.
- Make systems your top priority – the customer wants it to be right.
- Select the right people – make certain they fit in and are suited to the job.
- Learn from other companies.

Scottish Parliament values

In the Scottish Parliament one of the key values in the management plan is Client Focus, expressed as: 'We are responsive to the needs of members, the public and one another.'

The Lands' End approach

At Lands' End, the highly successful mail order clothing company, as reported by e-Research (5), one of the key values is expressed as: '*Put the customer first. Achieve an even higher level of customer service through personal attention and new technology.*' This is expanded by the following statement of 'what we believe in':

1. Satisfied customers and employees.
2. Integrity, honesty, friendliness, respect and trust.
3. The imperative to offer quality products and services at a fair price.

4. Lasting relationships with customers who appreciate our brand and its value.
5. Innovation in all we do.

The reason why the company wants to inspire staff is because it believes that the difference between doing something and doing it well comes down to the amount of effort people will put into their work. While an individual cannot be blamed for not taking an initiative or only working to their job description, their willingness to do that little bit extra is the difference between a good experience for customers and a poor one.

Lands' End staff are willing to make that extra effort because of their sense of pride in what the organization stands for: quality, service and value. Management believes that every employee wants to do a good job, and is motivated by doing so, but that being able to do this depends on the 'amount of space', in the sense of not being frantically busy the whole time, and the degree of responsibility that you give them. So, Lands' End ensures that staffing levels are such that employees have the time to offer a good level of service, which in turn creates greater pride and so on in a self-fulfilling cycle. The company takes a pride in its history of good service and publishes a book of 'great service stories' to help people understand how far they can go to help a customer.

Lands' End says that what front-line staff do has a far greater impact on customers than what the executive team does, which is why every staff member, including the managing director, works in a front-line job for four hours a week for the busy six weeks before Christmas. This reminds everyone of the importance of the front-line jobs and demonstrates to front-line staff that everyone else understands and values what they do.

Where jobs are repetitive or less challenging, it is particularly important to provide some challenge and fun, Lands' End believes. And if it isn't possible to give people a choice as to the type of work they do, they can be given a choice as to how they do it. So, for example, in the Lands' End call centre, unlike many others, good performance is not primarily measured by the number of calls, call duration or the amount of time a person is available to take a call. If a customer wants a service assistant to go to the distribution centre, pick the item they want to buy, call them back and describe the feel of the garment then that is what they should do. The company invests more heavily in staff training and giving people more responsibility than in putting in controls.

Steps to creating a customer-centric culture

1. Articulate the core values for service excellence that will be adopted by the organization.
2. Communicate those values to all staff.
3. Live the values at top management level – how they lead is how others serve.

4. Implement programmes of continuous improvement which provide for incremental but significant enhancements to service levels.
5. Implement total quality management or Six Sigma programmes (see Chapter 17) which provide for the achievement of high levels of product and service quality.
6. Focus on internal as well as external customers.
7. Define the attitudes and behaviours expected of all those dealing with external and internal customers.
8. Select people with the right attitudes, train them in the customer service skills they need and empower them to provide them with greater autonomy in relating to customers.
9. Monitor performance by reference to core customer service values and expected attitudes and behaviour.
10. Recognize and reward high levels of customer service achieved by individuals and teams.

DEFINE REQUIRED ATTITUDES, SKILLS, KNOWLEDGE, BEHAVIOURS AND COMPETENCIES

It is necessary to define the attitudes, skills and behaviours required of all those involved in customer service to provide a basis for managing customer service, recruitment, training, performance management and reward.

Attitudes

Customer service excellence is achieved by people whose attitudes can be summed up in the phrase 'put the customer first'. They must believe that they exist because customers exist and that being responsive to customer needs and expectations is a vital part of their role.

Skills

The main skills required are:

- interpersonal skills – ability to relate well to people during person-to-person contacts;
- listening skills – ability to pay attention to people, absorb what they are saying and react appropriately;
- communication skills – ability to explain matters to customers clearly and with conviction and to handle telephone conversations;
- complaints handling skills – ability to deal with complaints and handle angry customers.

Knowledge

Knowledge will be required of the product or service offered by the organization. This could be quite advanced knowledge enabling individuals to identify and deal with faulty equipment or provide technical advice. It will also be necessary to understand the customer service systems and procedures used in the organization.

Behaviours

The following are examples of the sort of behaviours typically required of anyone involved in servicing customers:

- Be helpful, polite, friendly and positive with customers.
- When dealing with customers, smile, make eye contact and look and sound enthusiastic.
- Speak clearly.
- Show personal interest.
- Show sympathy with customers making complaints – listen to what the customer has to say, establish the facts, agree what needs to be done, keep the customer informed.
- Provide information immediately or let customers know when they can expect it.
- Keep promises.
- Answer telephones promptly.
- Reply to letters, faxes, e-mails and voicemail messages quickly.
- Concentrate on the needs of customers, not on what is easiest to sell.

According to O'Connor (6) the top 10 behaviours are:

1. Takes time to understand the specific needs, requirements and any current pressures the customer may be under.
2. Shows an immediate understanding of the problem and the possible consequences.
3. Demonstrates empathy.
4. Generates a range of solutions to address a difficulty.
5. Uses organizational policy to guide the solutions rather than to act as blocks, or worse, reasons not to assist the customer.
6. Takes decisions quickly.
7. Is honest about the situation and what the organization can do to help.
8. Looks for ways to delight the customer.
9. Demonstrates an understanding of the commercial implications of decisions taken.
10. Seeks the appropriate guidance where required and does this efficiently, retaining ownership of the customer.

Competencies

Organizations with competency frameworks frequently use customer service as one of the headings. An analysis carried out by Rankin in 2002 (7) of the core competency frameworks of 40 employers showed that the second-equal most common heading was Customer Focus, used in 65 per cent of the organizations surveyed.

Defining competency levels for customer service is a good way of expressing the values and requirements of the organization for customer care. It provides the basis for recruitment, training and development programmes, and performance management and recognition and reward schemes. Two examples are given below.

Britannic Assurance

Table 15.1 Customer service competencies at Brittanic Assurance

Levels of performance in the customer service competency

LEVEL 1
- Take ownership of customer problems.
- Treat each and every customer contact as an opportunity to impress them with your professional service.
- Take care of your customers.

LEVEL 2
- Offer flexible service, taking time to build a rapport and assess customer needs.
- Present a range of alternative options to your customers.
- Put yourself in the customers' shoes.

LEVEL 3
- Are always prepared to go 'the extra mile' to deliver the highest quality service, on time, every time.
- Identify customer needs – beyond those expressly stated.
- Establish a personal relationship based on understanding their personality and individual traits.
- Offer a commitment to customer service excellence and can spot when things are going off track.

LEVEL 5
- Identify new and emerging areas of service and seize on these as opportunities.
- Conceive schemes which are mutually beneficial to the customer and other stakeholders.
- Act as the customers' champion, constantly driving the business forward in delivering service.
- Persuade others to see things from a customer's point of view.

Source: Customer Management, 12 (2), March/April 2004, pp 18–21. Reproduced with permission.

Peabody Trust

Table 15.2 Customer service competencies at the Peabody Trust

Manage customer service

Provide high levels of service to internal and external customers in accordance with exacting standards

Level Standard	Positive behavioural indicators	Negative behavioural indicators
1 Provide good services to internal and external customers.	• Meets expressed needs of customers.	• Has no appreciation of customer needs or pressures. • Doesn't listen to customers.
2 Build and maintain good relationships with customers.	• Handles customer queries effectively and knows where to channel queries in the organization. • Understands customer problems.	• Unaware of customer needs. • Passes enquiries when they should have taken action themselves.
3 Contribute to the development and maintenance of high standards of customer service.	• Identifies potential opportunities to help customers. • Asks customers how services could be improved.	• Fails to respond to customer requests or queries. • Does not deliver the standards of service customers have the right to expect.
4 Contribute to the development of customer service standards in the department and play an active part in achieving them.	• Builds collaborative relationships with customers. • Establishes high levels of trust amongst customers as witnessed by customer feedback.	• Customer enquiries and complaints are not attended to swiftly. • Gets negative feedback from customers.
5 Contribute to the development of customer services in the function and play an active part in achieving them.	• Develops extensive customer networks. • Sets standards of customer service and ensures they are met.	• Too little concerned with setting and monitoring customer service.
6 Lead and promote a culture which recognizes the importance of meeting the needs of both internal and external customers in key aspects of the Trust's operations.	• Actively involved in promoting high levels of customer service across the organization. • Continuously monitors customer service levels and takes swift corrective action when necessary.	• Takes a narrow view of customer service. Not concerned with wider issues.

DEVELOPING ATTITUDES, SKILLS AND BEHAVIOURS

The development of appropriate attitudes, skills and behaviours is achieved through recruitment, training, performance management and reward processes. But it is also generally accepted that if employees are satisfied then customers are more likely to be satisfied, which means paying close attention to their needs and measuring their attitudes through regular surveys such as those carried out by the Carphone Warehouse and GNER.

Recruitment

At the recruitment stage the aim should be to obtain people with the right attitudes to customer service who are potentially likely to behave effectively in delivering customer services. The role specification should indicate what attitudes and competencies are required and the interview plan should set out what evidence will be sought on behavioural patterns. This can form the basis for a behavioural-based structured interview in which candidates are asked to tell the interviewer how they would behave in situations that have been identified as critical to successful performance with regard to customer contacts, for example how they would deal with an angry customer, internal or external. Businesses such as Selfridges use psychological tests to provide additional information.

Training and development

At one time the 'big bang' approach to training in customer service was adopted, everyone in the organization from top to bottom being put through a one- or two-day course of 'smile training' as at British Airways. This method is now largely discredited because experience has shown that this 'one-off' method does not produce lasting changes in behaviour. The focus is now on formal induction training – getting the message across when people start, followed by continued learning on the job. Team leaders and supervisors are given the responsibility to ensure that learning does take place and that this results in the required behaviour. They require training and guidance on how to exercise this responsibility and in the skills they need to use. It should be emphasized that this is a key part of their role and that their performance in developing staff will be monitored and reviewed. This continuous development process can be supplemented by short training sessions to build knowledge, eg product knowledge, and skills, eg dealing with complaints.

NVQ/SVQ in customer service

Employees can be encouraged to take an NVQ/SVQ in customer service. The standards are set out below.

Key purpose

Deliver continuous improvement in service to achieve customer satisfaction.

Maintain reliable customer service

- Maintain records relating to customer service.
- Organize own work pattern in response to the needs of customers.
- Work with others to benefit the customer.

Communicate with customers

- Select information for communication to customers.
- Improve the flow of information between organization and customer.
- Adapt methods of communication to the customer.

Develop positive working relationships with customers

- Respond to the needs and feelings expressed by the customer.
- Present positive personal image to the customer.
- Balance the needs of customer and organization.

Solve problems on behalf of customers

- Identify and interpret problems affecting customers.
- Generate solutions on behalf of customers.
- Take action to deliver solutions.

Initiate and evaluate change to improve service to customers

- Obtain and use feedback from customers.
- Propose improvements in service delivery based on feedback from customers.
- Initiate change in response to customer requirements.
- Evaluate changes designed to improve service to customers.

Performance management

Competence frameworks such as those illustrated above can be used as the basis for performance management processes. Dialogues between managers or team leaders and their staff can take place which achieve understanding of customer service performance expectations and how they can be met. Periodic reviews take place (not just once a year) which refer to agreed expectations and how individuals have actually performed. The dialogue in review meetings covers any changes in behaviours required and how those changes should be achieved, by individuals with the support of their manager.

Reward

Rewards are used to recognize and motivate appropriate behaviour. They can be financial (some form of performance or contribution pay) or non-financial (some form of recognition). Formal recognition programmes can be more effective than awarding pay increases or bonuses. Programmes can provide for 'applause' which publicly recognizes exceptional performance in house journals, the intranet or notice boards. This can include naming people as 'employee of the month', or more comprehensibly, highlighting what they have actually done to achieve such recognition. Recognition programmes can include various forms of gifts, certificates, badges and appearance at presentations.

WORLD-CLASS CUSTOMER SERVICE EXAMPLES

A world-class organization will generally exhibit any or all of the following characteristics:

- market leader;
- high quality leadership;
- exceptional results;
- a leading employer of choice;
- meet highest standards of corporate responsibility – for stakeholders and the environment;
- meet demanding standards of customer service as indicated not by the rhetoric – what they *say* they do, but by the reality – what they actually achieve as measured against the highest standards elsewhere.

The following examples summarize the customer service practices at the world-class organizations of Audi, Britannic Assurance, Dell, Scottish Water, and Singapore Airlines (by courtesy of *Customer Management*).

Audi

Peter Brookes-Smith, Head of Customer Service for Audi UK, said that: 'In Audi, our vision is to make our customers our best salespeople and our goal is to develop our company's people, processes, systems and culture to ensure that every time we serve a customer, whether it's a managing director, a retired librarian or a school child wanting information for a project, they think we're great people and they tell their friends about it… . The principles that have guided us over the last two years are:

- if you want to make a change, start at the top;
- look to yourself to lead the way – practise what you preach;
- above all, know your customer;
- drive change through your business based on what they say;
- treat people as individuals, not groups;
- if you want to give the best service, you need the best people, processes and systems;
- care for your people and they will be more likely to care for your customers;
- investment is almost always required, both personal and financial.'

Apart from systematic programmes for getting to know customers, including the extensive use of focus groups and telephone customer satisfaction surveys, Audi has focused on people. Their 'Strategy for people' has four elements:

1. Recruit talented people.
2. Lead them with a clear and compelling vision.
3. Develop the talents into business competencies with a world-class training programme.
4. Keep people happy and motivated in the place of work.

Source: *Becoming Customer Driven*, 1999, Customer Service Management Journal. Reproduced with permission.

Britannic Assurance

At Britannic Assurance the customer service strategy incorporates a competency framework, much customer measurement activity, attention to individual and team performance and a focus on personal accountability for customer relationships. A 'coaching culture' to improve customer service has been developed which places real responsibility for learning on the individual. As described in the Britannic Assurance Coaching manual, coaching 'is not a way of someone else solving your problem for you. Coaching is based on the principle that an individual is ultimately responsible for their lives and the results they're getting. If we acknowledge that we are responsible for something it follows that we take power over it.'

Source: *Customer Management*, 12 (2), March/April 2004, pp 18–21. Reproduced with permission.

Dell

Dell is a classic example of an organization that has used customer participation to gain competitive advantage. It all began in 1981 when Michael Dell, a Texas University student, started a part-time business assembling and upgrading personal computers. In 1984 he founded Dell Computer on what is now known as the Dell Direct Model.

This afforded two key advantages. Bypassing the retail market meant no middleman margin and he could therefore undercut competitors. More importantly, by interacting directly with the customer, Dell received much more accurate and speedy intelligence about the demands and needs of the marketplace.

Dell quickly moved to its build-to-order process whereby the computer is only built after the customer has ordered it and to the customer's detailed specifications. Success followed success – aided further by the benefits afforded the direct method by the internet – and by 2000 Dell was clear market leader with a 20 per cent global share, and an operating profit greater than the sum of its next four competitors combined.

What Michael Dell did was understand the power of customer participation. His competitors were taken by surprise and have found it difficult to respond because of existing relationships with retailers and suppliers. And the brand continues to go from strength to strength.

Source: *Customer Management*, 11 (5), September/October 2003, p 16. Reproduced with permission.

Scottish Water

Scottish Water has launched a new online operation which is dramatically improving customer service and has saved £18 million in its first year. The project – Promise to Resolution – was developed along with Oracle Corporation and Celerant Consulting. The new way of working has resulted in one member of field staff now being able to execute eleven jobs a day as opposed to five. Customers now get an appointment time accurate to within an hour.

The new software, Oracle e-business suite, enables the contact centre to deal with customer calls much more quickly. The moment a customer contacts Scottish Water with a problem, the unique integrated system starts to respond. If the problem cannot be dealt with immediately, a customer adviser will book an appointment with the field operative. The system produced a significant rise in the number of customer calls resolved at the first enquiry. Scottish Water is on track to meet targets of 85 per cent compared to 53 per cent before the programme was developed. The new system means a customer adviser can tap into an online database containing details of the customer's previous calls, water service problems in the area, and the status of the current maintenance and repair projects. This means that more calls can be dealt with immediately – helping to cut the costs of dealing with repeat calls from frustrated customers.

Source: *Customer Management*, 12 (4), July/August 2004, p 16. Reproduced with permission.

Singapore Airlines (SIA)

As stated by Dr Ted Johns, Jochen Wirtz and Professor Robert Johnston (2):

> Companies that are authentically 'world class' are noted for the fact that they are continually restless, turbulent and dissatisfied with the status quo. Singapore Airlines certainly fits this description because its management, from the top down, pushes for all the company's processes and sub-processes to be focused on incremental improvements all the time, plus periodical major transformations in process design.

Singapore Airline's commitment to customers was described by Mr Yap Kim, Senior Vice president for Product and Service, as follows:

> When we were first started as a company by our former chairman, he drilled into us that regardless of whether you were a hanger assistant, a payroll clerk or an accountant, you are there because there's a customer who is willing to pay. This is our 'secret'. It is our culture.

As Ted Johns and his colleagues comment:

> What we can learn from Singapore Airlines, and from the ICS Template framework (see the beginning of this chapter), is something that we ought to know already, but something that evidently cannot be learned too often. It is this; service excellence requires (the following) total approach in which all the ingredients are mixed together harmoniously:

- The right strategic focus and service culture, though focused consistently on bottom-line results and customer retention.
- Top-down leadership and communication of consistent messages to every part of the structure.
- A clear understanding of what service means to the customers.
- Careful attention to the people issues: recruitment, selection, training/development, learning, recognition and reward.
- Systems and process that serve the customer rather than themselves; if they are clever, their cleverness is related to customer aspirations, not principally to the cleverness of their designers.

The three crucial messages delivered by Ted Johns and his co-writers are that:

1. SIA has created a culture which expects all staff to add value – to think about their processes, systems and routines all the time, to search for incremental improvements, even to develop radically different ways of delivering customer service enhancements to the customer.
2. SIA has achieved a balance between the need for consistency – the presentation of a single face to the customer – and the customer's need for customized, personalized service. This is an increasingly difficult balancing act, but Singapore Airlines shows that it can be done.
3. Not only does SIA simultaneously concentrate on service excellence and bottom-line profitability, but it has also pushed this trade-off to its front line, with spectacular success.

Source: *Customer Management*, 11 (5), September/October 2003, pp 40–41. Reproduced with permission.

SUMMARY

- High levels of customer service are achieved and maintained by developing and implementing a customer service strategy, building a customer-centric culture, defining the attitudes, skills and behaviours in relation to customers required by staff and ensuring that employees adopt those attitudes, possess the skills and behave appropriately when in contact with customers.
- A strategic approach to customer service is necessary to ensure that a longer-term view is developed on what needs to be done to develop effective, coherent and integrated policies, processes and practices.

- A customer-centric culture needs to be developed in which everyone in the organization is aware of the importance of customer service and works cooperatively with colleagues to achieve and exceed customer service standards.
- It is necessary to define the attitudes, skills and behaviours required of all those involved in customer service to provide a basis for managing customer service, recruitment, training, performance management and reward.
- The development of appropriate attitudes, skills and behaviours is achieved through recruitment, training, performance management and reward processes.

REFERENCES

1 Johnston, R (2002) Why service excellence = reputation = increased profits, *Customer Management*, 10 (2), March, pp 8–11

2 Johns, T, Wirtz, J and Johnston, R (2003) Singapore Airlines and the service template, *Customer Management*, 11 (3), May/June, pp 38–41 and 11 (5), September/October, pp 38–41

3 Cook, S and Bates, C (2002) How to create a customer orientated culture, *Customer Management*, 10 (2), pp 30–32

4 Customer Service Management Journal, ed P Douurado (1999) *Becoming Customer Driven*, Chapter 8, The next generation leadership, pp 25–28

5 e-Research (2004) *Research report on Lands' End*, e-Reward

6 O'Connor, Z (2003) The human touch, *Topics,* ER Consultants, pp 8–10

7 Rankin, N (2002) Raising performance through people: the ninth competency survey, *Competency & Emotional Intelligence*, January, pp 2–21

Part IV

Enabling continuous improvement

16

Continuous improvement

The notion of continuous improvement is based on the Japanese concept of *kaizen* which is a composite of the word *kai* meaning change, and *zen* meaning good or for the better. The kaizen management style relies on a foundation of gradual change, building up a culture of quality awareness and constant learning. This chapter starts by examining the nature of continuous improvement and continues by dealing in turn with its requirements, framework and programmes. The chapter ends with examples of approaches to continuous improvement.

THE NATURE OF CONTINUOUS IMPROVEMENT

Continuous improvement defined

Continuous improvement is a management philosophy which contends that things can be done better. It is a set of concepts, principles and methods developed from the quality principles proposed by the quality gurus W Edwards Deming, Joseph Juran and Philip Crosby. Continuous improvement is defined by Bessant *et al* (1) as 'a company-wide process of focused and continuous incremental innovation sustained over a period of time'. The key words in this definition are:

● *Focused* – continuous improvement addresses specific issues where the effectiveness of operations and processes needs to be improved; where higher quality products or services should be provided; and, importantly, where the levels of customer service and satisfaction need to be enhanced.

- *Continuous* – the search for improvement is never-ending; it is not a one-off campaign to deal with isolated problems.
- *Incremental* – continuous improvement is not about making sudden quantum leaps in response to crisis situations; it *is* about adopting a steady, step-by-step approach to improving the ways in which the organization goes about doing things.
- *Innovation* – continuous improvement is concerned with developing new ideas and approaches to deal with new and sometimes old problems and requirements.

Continuous improvement is closely associated with quality control and assurance as described in the next chapter but these are concerned more with prevention and cure than positive incremental improvements. However, the concept of continuous improvement is fundamental to the philosophy of total quality management as also described in the next chapter.

Although continuous improvement is essentially incremental, it can result in organizational transformation. This is the process of ensuring that the organization can develop and implement major change programmes that will ensure that it responds strategically to new demands and continues to function in the dynamic atmosphere in which it operates.

Aims of continuous improvement

Deming (2) considers that customers are the most important part of the production line. The ultimate aim of continuous improvement is to recognize this fact by developing operational and business processes which ensure that customer expectations are fully met, indeed exceeded. In achieving this ultimate aim it is also necessary to ensure that the organization is profitable (private sector) or is fulfilling its purpose effectively (public and not-for-profit sectors). The more detailed aims are to improve the quality and reliability of products or services and their customer appeal, enhance operational systems, improve service levels and delivery reliability, and reduce costs and lead times.

The importance of continuous improvement

Organizations that fail to pursue actively policies of continuous improvement will stagnate, decline and eventually die. All organizations have to exist in a constantly changing environment with new challenges and demands to meet from competitors, customers, clients, central or local government and regulatory bodies. They cannot afford to stand still. The importance of continuous improvement has been emphasized by Oakland (3) as follows:

Never-ending or continuous improvement is probably the most powerful concept to guide management. It is a term not well understood in many organizations, although that must begin to change if those organizations are to survive. To maintain a wave of interest in quality, it is necessary to develop generations of managers who not only understand but are dedicated to the pursuit of never-ending improvement in meeting external and internal customer needs.

The rationale for continuous improvement

The rationale for continuous improvement is the need to pay constant attention to what needs to be done to delight customers. As IRS (4) points out, the focus of continuous improvement 'is customer satisfaction, although resource utilization is just as important, since it enables an organization to bring a product or service to a customer at the lowest possible cost'.

A critical assessment of this proposition suggests that it is based on the notion that the only purpose of an organization is to serve its customers. But it could be argued that organizations exist to achieve other purposes, for example to be profitable, to increase shareholder value, to fulfil their obligations to their employees, their clients and the public at large, and to meet the requirements of government departments and statutory authorities. However, these purposes all embrace the notion of customer service. Profitability and increased shareholder value can only be achieved through customers and clients. All stakeholders – employees, boards, trustees, governors, public sector organizations and the recipients of aid and support – are customers of the organization. Their needs and expectations must be met and continuous improvement processes provide important means of doing so.

The rationale for transformation

Organizational transformation programmes are business-led. They focus on what needs to be done to ensure that the organization performs more effectively in adding value for its customers and owners and achieving competitive advantage. The rationale for transformation is that unless something is done about it, organizations typically follow a life-cycle pattern of growth, maturity and decline. It is all too easy for what was once a successful business to stagnate and then fail to arrest the decline because of consumer shifts in tastes, increased competition, the availability of substitute products, reluctance to take advantage of technological advances, complacency, and inability to spot and deal with process inadequacies. Faced with this situation, organizations often take drastic transformational steps. But it is much better to adopt the incremental approach of continuous improvement which can progressively lead to organizational transformation and continued success than to be forced to take precipitant action in a crisis.

The implications of continuous improvement

The pursuit of continuous improvement implies that the organization is fundamentally concerned with the achievement of excellence and therefore success. It specifically means that the organization intends to attain service excellence – delivering quality products or services to customers. It should be remembered that although continuous improvement is carried out by people working together, most problems, as Deming noted, are found in systems, not people. Continuous improvement seeks to find better ways of doing things, not to attach blame.

FOSTERING A CULTURE OF CONTINUOUS IMPROVEMENT

Continuous improvement requires concerted effort to enlist the ideas and enthusiasm of everyone in the organization to ensure that a steady stream of decisions are made which will generate incremental improvements to operational and quality performance and deliver increased value to customers. It is most effective when it becomes a natural part of the way everyday work is done. A culture of continuous improvement therefore needs to be fostered and this requires attention to many factors, including leadership, shared organizational values, the development of structures, processes and people, and, overriding all these, the establishment of a high performance culture incorporating challenging goals. Continuous improvement programmes must have a consistent focus which addresses these broad issues comprehensively as well as concentrating on particular requirements or problems.

Leadership

Top management provides the leadership and direction and ensures that their vision for continuous improvement is conveyed to everyone in the organization. They communicate the values underpinning continuous improvement as set out below and see that people live those values. Middle management and supervision support the concept of continuous improvement and are actively engaged in the programmes and processes involved.

Shared organizational values

Continuous improvement values are based on the belief that the achievement of customer satisfaction is crucial and that continuous improvement programmes are the best way to achieve this aim. The values that drive continuous improvement are essentially the values that impel the satisfaction of customers. This overarching value is supported by the following specific values:

- *Respect for people* – listening to their ideas and concerns, communicating with them openly and believing that they have the intelligence and expertise to contribute positively.
- *Trusting people* – management must trust employees to act independently and employees must trust management not to exploit their ideas to their detriment. This trust must be earned. Management must deliver their promises and employees, with guidance, encouragement and help, must show that they can be trusted to get on with it.
- *Cooperation* – Oakland (3) has stated that in an environment of cooperation a greater variety of complex problems can be tackled which are beyond the capability of any one individual or department. Processes and problems are exposed to a greater diversity of knowledge, skill and experience and are addressed more efficiently; this is particularly important when the problem extends across departmental boundaries.
- *Openness* – progress is more likely to be made if information is shared, opinions are voiced without fear or favour and people are honest with one another.

Structure

The organizational structure should support continuous improvement values. A rigid functional organization is likely to prevent this happening. A more flexible, team-based structure is likely to foster cooperation and ensure that the collective wisdom of a number of people is brought to bear on problems. These can be permanent teams within departments or, usefully, cross-functional teams. Groups can be assembled which are dedicated to reviewing the scope for improvements and making specific recommendations on what needs to be done. Extended teams can be set up which include customers and suppliers. Diverse contacts outside a person's own group can enhance innovation and the generation of ideas.

Process

Process is concerned with 'the way things get done around here'. It refers to how effort is directed and coordinated, how planning and control take place, how decisions are made and how influence is exercised. If they function effectively, all these processes can contribute to the achievement of continuous improvement.

Comprehensive people development

Continuous improvement programmes require people with the knowledge and skills needed to analyse opportunities and problems, innovate and reach practical solutions. They should be prepared to behave in a cooperative way, sharing knowledge and information and working effectively with others. Training programmes can help people to acquire the knowledge and skills, and performance management and personal development processes based on a competency framework can encourage and help people to behave appropriately as contributors to continuous improvement.

High performance culture

A high performance culture is conducive to continuous improvement. The characteristics of such a culture are:

- a clear line of sight exists between the strategic aims of the organization and those of its departments and its staff at all levels;
- management defines what it requires in the shape of performance improvements, sets goals for success and monitors performance to ensure that the goals are achieved;
- leadership from the top which engenders a shared belief in the importance of continuing improvement;
- focus on promoting positive attitudes that result in a committed and motivated workforce;
- performance management processes aligned to corporate objectives to ensure that people are engaged in achieving agreed goals and standards;
- capacities of people developed through learning at all levels to support performance improvement and they are provided with opportunities to make full use of their skills and abilities;
- people are valued, recognized and rewarded according to their contribution.

THE CONDITIONS AND BEHAVIOUR THAT PROMOTE CONTINUOUS IMPROVEMENT

Continuous improvement is promoted if people live the values and attention is paid to structural, process, people and cultural issues, as also mentioned above. The behaviours required for continuous improvement have been defined by the Peabody Trust in their competency framework as set out below.

Table 16.1 Continuous improvement compentencies at the Peabody Trust

Manage continuous improvement

Constantly seeks ways of improving the quality of services, the relevance and appeal of these services to the needs of customers/clients, and the effectiveness of support and operational systems

Level	Standard	Positive behavioural indicators	Negative behavioural indicators
1	• Take steps to improve task performance. • Improve work methods to achieve higher levels of efficiency. • Ensure that quality considerations are given proper attention.	• Continually strives to improve task performance. • Makes suggestions to manager on better ways of carrying out the work.	• Not interested in doing anything different.
2	• Develop new procedures and systems for carrying out work. • Identify areas for improvement and take action to achieve improvement plans. • Give close and continuous attention to the delivery of high quality services.	• Prepared to try doing things differently. • Aware of quality standards and takes steps to ensure service delivery.	• Complacent, believes that there is no room for improvement.
3	• Set targets for improvement. • Deliver and implement programmes for introducing change. • Contribute to the development of quality assurance and control processes and ensure they are implemented.	• Encourages the development of new ideas and methods, especially those to do with the provision of quality services. • Conscious of the factors that enable change to take place smoothly.	• Doesn't try anything that hasn't been done before.
4	• Develop and oversee the implementation of quality assurance and control processes. • Develop and monitor continuous improvement programmes and stimulate action as required.	• Discusses ideas with colleagues and customers and formulates view on how to improve services and processes. • Understands the need to seek ideas from outside own experience. • Takes action to ensure that	• Follows previous practices without considering whether there is any need for change.

(Continued)

Table 16.1 continued

Level	Standard	Positive behavioural indicators	Negative behavioural indicators
	● Contribute to the successful outcomes of the management of change.	change is accepted and implemented.	
5	● Contribute to the development of a culture which encourages innovation and continuous improvement. ● Manage major change programmes in areas of responsibility.	● Continually seeks to improve. ● Generates different options and assesses the risks and implications of pursuing them.	● Reluctant to admit that there is any need for change.
6	● Lead the development of a culture which encourages innovation and continuous improvement. ● Manage major change programmes affecting the Trust as a whole.	● Challenges people and inbuilt prejudices. ● Is prepared to take risks and challenge assumptions.	● Accepts the status quo. ● Risk averse.

THE FRAMEWORK FOR CONTINUOUS IMPROVEMENT

The framework for successful continuous improvement produced by The Continuous Improvement Research for Competitive Advantage (CIRCA) unit at Brighton University consists of five elements:

1. *Strategy* – Clear strategic goals need to be set for continuous improvement providing 'sign-posted destinations'. These goals should be communicated across the whole organization and translated into specific targets for teams and individual workers.
2. *Culture* – The culture of the organization should be developed to support continuous improvement and develop quality awareness. This means defining and communicating values about the need to persist in making incremental improvements to quality as perceived by customers, and about autonomy and empowerment for those involved in improvement on a continuous basis.
3. *Infrastructure* – As recommended by CIRCA, the type of organization-wide framework necessary for the successful development of continuous improvement

includes open management systems, cross-functional management and structures, teamworking, two-way communication processes, joint decision making and employee autonomy and participation. This framework depends largely on trust: 'Managers have to trust their workers if they are going to grant them greater responsibility and authority. Empowered employees, similarly, have to trust those in senior positions not to take advantage of employees' ideas to cut jobs. Information is a key component of the creation of greater trust.'

4. *Process* – The processes used in continuous improvement include individual problem-seeking activities, problem-solving groups, suggestion schemes and company-wide campaigns to promote continuous improvement. Continuous improvement does not simply happen by itself. It has to be encouraged and facilitated by management action.

5. *Tools* – Continuous improvement is enhanced by the use of the various problem-solving tools available for individuals and groups. These include Pareto diagrams, cause-and-effect diagrams and various statistical tools such as control charts and scatter diagrams. Benchmarking is another important tool to establish standards for continuous improvement. Groups can use brainstorming techniques to develop ideas.

CONTINUOUS IMPROVEMENT PROGRAMMES

Continuous improvement programmes need to be conducted within the framework of a strategy. This forms the basis for the development of an infrastructure of teams, processes and systems and for the conduct of the work of continuously reviewing and improving processes and systems and the ways in which they are managed.

The strategy for continuous improvement

A continuous improvement strategy needs to be formulated to provide a sense of purpose and direction. It will be concerned with how the organization intends to improve quality, processes and customer service. The strategy is produced in six steps: (1) establish corporate objectives, (2) determine the effects of current practices, (3) identify problems and their causes, (4) decide on actions, (5) prepare a programme for implementation, (6) define resources required, including the infrastructure.

The infrastructure for continuous improvement

The arrangements for implementing the continuous improvement strategy consist of the creation of an infrastructure of involvement processes, including suggestion schemes and improvement groups and the development of tools and assessment procedures. The infrastructure will be composed of people who have been given responsibility for promoting and coordinating continuous improvement programmes, and systems for analysing problems and recording outcomes and proposed actions, assessing results and ensuring that innovations are embedded. Self-managed teams are set up, procedures are developed for process mapping and problem solving and systematic benchmarking takes place. Although the ideas for continuous improvement may largely be developed by project teams or improvement groups, it is necessary to set up some form of coordinating body such as a steering group to oversee continuous improvement programmes and ensure that they are functioning properly in terms of implementation as well as the origination of practical and productive ideas. The steering group can be serviced by someone or a small team who will provide help and resources to improvement groups, monitor progress and maintain records.

Quality circles as a formal part of the infrastructure of continuous improvement achieved some popularity in the 1980s. They consisted of small groups of volunteers who carried out related work and who met regularly to discuss and propose ways of improving working methods or arrangements under a trained leader. Their aim was to tap the knowledge and experience of employees who may know more about work problems than their managers or supervisors. Quality circle members were trained in the use of analytical techniques such as cause-and-effect diagrams. They presented their ideas to management and were involved in implementation. Quality circles were based on what was assumed to be a Japanese technique and seemed to be a good idea at the time. Unfortunately, it was not appreciated that the approach to using such groups in Japan was only part of a much more comprehensive *kaizen* programme in which everyone was involved. In the UK, top management often either paid lip service to the idea or thought that it would solve all their problems, which of course it could not. Middle management were often overtly or, worse, covertly hostile because they saw suggestions coming from their staff as criticisms of them which trespassed on their prerogative. To get over the somewhat discredited image of quality circles, they were sometimes renamed 'improvement groups'. But as formal entities these often failed too, for the same reasons. The tendency now is to set up ad hoc groups to deal with specific problems, although these might and indeed should be treated as part of the infrastructure of a total continuous improvement programme. However, there is one important legacy of the quality circle movement. That is the emphasis of formal training for group leaders and members in analytical and problem-solving techniques as described later in this chapter.

Approaches to continuous improvement

Continuous improvement involves constantly adapting by getting and using information and by evaluating changes to make sure they are effective. It requires good information from a variety of sources to evaluate outcomes (what is achieved) and processes (how it is achieved). It is necessary to pull people together from different functions or disciplines and levels freely to discuss the information and issues involved, come up with ideas, critically evaluate them, ensure they are put into practice and measure progress and outcomes. The guidelines on improvement efforts are:

- Before you try to solve a problem, define it.
- Before you try to control a process, understand it.
- Before trying to control everything, find out what is important and work on the most important or on that process that makes the biggest impact.

Applications for continuous improvement

Continuous improvement is proactive – it explores new ways of doing things; it does not wait for a problem to emerge. It is about seeking opportunities, not fire-fighting. It can be intuitive, based on immediate apprehension or insight without empirically based reasoning. But intuitions have to be evaluated and for this purpose experimentation takes place to test the hypothesis that action will lead to improvement. Overall, the process of continuous improvement involves empowerment. Individuals and teams are empowered to investigate opportunities, solve problems, produce ideas and solutions and take action.

These applications need to be differentiated and evaluated in continuous improvement programmes. These ought to be proactive but there will be occasions where it is necessary to react to a pressing problem. Intuition has its place but it should not be allowed to go too far without proper testing. Experimentation is desirable but there will be times when something has to be done *now* – it can't wait. Empowerment is highly desirable but there will be occasions when management has to take the lead and make the decisions.

Continuous improvement techniques

Improvement is based on building knowledge of what works and does not work and then applying it appropriately. The three basic questions are: (1) What are we trying to accomplish? (2) What changes can we make which will result in an improvement? and (3) How will we know that a change is an improvement?

The plan–do–check–act cycle as set out by Deming (2) is used as the basis for developing and testing changes: *plan* the change strategy, including who will be involved, what data will be collected and when the data will be considered adequate for study, *do* the intervention, *check* the results, *act* on the knowledge gained from the data – maintain the plan, modify the plan, add to the plan. If the change is successful, embed it by expanding it to the rest of the system, establishing processes to support it and identifying ways in which further improvements can be made.

A number of analytical and problem-solving techniques are available as described below.

Problem solving

Problem solving is carried out in 10 steps:

1. *Define the situation* – establish what has gone wrong or is about to go wrong.
2. *Specify objectives* – define what is to be achieved now or in the future to deal with an actual or potential problem or a change in circumstances.
3. *Develop hypotheses* – develop hypotheses about what has caused the problem.
4. *Get the facts* – find out what has actually happened and contrast this with an assessment of what ought to have happened. Try to understand the attitudes and motivation of those concerned. Remember that people will see what has happened in terms of their own position and feelings (their framework of reference). Obtain information about internal or external constraints that affect the situation.
5. *Analyse the facts* – determine what is relevant and what is irrelevant. Diagnose the likely cause or causes of the problem. Do not be tempted to focus on symptoms rather than root causes. Test any assumptions. Dig into what lies behind the problem.
6. *Identify possible courses of action* – spell out what each involves.
7. *Evaluate alternative courses of action* – assess the extent to which the objectives are likely to be achieved, the cost of implementation, any practical difficulties that might emerge and the possible reactions of stakeholders. Critical evaluation techniques as described below can be used for this purpose.
8. *Weigh and decide* – determine which alternative is likely to result in the most practical and acceptable solution to the problem. This is often a balanced judgement.
9. *Plan implementation* – timetable, project management resources required.
10. *Implement* – monitor progress and evaluate success.

Critical evaluation

Critical evaluation techniques are used to assess the degree to which a proposal or a concept is appropriate or valid. There are five steps:

1. Analyse and describe requirement.
2. Identify alternative approaches to meeting requirement.
3. Assess the advantages and disadvantages of each approach.
4. Summarize factors influencing choice of approach.
5. Define criteria for determining the success of the selected approach.

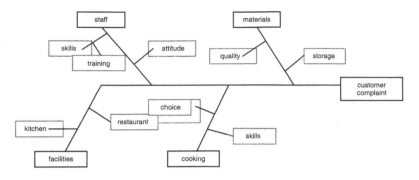

Figure 16.1 Cause and effect diagram

Cause-and-effect diagrams

Cause-and-effect diagrams are used to clarify the causes of a problem. They are sometimes called 'fishbone diagrams' (because of their shape) or 'Ishikawa diagrams' (after Kaoru Ishikawa, the Japanese quality expert who championed their use).

Suppose a customer complains at a restaurant. The fault may be caused by the raw materials, the cooking, the staff or the facilities. Problems with the raw materials may in turn be caused by suppliers, storage or costs. A cause-and-effect diagram draws these relationships as leading to spines like a fishbone as shown in Figure 16.1.

Pareto charts

Pareto charts are used to focus on key problems. They are based on Pareto's Law. Pareto, an Italian economist, observed that 20 per cent of the population owned 80 per cent of the wealth. Dr Joseph Juran (5) in the 1940s recognized a universal principle which he called 'the vital few and trivial many'. This principle – that 20 per cent of something produces 80 per cent of the results – became generally known as Pareto's Law. In his original work, Juran noted that 20 per cent of the defects caused 80 per cent of the problems. Many investigations have revealed that this law applies, for example 80 per cent of stock comes from 20 per cent of suppliers, 80 per cent of sales come from 20 per cent of sales staff. It is also sometimes argued that 20 per cent of an organization's staff will produce 80 per cent of the problems, but it works the other way round, ie another 20 per cent of staff will produce 80 per cent of added value. The principle has also been applied to the process of management, suggesting that people should identify the 20 per cent of the important things they do during a day and concentrate more on these than the remaining 80 per cent.

The problem is that of identifying the vital 20 per cent and Pareto charts are used for this purpose. They illustrate the relative importance of problems by showing their

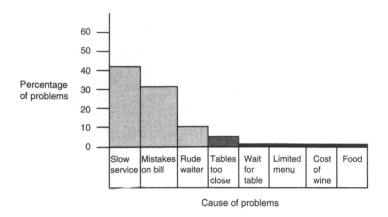

Figure 16.2 A Pareto chart

frequency or size in a descending bar graph as illustrated in Figure 16.2. They are constructed by listing the problems and then assessing how significant they are in relation to one another.

Brainstorming

Brainstorming gets a group to generate as many ideas as possible without pausing to evaluate them. The rationale for the process is that people are more likely to come up with ideas if they are not subjected to criticism or even ridicule. Any idea goes and no one is allowed to comment on what others say. The aim is to produce as many ideas as possible. The majority (possibly 80 per cent) are likely to be useless, but some possible ideas (20 per cent perhaps) will emerge. Evaluation of the ideas only takes place after the session has finished and no one gets the credit for any accepted ideas or the blame for any of those rejected.

Nominal group technique

The nominal group technique gets a group to achieve consensus on the ranking of problems, issues or solutions in order of importance.

Benchmarking

Benchmarking involves identifying good practice in other organizations, comparing them with practices within the benchmarker's organization and drawing conclusions on the lessons learnt from good practice elsewhere which can be applied within that organization. The comparisons concentrate on the areas for improvement that have been identified and the aim is to learn as much as possible about how other organizations have tackled similar problems, bearing in mind that what works well in one organization does not necessarily work well in another.

Continuous improvement programmes

Continuous improvement programmes can take place in the following stages:

1. *Set up project teams* – they will consist of people who have the knowledge required to address continuous improvement issues. The members will be trained in analytical and problem-solving techniques and the leader will be trained in facilitation skills.
2. *Define terms of reference* – the terms of reference define the scope of the project which includes a statement of the issue or problem, a definition of the boundaries, a target date for completion and an indication of the resources available.
3. *Set objectives and targets* – goals for improvement are set with an indication of their size and a description of the context in which they are to be achieved. The broad areas covered may include increasing customer satisfaction and therefore retention by means of specific improvements to quality and levels of service, improvements to the efficiency and effectiveness of selling, production and distribution processes, reduction in defects or errors and the achievement of 'right first time', improvements in productivity and the use of value analysis (a cost reduction technique which uses organized procedures for the identification of unnecessary cost elements in a component or product by the analysis of its function and design – function being defined as that aspect of the product which makes it work or sell). These broad areas may be defined more closely in terms of specific targets for such requirements as reducing errors, speeding up processes or responding to customer complaints.
4. *Plan the project* – this involves fact collection and analysis, diagnosing the causes of problems, developing solutions, implementing the changes and reviewing the results.
5. *Fact collection and analysis* – the aim is to understand the process or system – this means getting the facts about how it works (or does not work). The questions asked at this stage include: What does the process do? What are the stages of the process? What are the inputs and outputs from the process? Who are the suppliers and customers (internal and external) of the process? Are there any problems with the process? Use is made of flow charts which provide a picture of the process by tracing each of its stages and their interconnections.
6. *Define the problem* – on the basis of the analysis, describe what the problem is and what impact it makes. Use Pareto charts to describe the relative significance of the problems so that attention can be focused on them during the diagnostic stage.

7. *Diagnose causes* – use problem-solving techniques and cause-and-effect diagrams to establish the cause or causes of the problems.
8. *Develop solutions* – ideas are generated for solution by studying the facts and the diagnosis and by investigating alternative ways of doing things based on the group's experience supplemented by specific enquiries and reading appropriate literature. Critical evaluation techniques are used to identify solutions. The group may decide at this stage to benchmark, ie find out how other organizations are tackling the problem (problems are seldom unique).
9. *Implement the solution* – the plan–do–check–act sequence described earlier in this chapter is adopted to implement the selected solution. Define exactly what changes need to be introduced, the sequence of activities required to make them, the responsibilities for implementation, the resources required and the timetable.
10. *Monitor* – review and evaluate the impact of the changes, answering the following questions: Were the expected benefits achieved? If not, what needs to be done about it? What lessons can be learnt? How can we ensure that the improvements are maintained (hold the gains)?

Barriers to continuous improvement

The main barrier to continuous improvement is complacency on the part of management. If they believe that everything is fine, it is unlikely that any serious attempt will be made to do things better. The other barrier is indifference or lack of cooperation from staff.

Complacency is difficult to deal with if it is ingrained into the culture of the organization. It can be shaken if major problems of performance or profitability arise but it may then be too late. If it exists amongst top management it can only be hoped that there are some people in the organization who are armed with the facts and are determined enough to pressurize management into taking action. If not, management complacency may only be shattered when shareholders, government departments, governors or trustees make their concerns felt. And it may then be too late.

Indifference or hostility to continuous improvement changes from staff can be countered by recognizing that it is the situation which requires systematic change management approaches, including communication, involvement and training. These are considered in Chapter 12.

Holding the gains

It is necessary to ensure that the outcomes of a continuous improvement programme should be embedded to become a permanent and effective part of the organization's processes. Juran (5) used the phrase 'holding the gains' to emphasize this requirement. Holding the gains begins when a solution is developed to develop better practices and processes, produce cost savings or deliver improved customer service. It must be a solution which is not only practical in terms of its immediate implementation but is also sustainable without undue effort. The momentum created by the change should continue. Quality assurance techniques can be introduced to keep the process under continuous review so that any failings can be identified quickly and dealt with. It must never be assumed that a changed process will go on operating as planned under its own volition. Continuous effort is required to ensure that incremental gains are consolidated and become part of normal working practices to the benefit of customers and, therefore, the organization.

EXAMPLES OF APPROACHES TO CONTINUOUS IMPROVEMENT

The following examples illustrate the imperatives for and application of continuous improvement in a sample of different organizations and sectors.

Higher education – The University of Sydney

The University of Sydney states that its approach to continuous improvement is to learn from best practice, locally and internationally, and benchmark against leading research universities. It claims that its quality assurance processes are evidence based and intrinsic to the work of all staff. The features of its policy are critical self-evaluation, methodical collection of evidence about service satisfaction and student experience and a 'focus on efficient planning, management and resource processes to achieve excellence and ensure continuous improvement'. A process of cyclical reviews (five years) is followed to assist in safeguarding and enhancing the quality of its core activities, ie teaching, learning and research. These include reviews of administrative services to identify, evaluate and appraise the quality of deliverables and to implement improvements in a planned, timely and effective manner.

Finance – Mortgage Express

Mortgage Express is committed to the principles of the EFQM Excellence Model (see Chapter 17). Self-assessment against the model revealed a number of areas for improvement, including a review of mission, vision and values, the need to provide better training on customer service, a need to develop staff communications, a new process to capture improvement ideas from staff, a system for getting regular feedback about staff satisfaction and a requirement to train management in facilitating change skills. An 'Exceeding Expectations' programme was introduced to support the

'Customer Value Proposition' for the achievement of outstanding customer service. A database was launched to record staff improvement ideas. This comprised IF and DONE processes. IF is the name given to an ideas forum and DONE refers to the actions taken to evaluate and implement improvements.

Local authorities

Merthyr Tydfil County Borough Council has set up a continuous improvement programme to achieve excellence by encouraging staff to make improvement suggestions. There are about 50 teams working to suggest and create improvements.

One of the four key corporate priorities at North Somerset Council is 'to ensure that the customer is at the heart of the Council's approach to service delivery'. The aim is to improve the Audit Commission's Performance Assessment. Indicators have been developed, such as the proportion of people who say that they received friendly and polite service when they approached the Council, the percentage of telephone calls answered within 15 seconds, the number of people who think the Council keeps them well informed, the percentage of invoices that were paid promptly.

Public utility – Severn Trent Water

As reported by Tennant, Warwood and Chiang (6), Severn Trent Water conducted in-company research to identify the main barriers to continuous improvement in the areas of leadership, training, communication, motivation, teamwork and change management. The study concluded that the company should develop an organization culture and management style to support continuous improvement of daily working processes, and that change should be managed against the achievement of appropriate quality targets. A continuous improvement process was introduced based on a structured problem-solving model incorporating the application of established quality tools, to be applied by trained problem-solving teams from the Customer Relations Department.

In their comments on this case, Tennant *et al* noted that:

- 'Targets should be clearly defined and refined for the whole organization down to individual levels to enable activities to be designed and controlled to reach the predicted achievement for productivity, profitability, responsibility, workforce achievement, management development and innovation.'
- Targets should be 'formulated in a team environment to achieve consensus and achieve a mutual commitment to them'.
- Cross-functional teams should be set up to review higher-order targets to develop local targets and means. The basis should be the Japanese process known as *Hoshin Kanri* which focuses on the improvements required to meet the targets rather than the targets themselves.

- 'To be effective, a continuous improvement process needs to be delivered through rapid resolution of problems which represent a concrete improvement activity.'
- The best problem-solving methods are simple ones that can be applied at all levels from senior management to junior staff.
- A 'bottom-up' approach to problem solving is the more natural and effective way for achieving continuous improvement, as it is the workforce that can 'understand, contribute, generate and manage change'.

Manufacturing – The Boeing Company

The Boeing Company lays down that the organization: 'Shall develop and document a continuous improvement system. This system is to include performance measures, such as measures of waste, quality, cycle time and customer satisfaction. The organization shall conduct periodic management reviews of the system, paying close attention to the performance measures and modifying improvement activities as necessary.' The requirement is that: 'Procedures are coordinated enterprise-wide for consistency and standardization, so that all departments practice continuous improvement.'

Service – Serco

As one of the world's leading service companies, Serco has defined its approach to continuous improvement as follows: 'Competitive pressure creates a continuous challenge to generate fresh ideas to win and retain contracts. The challenge is to create an environment and culture that recognize the need for continual improvement and innovation in the way we develop our service throughout the life cycle of each contract.' The following elements drive continuous improvement:

- *Strategic planning* – the contract development plan, cost reduction strategy and procurement strategy.
- *Service management* – manage customer expectations (demand) and the delivery process (service), improve user interface and communications, introduce better financial control.
- *Operational delivery* – introduce and monitor systems that define service requirements such as service level agreements, produce performance standards and measurements for incorporation into contracts and in-service appraisals and continued development of procedural and operating manuals.

External benchmarking is used to gain understanding of how Serco is performing in different areas in comparison to other operations. Internally, the Serco Best Practice Centre has been set up to evaluate the needs of the business, design tools and processes to improve effectiveness and provide training. It is also responsible for identifying the intellectual property in the organization, capturing that knowledge and using it in the business.

SUMMARY

- Continuous improvement is defined as 'a company-wide process of focused and continuous incremental innovation sustained over a period of time' (1).
- Continuous improvement is closely associated with quality control, assurance and total quality management.
- The ultimate aim of continuous improvement is to develop operational and business processes which ensure that customer expectations are fully met, indeed exceeded.
- Organizations that fail to pursue actively policies of continuous improvement will stagnate, decline and eventually die.
- The rationale for continuous improvement is the need to pay constant attention to what needs to be done to delight customers.
- The pursuit of continuous improvement implies that the organization is fundamentally concerned with the achievement of excellence and therefore success.
- Continuous improvement requires concerted effort to enlist the ideas and enthusiasm of everyone in the organization to ensure that a steady stream of decisions are made which will generate incremental improvements to operational and quality performance and deliver increased value to customers.
- Continuous improvement values are based on the belief that the achievement of customer satisfaction is crucial and that continuous improvement programmes are the best way to achieve this aim.
- A continuous improvement strategy needs to be formulated to provide a sense of purpose and direction. It will be concerned with how the organization intends to improve quality, processes and customer service.
- The infrastructure for continuous improvement consists of the creation of involvement processes, including suggestion schemes and improvement groups and the development of tools and assessment procedures.
- Continuous improvement involves constantly adapting by getting and using information and by evaluating changes to make sure they are effective. It requires good information from a variety of sources to evaluate outcomes (what is achieved) and processes (how it is achieved).
- Improvement is based on building knowledge of what works and does not work and then applying it appropriately.
- The plan–do–check–act cycle as set out by Deming is used as the basis for developing and testing changes: *plan* the change strategy, including who will be

involved, what data will be collected and when the data will be considered adequate for study, *do* the intervention, *check* the results, *act* on the knowledge gained from the data – maintain the plan, modify the plan, add to the plan.

- A number of analytical and problem-solving approaches are available such as problem-solving techniques, critical evaluation, cause-and-effect diagrams, Pareto charts, brainstorming, nominal group technique and benchmarking.
- Continuous improvement programmes can take place in the following stages:

1. *Set up project teams*
2. *Define terms of reference*
3. *Set objectives and targets*
4. *Plan the project*
5. *Collect and analyse facts*
6. *Define the problem*
7. *Diagnose causes*
8. *Develop solutions*
9. *Implement the solution*
10. *Monitor.*

- The main barriers to continuous improvement are complacency on the part of management and indifference or lack of cooperation from staff.
- It is necessary to 'hold the gains' – ensure that the outcomes of a continuous improvement programme are embedded to become a permanent and effective part of the organization's processes.

REFERENCES

1   Bessant, J, Caffyn, S, Gilbert, J and Harding, R (1994) Rediscovering continuous improvement, *Technovation*, 14 (3), pp 17–29
2   Deming, W E (1986) *Out of the Crisis*, MIT Centre for Advanced Engineering Study, Boston, MA
3   Oakland, J S (1998) *Total Quality Management: The route to improving performance*, Butterworth-Heinemann, Oxford
4   Industrial Relations Services (1997) Variety through continuous improvement, *IRS Employment Trends No. 624*, pp 8–16
5   Juran, J M (ed) (1988) *Quality Control Handbook*, McGraw-Hill, Maidenhead
6   Tennant, C, Warwood, S J and Chiang, M P P (2002) A continuous improvement process at Severn Water, *The TQM magazine*, 14 (5), pp 284–92

17

Quality management

Continuous improvement as described in the last chapter is closely associated with quality management. They both aim to deliver excellence to the customer by attaining high quality standards. The difference is that quality management as discussed in this chapter is concerned more with the assurance and control of quality rather than the achievement of incremental improvements by developing new approaches to managing processes and systems.

This chapter starts by defining the concepts of quality and quality management and describing the contribution of the quality 'gurus' to it. It continues with a description in turn of the main approaches to quality management: quality assurance, quality control, total quality management, 'Six Sigma', quality issues and the use of quality standards.

QUALITY DEFINED

There are two views of quality: the traditional *internal* view which indicates that a product that meets the standards of the organization should meet the needs of customers, and the more acceptable current *external* view that it is customers who decide when a product meets their expectations. These broad descriptions of quality can be expanded as indicated below.

Quality can be defined and assessed in the following terms:

- innate excellence;
- convenience of use;

- performance;
- reliability;
- value for money;
- level of customer service;
- fitness for purpose;
- attractive appearance or style;
- durability;
- conformance to design specifications;
- uniformity, with small variability.

These characteristics refer to two aspects of product quality: *designed* quality, which sets the quality that a product is designed to have; and *achieved* quality, which shows how closely a product comes to meeting the designed quality standard.

QUALITY MANAGEMENT DEFINED

Quality management is concerned with all the activities required to ensure that products and services conform to the standards set by the organization and meet expectations of customers. These activities include the steps taken to ensure that high quality is achieved (quality assurance), and the actions taken to check that defined quality standards are being achieved and maintained (quality control).

CONTRIBUTION OF THE QUALITY GURUS

The approach to quality management generally used today owes much to the contributions of the quality gurus, especially Deming, Juran and Crosby who spelt out the conditions and behaviour that promote quality as summarized below.

W Edwards Deming

Deming (1) emphasized the importance of customers, the significance of continuous improvement and the fact that quality is determined by the system. He believed that customer satisfaction is created by a combination of responsiveness to customers' views and needs and continuous improvement of products, services and operational systems. He summarized his views in 14 principles:

1. Create constancy of purpose towards product quality.
2. Refuse to accept customary levels of mistakes, delays, defects and errors.
3. Stop depending on mass inspection and build quality into the product in the first place.

4. Stop awarding business on the basis of price only – reduce the number of suppliers and insist on meaningful measures of quality.
5. Develop programmes for continuous improvement of costs, quality, productivity and service.
6. Institute training for all employees.
7. Focus supervision on helping employees to do a better job.
8. Drive out fear by encouraging two-way communication.
9. Break down barriers between departments and encourage problem solving through teamwork.
10. Eliminate numerical goals, posters and slogans that demand improvement without saying how it should be achieved.
11. Eliminate arbitrary quotas that interfere with quality.
12. Remove barriers that stop people having pride in their work.
13. Institute vigorous programmes of lifelong education, training and self-improvement.
14. Put everyone to work on implementing these 14 points.

Deming suggested that managers are in control of the organization and are responsible for its performance. The quality process is in two parts: the *system* over which managers have control and which contributes 80 per cent of the variation in quality, and the *workers* who are under their own control and who contribute 20 per cent of the variation in quality. Major variations in quality therefore come from managers improving the system rather than workers improving their performance.

J M Juran

Juran's (2) main contribution to the philosophy of total quality was his concept of managerial breakthrough. In the traditional control situation, the typical managerial attitude is that the present level of performance is good enough or cannot be improved. The aim is therefore to perpetuate performance at that level. Management attempts simply to identify and eliminate short-term deviations from the usual performance.

Juran stated that in the breakthrough situation management adopts a completely different attitude. The belief is held strongly that change is desirable and possible in all aspects of operation. It is up to managers to make the 'breakthrough'. They must recognize and act on the need for what is, in effect, continuous improvement.

Philip B Crosby

Crosby (3) emphasized that 'in discussing quality we are dealing with a people situation'. He suggested five factors which govern the management of quality:

1. Quality means conformance not elegance.
2. There is no such thing as a quality problem.
3. There is no such thing as the economics of quality. It is always cheaper to do the job right first time.
4. The only performance measurement is the cost of quality.
5. The only performance standard is zero defects.

QUALITY MANAGEMENT APPROACHES

Quality management systems and techniques aim to deliver excellence to customers and thus make a major contribution to organizational success. The quality management approaches as described below are the standardized techniques of quality assurance and quality control, and the holistic concepts of total quality management and Six Sigma.

Quality assurance

Quality assurance aims to build quality into the system. It is based on procedures designed to ensure that the activities carried out in the organization such as design, development, manufacturing, and service delivery result in products, services or other outcomes which meet the requirements and needs of customers. The underpinning philosophy of quality assurance is that right methods will produce right results (quality products or services).

Quality is also achieved by ensuring that individuals have the skills required to do their jobs. Careful selection, skills training and appropriate allocation of people to jobs are therefore important aspects of quality assurance. Job design is another key aspect of quality assurance. The jobs people do and the level of responsibility they are given must enable them to manage the quality of their outputs themselves without relying on other people, eg inspectors, to do it for them. As Maslow (4) said: 'If you want people to do a good job, give them a good job to do' and 'A job that isn't worth doing isn't worth doing well.'

Quality control

Quality control involves the application of data collection and analysis to monitor and measure the extent to which quality assurance requirements have been met in terms of product or service performance and reliability. It can involve detailed procedural documentation which spells out how quality should be achieved and measured. The traditional approach to controlling quality is inspection. Control can be exercised more scientifically by means of statistical techniques.

Statistical quality control

Statistical quality control uses sampling techniques and mathematical analysis to ensure that during design, manufacturing and servicing, work is carried out and material used within the specified limits required to produce the desired standards of quality, performance and reliability. The main techniques used in statistical quality control are:

● *Acceptance sampling*, which ensures that items do not pass to the next stage in the process if an unacceptably high proportion of the batch is outside the quality limit. Sampling consists of taking a representative number of examples from a population and drawing conclusions about the behaviour of the whole population from the behaviour of the sample. Sampling techniques are based on statistical theory, including probability theory.
● *Control charts*, on which the results of the inspection of samples are compared with the results expected from a stable situation. If they do not agree, then action may be necessary. These comparisons can be recorded graphically on control charts on which warning and action levels are marked. Control charts set out the control limits which either warn that a problem exists or indicate that action needs to be taken (warning and action limits).
● *Control by attributes* – attributes have only two states, ie whether an article or service is acceptable or not. The information required for control purposes compares the number of defects and/or the number of defects per unit, which are compared with the desired level of quality – the acceptable quality level (AQL).
● *Control by variables* – variables can have any value on a continuous scale. Control by variables therefore takes place when there is a distribution of the features being measured rather than a go or no-go position as in attribute control. Variables are therefore measured, in contrast to attributes, which are counted.

Total quality control

Total quality control takes a comprehensive view of all aspects of quality through techniques such as zero-defects programmes or Taguchi methodology.

Zero-defects programmes

Zero-defects programmes aim to improve product quality beyond the level that it might economically be achieved through statistical procedures. The ultimate aim is to eliminate defects so far as that is conceivably possible.

The principal features of such programmes are:

- Agreement is reached with all concerned on the quality goals to be attained and the quality problems which prevent their achievement.
- The participation of all those involved in establishing and running the quality programme is organized.
- Clear targets are set against which improvements can be measured.
- Procedures are established for providing prompt feedback to employees on their quality achievements.
- Provision is made for rewards to be given for achieving high quality standards.
- Employees are encouraged to make suggestions on causes of errors and remedies and arrangements are made for ideas to be implemented jointly.
- Work is organized and jobs designed to facilitate all of the above.

Taguchi methodology

This methodology was developed by the Japanese engineer, Taguchi. Its main features are to:

- push quality back to the design stage because quality control can never compensate for bad design;
- emphasize design rather than inspection for control of production;
- produce robust products with intrinsic quality and reliability characteristics;
- prototype product designs and production processes;
- concentrate on the practical engineering, not the statistical niceties of quality control theory.

Total quality management

Total quality management (TQM) is a systematic method of ensuring that all activities within an organization happen in the way they have been planned in order to meet the defined needs of customers. Its approach is holistic – quality management is not a separate function to be treated in isolation, but is an integral part of all operations. Everyone in the organization is concerned with quality. Its philosophy is that it is necessary to be 'right first time', ensuring that no defective systems are in use and that no defective units are made or inadequate services delivered.

TQM involves a change of focus from inspections at the end of a process to an emphasis in the planning stage on ensuring that the design allows high quality and in the operations stage that no defects are produced. During the process, operations departments take responsibility for their own quality. There is no separate inspections function. Each person is responsible for passing on units that are of perfect quality. This is quality at source, with job enlargement for operatives who are now responsible for both production and quality management and are rewarded accordingly.

The steps for introducing TQM are:

1. *Get top management commitment.* This is a key feature of TQM. Managers have control of the organization and they must realize that TQM is not another fad that will disappear in a few months, but is a way of thinking that improves long-term performance.
2. *Find out what customers really want.* Without knowing exactly what customers want it is impossible to design products or offer services that satisfy them. This goes beyond simply asking for opinions, and gets customers involved in the process, perhaps discussing designs in focus groups.
3. *Design products with quality in mind.* Organizations must design products that are robust and satisfy both internal and external demands.
4. *Design the process with quality in mind.* The quality of the product depends on the process used to make it, so this must work effectively and efficiently to produce perfect quality.
5. *Build teams of empowered employees.* Quality depends on everyone in the organization, so they should be recognized as the most valuable asset, with appropriate training and motivation.
6. *Keep track of results.* TQM looks for continuous improvement, with the adjustments to products having a cumulative effect over time.
7. *Extend these ideas to suppliers and distributors.* Organizations do work in isolation but are part of a supply chain, with the quality of the final product depending on every link in the chain.

Six Sigma

The main cause of quality problems is variation. To improve quality, variation must be measured, reduced and eventually prevented. Six Sigma, a name coined by Motorola Inc, is a statistical approach to the measurement of variations which has been expanded holistically to cover all aspects of quality in an organization. The Greek letter sigma (() is used as a symbol to denote the standard deviation or the measure of variation in a process. Statistically, six sigmas represent the range of values of a population with a normal distribution. Operations can be calibrated in terms of sigma level and the greater the number of sigmas, the fewer the defects. The aim is to achieve a quality level of six sigmas. Businesses that want to impress their customers label themselves as 'Six Sigma organizations'.

General Electric Co has carried out an ambitious five-year programme to promote the quest for Six Sigma in all its business activities. The customer satisfaction objective is highly interdisciplinary, encompassing all activities in a modern enterprise. General Electric refers to Six Sigma as a product of learning. In a recent annual report the company stated that: 'We have invested more than a billion dollars in effort and the financial returns have now entered the exponential phase.'

Six Sigma uses a range of quality management and statistical tools to construct a framework for process improvement. The aim is to achieve the sigma level of 'critical to quality' performance measures that meet the needs of customers. This is done by following the sequence define–measure–analyse–improve–control (DYMAIC).

Commentary

Quality management must start with quality assurance, and statistical quality control techniques can be used to check on the standards achieved and indicate where action is required. But quality assurance and quality control methodologies are best carried out within an holistic framework – TQM or Six Sigma. The problem with both these approaches is that they depend on strong top management, committed line managers and a continuing programme of communication, encouragement and training to achieve general commitment to the philosophies upon which these are based. This can be difficult to achieve, and if it is not, the impetus for total quality may not be sustainable.

QUALITY STANDARDS

Quality standards provide the basis for developing and measuring the effectiveness of a quality system. Their aim is to encourage organizations to think about their management processes and react to the changing demands placed upon them. The international standard ISO 9000 is the one most generally used. In addition, an important quality standard has been produced by the European Foundation for Quality Management – the EFQM model.

ISO 9000

The requirements of ISO 9000 are structured under four headings:

- management responsibility – this includes particular responsibilities for ensuring continuous improvement, benchmarking and management review;
- resource management – this focuses on the effective use of resources, especially matching the skills of individuals to the demands of their jobs (the skill-based rather than procedural documentation approach);
- process management – this includes a requirement for risk analysis, recognition of the interactions between departments (the internal customer chain), capacity to

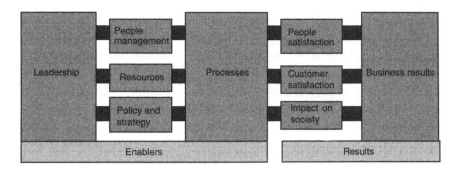

Figure 17.1 The EFQM model

respond to changing customer expectations, formal and documented reviews of capabilities and a focus on the delivery and post-delivery activity (organizations are expected to 'deliver it right' as well as 'make it right');
● measurement, analysis and improvement – this requires an appropriate measurement system to be in place which captures the adherence, or otherwise, of the product to the standards specified.

The EFQM model of quality

The European Foundation for Quality management (EFQM), as shown in Figure 17.1, indicates that customer satisfaction, people (employee) satisfaction and impact on society are achieved through leadership. This drives the policy and strategy, people management, resources and processes required to produce excellence in business results.

The nine elements in the model are defined as follows:

● *leadership* – how the behaviour and actions of the executive team and all other leaders inspire, support and promote a culture of total quality management;
● *policy and strategy* – how the organization formulates, deploys and reviews its policy and strategy and turns it into plans and actions;
● *people management* – how the organization realizes the full potential of its people;
● *resources* – how the organization manages resources effectively and efficiently;
● *processes* – how the organization identifies, manages, reviews and improves its processes;
● *customer satisfaction* – what the organization is achieving in relation to the satisfaction of its external customers;
● *people satisfaction* – what the organization is achieving in relation to the satisfaction of its people;

- *impact on society* – what the organization is achieving in satisfying the needs and the expectations of the local, national and international community at large;
- *business results* – what the organization is achieving in relation to its planned business objectives and in satisfying the needs and expectations of everyone with a financial interest or stake in the organization.

Organizations that adopt the EFQM model accept the importance of performance measurement and work all the time to improve the usefulness of their measures, but they also recognize that simply measuring a problem does not improve it. Managers can often devolve their best energies to the analysis, leaving little left for the remedy. It is important to focus on both the *enablers* and the *processes*.

QUALITY MANAGEMENT ISSUES

The principal issues that affect quality management are:

- sustaining interest and maintaining momentum;
- developing the conditions and behaviour that promote quality;
- resolving the conflict between quality assurance and production or delivery targets;
- ensuring process compliance.

Sustaining interest and maintaining momentum

Total quality management or Six Sigma initiatives usually start on a wave of enthusiasm. This may originate from top management but it frequently happens as a result of the messianic zeal of a middle manager who convinces everyone from the top downwards that priority should be given to quality management.

A comprehensive programme then emerges involving communication, training and any other devices that will ensure commitment and engagement. Systems are designed, procedures are created and an infrastructure of full-time quality specialists, steering committees and improvement groups is set up.

The problem is sustaining interest and engagement after the first waves of enthusiasm have died down. Some people can become indifferent to quality, seeing it as an abstract concept and nothing to do with them. Others pay lip service to it but don't try very hard. Yet others resent the perceived bureaucracy of quality assurance and quality systems because they see them as taking up unnecessary time and interfering with their work.

If interest is not maintained, momentum will cease. So what can be done about it? The first step is to involve everyone from the start and keep them involved. Contributions to improving quality should be recognized and rewarded. Roles should be designed which emphasize responsibilities for quality and encourage people to be quality conscious. Competence frameworks should include quality and continuous improvement as a major heading, and performance management processes should ensure that the delivery of quality is specifically reviewed and assessed. Induction courses should emphasize the importance of quality and continuous learning programmes should equip people with the skills to produce quality performance. Bureaucracy should be kept to a minimum. If there are designated quality assurance or quality control specialists, they should act on the principle that their job is to help people to deliver quality, not to police their performance.

Developing the conditions and behaviour that promote quality

The activities set out above will all contribute to the development of the conditions and behaviour that promote quality. This is essentially a matter of creating and maintaining a quality-orientated culture. Such a culture will be defined in terms of values and norms. The core values of the organization should give prominence to quality. The behavioural norms that characterize quality performance should be recognized, encouraged and rewarded. It is not enough just to espouse values. They must become values in use – accepted by everyone as governing behavioural norms in the realm of quality.

Resolving the conflict between quality assurance and production or delivery targets

Quality assurance requirements may appear to restrict the scope for departments and individuals to pursue what they believe to be the best routes to achieving their production or delivery targets. There are three ways of dealing with this problem. The first is to ensure, when setting quality assurance standards, that they are relevant and realistic. The second is to involve line managers in setting and regularly reviewing the standards so that they can have their say on what they should be and how they should be applied. Third, quality assurance should monitor the application of their standards not only to achieve compliance but also to discuss with line managers any problems they create that interfere with their production or delivery responsibilities.

Ensuring process compliance

The aim of quality assurance is to set guidelines and standards for the levels of quality required. These are integrated within the total quality management or Six Sigma framework. There is clearly no point in having guidelines or standards unless they are complied with. Compliance is achieved by monitoring performance using, as appropriate, quality control techniques. But ensuring compliance should not be a mechanical 'policing' process which relies on extensive procedural documentation. Quality management is the responsibility of line managers; it cannot be imposed by a quality management function. In other words, it should be a self-managed process. This does not mean that line managers should be left to their own devices. Monitoring is still necessary but it should be monitoring with a light touch in line with the total quality management philosophy that quality is everyone's business.

SUMMARY

- Quality can be defined and assessed in terms of innate excellence, convenience of use, performance, reliability, value for money, level of customer service, fitness for purpose, attractive appearance or style, durability, conformance to design specifications, and uniformity, with small variability.
- Quality management is concerned with all the activities required to ensure that products and services conform to the standards set by the organization and meet expectations of customers.
- Quality assurance aims to ensure that the activities carried out in the organization (design, development, manufacturing, service delivery) result in products or services that meet the requirements and needs of customers.
- Quality control involves the application of data collection and analysis to monitor and measure the extent to which quality assurance requirements have been met in terms of product or service performance and reliability.
- Total quality management (TQM) is a systematic and holistic method of ensuring that all activities within an organization happen in the way they have been planned in order to meet the defined needs of customers.
- TQM involves a change of focus from inspections at the end of a process to an emphasis in the planning stage on ensuring that the design allows high quality and in the operations stage that no defects are produced.
- Six Sigma uses a range of quality management and statistical tools to construct a framework for process improvement. The aim is to achieve the sigma level of 'critical to quality' performance measures that meet the needs of customers. This is done by following the sequence define–measure–analyse–improve–control (DYMAIC).
- Quality standards provide the basis for developing and measuring the effectiveness of a quality system. Their aim is to encourage organizations to think about their management processes and react to the changing demands placed upon them. The international standard ISO 9000 is the one most generally used. In addition, an important quality standard has been produced by the European Foundation for Quality Management – the EFQM model.

- Interest in and enthusiasm for quality can be sustained by involving everyone from the start and keeping them involved. Contributions to improving quality should be recognized and rewarded.
- Developing the conditions and behaviour that promote quality is a matter of creating and maintaining a quality-orientated culture.
- Resolving the conflict between quality assurance and production or delivery targets can be achieved by (1) ensuring when setting quality assurance standards that they are relevant and realistic, (2) involving line managers in setting and regularly reviewing the standards and (3) monitoring the application of standards not only to achieve compliance but also to discuss with line managers any problems they create that interfere with their production or delivery responsibilities.
- Compliance is achieved by monitoring performance using, as appropriate, quality control techniques. But ensuring compliance should not be a mechanical 'policing' process which relies on extensive procedural documentation. Quality management is the responsibility of line managers; it cannot be imposed by a quality management function.

REFERENCES

1   Deming, W E (1986) *Out of the Crisis*, MIT Centre for Advanced Engineering Study, Boston, MA
2   Juran, J M (1988) *Quality Control Handbook*, McGraw-Hill, Maidenhead
3   Crosby, P B (1978) *Quality is Free*, McGraw-Hill, New York
4   Maslow, A (1954) *Motivation and Personality*, Harper & Row, New York

Appendix

GUIDELINES FOR MANAGING FOR RESULTS STUDENTS

The following guidelines are for use by students taking the CIPD Managing for Results examination. They are set out under the following headings:

- General guidance
- Guidance on tackling Section A of the examination
- Guidance on tackling Section B of the examination

GENERAL GUIDANCE

Professional standards

Study the Managing for Results Professional Standards as summarized below. The figures in brackets indicate the page numbers in which the subject is covered in the text.

The practice of management

- The role of the manager in a variety of contrasting contexts (21–22, 24–26).
- The contribution of managers and management to the effectiveness of the organization and organizational success (22).
- The nature of management (3–11).

- Management standards (7).
- Management styles (14).
- Similarities and differences between managers and leaders and the potential conflict and tension between them (5–6).
- Planning, organizing, setting targets and agreeing objectives (31–39).
- Managerial approaches: leading, coaching, facilitation, delegation (13–16, 45–48, 50–52, 52–53).
- Developing and operating a network of functional and vertical relationships with colleagues, teams, individuals and internal and external organizations (53–56).
- Communicating persuasively and convincingly (39–43).
- Understanding organizational policies and influence, authority and power (54, 55–56, 56–57, 57–58, 115–116).
- Systems and process management and the conflict and challenges that these may present (73–79, 112).
- Assessment of working conditions and remedies to address unsatisfactory situations (158).
- Industrial and professional codes of practice, procedures, organizational and legal requirements (8–10).
- Developing self through the identification of individual potential value, motivation capabilities and capacity (86–87).
- Knowing how to give, receive and act on feedback (49–50).
- Methods of management development: self-development, executive coaching, mentoring, personal network, action learning sets (81–83, 84–86).
- Factors affecting 'added value' contribution (22–23).
- Significance of strategic and visionary thinking (26).
- The pivotal contribution of the line/middle manager in promoting appropriate behaviours, role model, exemplar, guide, coach and mentor (27, 52, 84).
- Developing a shared vision and providing direction (70, 131).
- Gaining support for the organization's vision and strategy (77).
- Refining strategy and gaining support for plans (69, 77).
- Inspiring and motivating others to make their full contribution (48–49).
- Self-management strategies and opportunities – seeking out opportunities for development (86–87).
- Evaluating the impact of own performance (86–87).

Delivering change

- Planning and monitoring a programme of change (122, 127–29).
- Development and maintenance of organizational structures and systems (94–95, 108–11, 112).
- How organizations grow and change (99–100).

- Elements leading to the successful implementation of change (130–31).
- Organizational dynamics (98–99).
- Comparative organization types and structures (104–08).
- Comparative organization functions (113–15).
- Comparative organization cultures (115).
- Developing a change culture (96–125).
- Fostering innovation and risk (130).
- Assessing the organization's current position in the market (93, 125–26).
- Embracing a change culture when there is no obvious competition for the purpose of providing more efficient, effective services (125).
- Models and theories of change management (119–21).
- Corporate culture (95–96).
- Identifying the need for change (125–26).
- Proactive intervention (129).
- Reactive/remedial recovery (126).
- Equilibrium, disequilibrium and stability (99).
- Making the business case for change; identifying the drivers, benefits and risks (126–27).
- Realizing short-term gains as well as longer-term deliverables (130).
- Planning for change; identifying barriers and solutions (127–28).
- Communicating plans for change (124).
- Promoting understanding and showing empathy with other needs, feelings and motivation (130).
- Taking personal responsibility for making things happen (61–65).
- Agreeing goals and objectives (110, 127–28).
- Monitoring and evaluating progress (129).
- Ensuring flexibility of response and making adjustments while not losing sight of long-term goals (130).

Enhancing customer relations

- Nature and importance of customer service (137–38).
- Priorities of customer service (139).
- Approaches to measuring customer satisfaction (153–55).
- Assessing customer needs (148–49).
- Keeping customers (161).
- Infrastructure factors essential to good customer service (157).
- Distinction between customers, users, payers and clients (137).
- Evaluating models of customer service – service level agreements, preferred supplier status, telesales, help lines, accounts management, call centres (157–59).
- Elements of customer satisfaction (140–41).

- Establishing and maintaining good relationships with customers – installing confidence that their requirements will be met, on time with cost-effective solutions and adequate support availability (161).
- Meaning of customer service reliability: responsiveness, competence, credibility, access (141).
- Mechanisms for dialogues with customers: surveys, questionnaires, focus groups (150).
- Application of customer service values to internal customers (161–62).
- Changing customer dynamics and the need to go beyond satisfaction (141–42).
- Creating a customer-centric culture (167–70).
- Critical evaluation of the factors behind the creation of such a culture: attitudes and behaviours for individuals, units, functions and organizations (170–74).
- Ensuring the competencies, creative and innovative skills are available to design and develop products and services to meet customer needs (170–73).
- Identifying target customers for goods and services (151–52).
- Communicating availability and benefits (152).
- Helping customers select the products and services that best suit their needs (152, 155).
- Assessment of the contingent lessons to be learnt from 'world class' service enterprises (176–80).

Enabling continuous improvement

- Advise on the importance, requirements and implications of continuous improvement from quality control and assurance through to transformation (187).
- Foster a culture of continuous improvement (188).
- Quality and continuous improvement techniques (195–99, 201–204).
- Conditions and behaviour that promote quality and continuous improvement (190–92, 216).
- Critical assessment of the rationale for continuous improvement and transformation (187).
- The continuous improvement framework, strategy and infrastructure (192–95).
- Problem-solving activities, problem-solving groups, problem-solving tools (195–99).
- Evidence-based review of infrastructure models of continuous improvement (202–04).
- Quality management systems and their contribution to organizational goals and objectives (210–14).
- Process compliance – auditing process compliance of systems (217–18).
- Tension and conflict between quality assurance and production/delivery targets (217).

- Evaluation of differentiator applications for continuous improvement: proactive, opportunity seeking, intuitive experimentation, empowerment (195).
- Methods of identifying and overcoming the barriers to continuous improvement (200).
- Assessment of the internal/external imperatives for continuous improvement in specific organizations and sectors (201–04).
- Critical evaluation of the standardized/holistic approaches to quality rectification, maintenance and for quality improvement (210–14).
- Assessment of the factors that generate a continuous improvement/transformation culture: top-down management, leadership, consistent focus, challenging goals, comprehensive people development (188–90).
- 'Holding the gains'; identifying and maintaining better practices and processes, cost savings, improved customer service (200–01).

Approach to learning and revision

- Ensure that where appropriate you can at least define any key concept or practice succinctly (up to 50 words) so that when it comes to the exam you can start impressively when dealing with a particular question.
- Make sure that you know at least 50 per cent (preferably 75 per cent) of the key headings or features of any of the main areas covered by the standards.
- Supplement the basic information provided in this text by reading about the subject in greater depth in journals such as *People Management* and the *Harvard Business Review*, and the publications of the CIPD and key writers on management and leadership such as John Adair, Peter Drucker, Rosabeth Moss Kanter, John Kotter, Daniel Goleman, Gary Hamel, Charles Handy, Henry Mintzberg, Tom Peters and Rosemary Stewart. Where appropriate, refer briefly to any relevant concepts, practices or research you have learnt about in your answers.
- Get to know the key management practices in the areas covered by the standards in your own organization or any organization with which you are familiar so that you can illustrate and support your answers with examples.

MANAGING FOR RESULTS EXAMINATION PAPER

Section A

Purpose and features

Section A of the Managing for Results paper offers four questions, two of which must be attempted. The questions in Section A focus on the performance differentiators. They may generally address the entire range of the standards, or be based on specific areas. This means you need to have breadth and depth of knowledge. Each question is based on recently published material from readily accessible sources. Even if you have not studied that specific source, you should still be able to critically evaluate and write about the concepts and ideas behind what is being said. Critical evaluation involves demonstrating that you understand the concept and can evaluate its pros and cons and come to a justified conclusion about its relevance and use. You will be expected to demonstrate that you understand how managers think and act to improve both their own and their organization's performance. The purpose is to ensure that managers, their staff and their organizations become the best at what they do.

Tackling Section A

As in real life, the situations require you to adopt an analytical and diagnostic approach to answer the questions. You will normally be asked to comment initially on the subject matter and to further show your understanding by giving examples of where the ideas could or should apply in organizational practice. Whatever the setting, and whatever aspect of the standards it addresses, it is essential to adopt the perspective of someone who is acting as a 'business partner' and 'thinking performer'. If your work experience to date has not been at a senior level, you need to develop a more strategic approach to your analysis and writing.

Always take time to read all four questions carefully before choosing which ones to answer. You may be familiar with the subject matter, but uncomfortable with the tasks you are asked to carry out, or the approach you need to take. It is very easy to gravitate towards a topic area that is familiar to you, or an extract from a text that you have read, only to find yourself writing at length everything and anything that is in the least way connected.

The question will ask you to do quite specific things. It is for doing what the question asks that you are awarded marks, not for being able to recall six pages of associated facts, examples and opinion.

Example of a question paper Section A

Here are some examples of the type of question typically found in Section A. They include one drawn from a journal article, two based on extracts taken from recently published texts and one that refers to data published following a recent survey. In this instance these are: *Harvard Business Review*, 2001, texts by A Baron and M Armstrong, and G Smith and survey data from 'The Sunday Times 100 Best Companies to Work For in 2004'.

Questions

1 'The fact that success has become less persistent strongly suggests that momentum is not the force it was. To be sure there is still enormous value in having a coterie of loyal customers, a well known brand, deep industry know-how, preferential access to

distribution channels, proprietary physical assets, and a robust patent portfolio. But that value has steadily dissipated as the enemies of momentum have multiplied... In the past, executives had the luxury of assuming that business models were more or less immortal. Companies always had to work to get better, of course, but they seldom had to get different. Today getting different is the imperative!!' (Primal leadership: the hidden driver of great performance, D Goleman, R Boyatsis and A McKee, *Harvard Business Review*, 2001)

Critically discuss the actions that, in your view, an organization needs to embrace and adopt to 'get different' and taking as an example any organization of your choice, evaluate how it has already achieved this, or how it might do so in the future.

2 'The panacea to most workplace ills continues to be home working. The 2003 survey established that home workers were much better disposed, overall, to their bosses, colleagues and company. More detailed research in 2004 shows that among those working home for up to 30% of their working week, only 11% would leave tomorrow for another job, compared with 18% among those working only in an office. More than 50% of those who do some homeworking think they have a dream job, compared with an average of 31.5% who do less of their work at home.' (From The Sunday Times 100 Best Companies to Work for 2004)

Critically evaluate the business benefits of enabling employees to work from home and the challenges that such arrangements present for line managers.

3 'Interviewees from other organizations described the performance management process as being about "coaching, guiding, appraising, motivating and rewarding colleagues to help unleash potential and improve organizational performance". One said: "Where it works well it is built on excellent leadership and high quality coaching relationships between managers and teams."' (A Baron and M Armstrong, Managing performance, *Performance Management in Action*, CIPD, 2004)

Comment briefly on these observations about Performance Management and evaluate, with recommendations for improvement, the approach taken in your own organization or department.

4 'Owing to the nature of their work and training, many professionals prefer to do things in their own way. They are knowledge workers or conceptualists who rely heavily on their own expertise. Wherever they work they seek both to use and to expand the existing knowledge base. Although they have to work in teams, they are often unenthusiastic about it. They certainly resist being over managed. The challenge for their leaders is to foster and maintain well co-ordinated, high performing reams, capable of achieving clear business objectives, but with a light touch.' (*Leading the Professionals*, Geoff Smith, Kogan Page, 2004)

Imagine you are about to be appointed to lead and manage a team of professionals.
Identify the major management competencies and skills that you will need in this new role and the methods you will employ to acquire or enhance these in yourself.

Points for inclusion in answers to Section A

1   This extract from the *Harvard Business Review* formed the background to Gary Hamel's opening keynote presentation at the 2004 CIPD National Conference. Even if you were not able to attend the conference, reports of the major presentations are available in *People Management* and on the CIPD website. Hamel is telling us that 'in the past companies always had to work to get better, but they seldom had to get different – not at their core, not in their essence'. Today he proposes getting different is the imperative. Gary Hamel calls this the resilience gap.

The nub of the argument or concept lies in thinking strategically and constantly engaging in creative and innovative thinking and new practices. The use of an example here is important because it will demonstrate an understanding (or not!) of the concept. Hamel himself cites many US-based organizations who find themselves faced with the challenge, including Coca-Cola, McDonald's, Dell, Motorola, Gap and CNN. UK examples might include M&S, Sainsbury, MG Rover and Royal Mail. Whatever the example, answers should go some way to explaining the background situation of the company and include evidence-based discussion regarding how to foster innovation and creativity. Typically these might be simple but well-rewarded suggestion schemes, 'internal' venture capital and other resources to support new ideas. You might include in your answer consideration of how to develop a culture of innovation and creativity that means constant regeneration rather than response to a crisis.

The need for organizations to have a strategic vision is also an important dimension. If you do not operate at a strategic level in your organization, it is important that your awareness of holistic and longer-term thinking is developed through reading and the study or shadowing of role models at a senior level.

2   This question addresses the tensions presented to managers who must manage at a distance. These may be experienced because the organization wants to do it, but managers do not, or cannot, manage this way or because managers want to do it, but their organizations won't let them. Research indicates that more homeworking is likely and good answers will cite evaluated examples of where this already happens, how it is practised, why and with what degree of success.

The answers should spotlight the debate on the changing role for the manager and the need for organizations who wish to foster homeworking to provide development, support communication vehicles, etc for such practices to be successful. It is helpful to highlight the specific management competencies most needed for managing at a distance, but this alone would not gain a pass.

3   Whatever level of experience you have as a manager you should be able to realize the importance of Performance Management to organizational success. Case studies, articles and texts abound giving plenty of advice and guidance. The CIPD 2004 survey said that 87 per cent of organizations use a formal Performance Management process and 94 per cent see it as an essential tool in the management of organizational culture. In answering the question, it is important to focus on the main criteria for successful Performance Management:

● strategic;
● integrated;
● concerned with improvement and development;
● owned by employees and operationalized by line management;
● part of the culture;

and then to evaluate that particular student's organization. By making recommendations for improvement the candidate will assure the examiner of their knowledge and understanding and their ability to apply that knowledge. In justifying your recommendations, you should highlight the achievement of organizational objectives and success.

4   'The challenge for the leaders of professionals is to foster and maintain well co-ordinated, high performance teams capable of achieving clear business objectives' is the key to what is required in the answer. It is about encouraging and supporting rather than directing and controlling.

Digby Jones (Director General of the CBI) believes that 'Leadership of professional teams is much the same as team leading in other walks of life. It brings similar responsibilities and similar skills. However, leading professionals can be much tougher than many people realize. Professional people generally have had a rigorous training before they start work and tend to have a sceptical turn of mind. They enjoy challenging received wisdom and trying to reach a consensus is often quite difficult. Many of them prefer to work alone so getting teams to work together can be a tough proposition. The bottom line is that professionals value their independence and judgement so their team leaders usually have to work doubly hard, often in quite subtle ways to achieve accountability.'

Better answers will allude to this situation and focus on management competencies related to interpersonal skills, morale boosting, communications and maintaining standards. Examples will serve to strengthen your answers. The development of those people who manage such professionals should then be related to the competencies described. Useful techniques might include some self-assessment in these skill areas through published tools such as *Self Development for Managers* by M Pedler, J Burgoyne and T Boydell (McGraw Hill, 2001).

As much of the role is interpersonal and related to individuals in a fairly untypical situation, a mentor for the manager would be a good method to recommend for development. It is essential to explain briefly why that is the choice, how you might identify someone suitable and what you could expect to get from the relationship.

Section B

Points to bear in mind

To do well in answering the seven out of ten questions you must:

- Answer the question – this may sound like boringly familiar advice but it is astonishing how often candidates fail to do so. You must look at questions and ask yourself: 'What is the examiner getting at?' 'What is wanted in the reply?' 'If this is a question asking me to respond to a request for information or advice, how do I express my reply in a way which meets this requirement?'
- Ensure that you adopt a realistic approach and show that you understand the business considerations relevant to the question.
- Emphasize the practicalities in terms of what impact this particular aspect of managing for results makes on the motivation, commitment, morale and performance of employees and on organizational effectiveness.
- Define briefly any terms or concepts to which you refer.
- Show that you understand the key features of any of the key leadership and management policies or practices you are asked to comment on and how they can be applied by setting out your knowledge of the major theories, concepts and research findings. This should be based on information gained by studying the literature.
- Refer briefly wherever possible to effective and relevant leadership and management practices in your own and other organizations. If appropriate, you should take pains to understand thoroughly the policies of your own organization by studying them and talking to HR people and line managers who are involved. You can build up some useful examples of good and, sometimes, not so good practice in this way. Read any case studies you can get hold of from journals, magazines and books, including this one. They will provide you with a view of leadership and management in action which is an essential part of this highly practical subject.
- Present your arguments for a particular approach or practice in a clear and persuasive way.
- When answering a typical contextualized question involving action (eg questions 3, 5 or 9 below), remember to ask, and answer, the questions: 'Who am I?' and 'What am I doing for whom?'

Example of a question paper – Section B

(seven to be answered out of ten)

1 Drawing on your knowledge of published research and organizational practice, show how two apparently different management styles can be effectively deployed in the same organization.

2 Draft a short article for your local CIPD branch newsletter entitled 'Visionary leaders – why do we need them?'

3 You have received an e-mail from your newly appointed quality supervisor. She wants to know what is meant by 'zero defects' and whether, realistically, it can ever be achieved. She also wonders if you would be able to suggest a comparable alternative quality assurance model. Draft your comprehensive, but concise, reply.

4 Drawing on your knowledge of published research and models of change, explain, with examples, the term transformational change.

5 Your new CEO is asking for ideas that would really improve your organization's service to external or internal customers. What three suggestions will you e-mail to her and why?

6 Team leaders in your call centre are furious that staff are being 'taken out' to undergo health and safety training as this is affecting call rate targets. Outline and explain the arguments you will use to reassure the team leaders and to reinforce the importance of such training.

7 You are acting as a consultant to a local taxi firm that wants to improve its customer relations in order to increase market share. Explain and prioritize the mechanisms that you will suggest are available for them to use to evaluate customer service.

8 A colleague, who is seeking promotion, asks your advice on choosing a coach to help her to improve her management skills. She wishes to know what are the important qualities to look for in a coach and also wants to know what being coached is likely to entail. Outline your advice to her.

9 Outline the main points you would want to make in a short presentation to senior managers entitled 'Change, maximizing the benefits – minimizing the pain'. In view of the fact that they are bound to want to know more about the subject, you are also asked to make recommendations for further reading and/or examples of good practice.

10 Distinguish between the roles of internal and external change agents. Give an example from your own organization that shows how one of these has been, or could be, used to good effect.

Points for inclusion in answers

1   You have a wide choice here when it comes to management style, but you should try to refer to at least one published writer or piece of research. Drucker, Handy, Stewart, Goleman or any similar writer would be fine. The arguments you make to support the proposition must show how more than one management style can work within the organization based on:

- the sector/industry expectations;
- the nature and expectations of staff;
- the task itself – urgency and magnitude.

You are required to show your knowledge of the theory and apply it to practice.

2   This answer should be drafted as a newsletter article – opening and closing comments with main points in between and no more than one side of A4 in length. You will need to include a definition or explanation of visionary leadership and how such leaders contribute to organizational success. An example would be a good way to enhance understanding. You must address the 'why do we need them' angle as well – they are needed because they give direction and focus, they keep the organization motivated and moving, they champion and drive change. These are all essentials for organizations to be successful in the 21st century.

3   This answer requires knowledge and understanding of two models for quality assurance; there is quite a wide range to choose from. Zero defects is attainable in some environments, especially highly automated ones. Six Sigma has found favour with many organizations; this statistical technique is popular in engineering and construction. Other models such as EFQM or ISO 9000 could be used also for a comparison.

4   Transformational change is an important concept in Managing for Results. Your answer *must* draw on research and change models. Gary Hamel refers to transformation in terms of innovation, regeneration and resilience, Tom Peters advises firms to stick to the knitting. Jack Welch talks about 'going for the leap' and Purcell confirms that successful companies possess 'the big idea'.

5   You might choose to answer this from a strategic or an operational perspective, or you could offer a mixture of both. Don't try to deal with external and internal customers though, as the question asks you to pick only one type.

Sometimes a quick fix/impact suggestion goes down well with senior management followed by suggestions for the longer term. The CEO will be seeking solutions that work, so ideas and examples from successful organizations/competitors could help the 'why' dimension. This e-mail should be short, sharp and to the point.

6   The tension between productivity and health and safety will never go away. Managers need to deal with balancing the two and the question wants you to give arguments relating short termism and organizational success. A good argument incor-

porates the legal and ethical issues and is backed by data and statistics. Your best argument would initially sympathize with the manager's point of view but then relate to longer-term survival.

7   This question has two key words, 'mechanisms' and 'prioritize'. You need to identify the mechanisms and by prioritizing these you will indicate what is best for this taxi firm and why. This company does not just want to know about now; they are looking to improve, to gain market share. You might want to include buying behaviour analysis or market research, customer relationship management or customer analysis. The briefest of definitions of these is all that will be expected, just enough to communicate the 'why'.

8   Coaching comes in many forms and is done for many reasons. Here it is one to one to improve management skills. You should explain that a good coach is trained, able to listen, guide and prompt. He or she may not be someone you already know, but will be work focused, inclusive and help the colleague to do things differently. Your colleague has already decided on what she wants the coaching to achieve; she will need to listen, think about and analyse her own behaviours and try out new approaches.

9   Here's your chance to fall into the trap of writing everything and anything you can remember about change. Keep the answer short and to the point – focus on the practical aspects that have been shown to work in theory and practice.

Focus on commitment, shared vision, consensus, consolidation and monitoring and review. You must include the further information sources to maximize marks. You might include: Texts, eg Moss Kanter's *The Change Masters*, CIPD publications like *The Change Agenda* and any of the many case studies in *People Management*.

10   A straightforward question; you can answer with a matrix if you want to. You ought perhaps to say what a change agent is, then list their qualities, for example:

Table 18.1

Internal	External
Existing member of staff	Consultant/expert with wide experience
Wholly seconded or doing this as part of own job	More objective
Less expensive	More credibility with senior managers
Variable credibility, better with staff than senior management	Less credibility with other staff as they don't have to live with the consequences of their actions

Choose one type of change agent for your example. Writing something for both will not maximize your marks because only one part of the answer will be taken into account.

Index

ACAS 10
accident prevention 75–76
accountability 21
accounts management 159
achievers 62–63
action learning 85–86
Adair, J 14, 16
added value 22, 23
added value contribution 22
affiliation 62
AIDA sequence 149
Audi 177
authority 21, 56–57, 116

Bandura, A 121
Bartlett, C A 94
Bates, C 167
Beckhard, R 120
Beer, M 122
behavioural change 96–97
behavioural commitment 97
behavioural modification 97–98

Bennis, W G 5
Bessant, J 185
big idea, the 95–96
Britannic Assurance 172, 177
British Computer Society 9, 76
British Gas Trading 160
business process re-engineering 112
buyer/decision sequence 149
buying behaviour 148–49

call centres 158, 160
cause and effect diagrams 197
change
    agents 128, 129
    barriers to 128
    behavioural 96–97
    benefits of 126
    cultural 95, 96
    drivers of 126
    environmental 125
    how it happens 98
    how people change 121

identifying need for   125–26
and market position   125–26
models   119–21
resistance to change   122–24
risks of   127
types of   91–92
change culture, development of   125
change management
    communicating plans for change   124
    defined   119
    defining objectives of change   127–28
    flexible response   130
    long-term goals   130
    monitoring and evaluating progress
        129
    planning the change programme
        127–30
    project planning   129
    requirements for success   129–30
    responsibilities for   128–29
    steps to change   122
    successful implementation   130–31
Chartered Institute of Personnel and
    Development (CIPD)   xi, 9
Chartered Management Institute   8
Child, J   93
coaching
    aims of   51
    defined   50–51, 84
    and development   84
    effective coaching   52
        executive coaching   84
    need for   51
    planned coaching   52
    process   84
    sequence of   51–52
codes of practice
    defined   8
    industrial codes of practice   9
    official codes of practice   10
    professional codes of practice   8–9

commitment   95, 97
communicating
    barriers to communication   40–42
        managers as communicators   39
communities of interest   54
competencies
    leadership   16
    managerial   28–29
competency frameworks   28–29, 86
competitive edge   151
competitor research   151
complaints   160
computer-integrated manufacturing
    system   78–79
consequence management   65
consideration   15
consumer buying behaviour   148–49
continuous improvement
    aims of   186
    applications of   195
    approaches to   194–95
    defined   185–86
    framework for   192–93
    and a high performance culture   190
    implications of   188
    importance of   186–87
    programmes   193–94, 199–200
    and quality management   207
    rationale for   187
    requirements of   188–90
    techniques   195–99
    and total quality management   186
    and transformation   187
    values 188
Cook, S   167
corporate culture
    cultural change   95–96
    defined   95, 115
    types of   115
corporate governance 10–11
critical evaluation   196

Crosby, P B   185, 209–10
cultural change   95, 96
culture *see* corporate culture
customer care   139
customer-centric culture   167–70
customer dynamics   141–42
customer relationship management
     149–50
customer satisfaction
   elements of   140–41, 142
   measurement of   153–55
customer service
   activities   140
   aims of   138, 140
   approach to   145
   attitudes   170
   behaviours   171
   competencies   172–73
   concern with product and process
      138
   and continuous improvement   187
   defined   137–38
   importance of   138–39
   knowledge   171
   levels   159–60
   managing relationships with
      customers   145
   models of   157–59
   priorities   139
   quality   140
   skills   170
   standards   159–60
   strategy   167
   world-class customer service examples
      176–80
   world-class service excellence   165–66
customer service or contact centres   140,
   157–58
customers
   building satisfaction   161
   and clients   137

communicating on availability of
     goods or services   152
creating a customer   xi
customer questionnaires   153
customer surveys   153–52
defined   137
expectations   148
external customers   138
helping to select the products or
     services they need   152
internal customers   138
keeping   161
needs   148
and payers   137
questionnaires
target customers, identification of   15
and users   137

decentralization   35
decentralized organizations   106–07
decisiveness   64–65
delayering   27, 35
delegation   45–47
deliverables, customer service   148
Dell   178
Deming W E   185, 195, 208–09
Devenna, M A   69
Digman, L A   68
disequilibrium   99
Drucker, P   xi, xii, 23, 81, 126, 130

effectiveness   22
efficiency   22
EFQM model of quality   215–16
Eliot, T S   115
emotional intelligence   17
Equal Opportunities Commission   10
equilibrium   99
exception report   48
executive coaching   84
external customers   138–39

facilitation
  defined 52
  of groups 53
  of individual learning 52
Faulkner, D 68
Fayol, H 4
feedback
  aim 49
  giving 49–50
  receiving and acting on feedback
    50
Fiedler, F E 15
fishbone diagrams 197
flexibility 35
focus groups 151
followers and leaders 17–18
Fombrun, C J 68
fragmentary nature of managerial work
  25–26

General Electric 130, 213
Ghoshal, S 94
Goleman, D 17
Gratton, L 96
Graves R 17
group discussions 154
group facilitation 53

Halpin, A W 15
Hampel Committee 10–11
Handy, C 15, 56, 115
hard delegation 48
Harvey-Jones, J 61
health and safety audits 75
Health and Safety Authority 10
health and safety system 74–76
Heller, R 68
Heraclitus 91
high achievers 63
high performance culture 190

improvement groups 194
incremental change 92
industrial codes of practice 9
influence, exerting 55–56
information technology 76–77
initiating structure 15
internal customers
  applying customer service values to
    161–62
  defined 138, 161
involvement 124
ISO 9000 214–15

jobs 24
Johns, T 167, 179, 180
Johnson, G 68
Johnston, R 167
Juran J M 162, 185, 209

Kaizen 185
Kanter, R M 69, 98
Kelley, R E 18
Kelly repertory grid 151
knowledge management 54
Kotter, J P 5, 57–58
Kreitner, R 97

Lands' End 168–69
leaders
  and followers 17–18
  as managers 6
  qualities of 15, 16
  roles 13–14
  situational leadership 14–15
  task-orientated approach to 14
leadership
  behavioural requirements 16
  characteristics 15–16
  competencies 16
  and continuous improvement 188

defined   13
description of   6
and emotional intelligence   17
exercise of   15
and management   5–6
performance   15
purpose   ix, 3
qualities   16
leadership style   14, 15
legal requirements   10
levels of customer service   159–60
Levitt, T   146–47
Lewin, K   119–20
line managers
    contribution of   27
logical incrementalism   92
Luthans, F   97–98

making things happen
    how to make things happen   61–62
    improving ability to make things
        happen   65
    and management   xi
management
    by agreement   56
    by control   56
    defined   3
    description of   6
    influences on   6
    and leadership   5–6
    process of   4
    purpose   xi, 3
management standards   7
Management Standards Centre   7
management style   14
managerial activities   31
managerial work, fragmentary nature of
    25–26
managers
    added value contribution of   22–23

attributes of   28
being authoritative   56–57
as coaches   27, 52
as communicators   39
competency frameworks   28–29
contribution of   22
described   21–22
how managers work   25
as leaders   6
line managers   27
as mentors   29
as role models   27
roles   24–25
as strategic thinkers   26
and strategy   68
as visionary thinkers   26
what managers do   25–26
managing for results   xi
Managing for Results examination paper
    225–33
managing systems and process – conflict
    and challenge   79
marketing research   150
Maslow, A   210
matrix organizations   107–08
McClelland, D   62
measurement of customer satisfaction
    153–55
mentor   82
mentoring   84–85
middle managers   27
Mintzberg, H   4, 68–69
motivating
    achieving high levels of motivation
        48–49
    motivation defined   48
mystery shopping   141

Nadler, D A   124
Nanus, B   5

networking   53–54, 82–83
norms   95
NVQ/SVQ in customer service   175

Oakland, J S   186–87
objectives
    defined   36
    defining objectives of change   127–28
    defining work objectives   38
    good work objectives   37–38
    personal objectives   36
    SMART objectives   38
    standing objectives   37
    work objectives   36–37
O'Connor, Z   171
official codes of practice   10
OFTEL   9
open systems theory   104
order processing   160
organizations
    defined   103
    as open systems   103
organizing   33
    defined   104
    process of   104–05
organization analysis   109–10
organization design   33–34, 111
organization diagnosis   110–11
organization dynamics   98–99
organization functions   113–14
organization guidelines   34–35, 111
organization planning   111
organization reviews   108–09
organization structures
    centralized   105–06
    decentralized   106–07
    defined   104
    matrix   107–08
    process-based   108
    unitary   05
organizational change   93–94
organizational culture   95, 115

organizational development   98
organizational policies   53
organizational requirements   10
organizations
    stages of development   99–100
    types of   105–08

Pascale, R   92–93, 94
Peabody Trust   173
Pedler, M   28, 82
performance management   82, 86
performance review   86
performance standards   39
personal development plans   83
personal objectives   36
persuading
    and communicating   43
    and influence   55–56
Pettigrew, A   98
planning
    activities   32
    aim of   31
    defined   31
    ingredients   32
policies
    areas of   54–55
    formal and informal   55
    organizational policies   53
    reason for   54
Porter, M   147
power
    defined   57
    exercise of   57–58
    in organizations   115–16
preferred supplier status   159
problem solving   58, 64, 196
procedures   10
process   189
process-based organizations   108
process consulting   129
process management   78–79
processes

defined   73
   managing processes   74, 79
processes of management   4
product life cycle   155–57
product planning   155
professional codes of practice   8–9
Pugh, D   123–24, 128
Purcell, J   27, 95–96

quality
   in customer service   140
   defined   207–08
quality assurance   210
quality circles   194
quality control   210
quality management
   approaches   210–14
   defined   208
   issues   216–18
quality standards   214–16
quantitative performance standards   39
Quinn, J B   92

Recruitment and Employment
   Confederation   9
relationship management   146–48
results   48
Revans, R W   85
reward systems   77–78
right first time   212
risk assessments   75
role clarification   35
role model   82
roles   24

Schein, E H   129
Scottish Parliament   97, 168
Scottish Water   178–79
self-development
   defining how to satisfy needs
      82–83
   identifying needs   82

process of   81
   strategies   86–87
self-managed learning   81–82
self-management   86–87
service centres   157–58, 160
service delivery   148
service level agreements   158–59, 162
Sewell Cadillac   168
shared vision   70
Singapore Airlines   179–80
Six Sigma   213
Sloan, A P   91
SMART objectives   38
socio-technical model of organization
      103–04
soft delegation   49
stability   99
stakeholders   70, 187
standards of customer service   159–60
standards of performance   86
standing objectives   37
statistical quality control   211
Stewart, R   4
Stone, M   139
strategic change   93
strategic management   69
strategic planning   70, 125
strategic thinking   26
strategy
   defined   67
   development of   68–69
system
   defined   73
   development of   112
   managing systems   73–74, 79
systems management   74, 74–79

Taguchi methodology   212
target customers, identification of   151–52
targets   37, 38–39
telesales   159
Thurley, K   120–21

Tichy, N M   69
Total quality control   201
total quality management
    and continuous improvement   186
    defined   212
    focus   212
    introduction of   213
    philosophy   212
transactional change   92–93
transformation and continuous
    improvement   187
transformational change   92–93
twelve pillars of world-class customer
    service excellence   165–66

unitary organization structures   105
unsatisfactory conditions, dealing with   58

value chain   147
values   95, 96, 97, 188
vision   5, 70
visionary management   69
visionary thinking   26

websites   158
Welch, D   64, 93
Whipp, R   98
Winer, B J   15
Wodehouse, P G   22
Woodward, J   123
work objectives   36–37, 38
working conditions   58

Zaleznik, A   5
zero defects programmes   211–12

FURTHER READING FROM KOGAN PAGE

Leading the Professionals
How to inspire and motivate professional service teams
Geoff Smith

"A fascinating insight into leadership in practice and in context – that of the professional service firm... offers perceptive analysis, thoughtful guidance and practical illustration."
— Professor Michael Osbaldeston, Director of the Cranfield School of Management

The Healthy Organization
A revolutionary approach to people and management
Brian Dive

"The book is a must-read for business leaders and educators, senior HR professionals and consultants." — Business World

Hard Core Management
What you won't learn from the business gurus
Jo Owen

"Jo Owen has mined a rich seam of valuable and pragmatic insight to bring some real sense to the complexities of our modern businesses." — Peter Dixon, Director of Strategy, Deloitte Touche Tohmatsu

The Leader's Guide to Lateral Thinking Skills
Powerful problem-solving techniques to ignite your team's potential
Paul Sloane

"Sloane delivers rocket fuel for the business brain." — Bill Penn, CEO, Sparx Group

The Instant Manager
Tools and ideas for practical problem solving
Cy Charney

"Loaded with practical hints." — Business Life

Shut up and Listen
The truth about how to communicate at work
Theo Theobald and Cary Cooper

"Concise and practical, it offers plenty of nuggets of advice from the people interviewed, in addition to may case studies and authors' own stories." — Commerce and Industry

Kogan Page publishes books on Business, Management, Finance, Marketing, HR, Training, Careers and Testing, Transport and Logistics and more.

Visit our website for our full online catalogue:
www.kogan-page.co.uk

Also by **Michael Armstrong**

"The undisputed 'bible' on the topic."
—Administrative Management

Hardback 704 pages
0 7494 3984 X

"Offers both specialist reward practitioners and generalist HR personnel essential material."
—**John Martin, Associate Examiner (Employee Reward) CIPD**

Paperback 496 pages
0 7494 4343 X

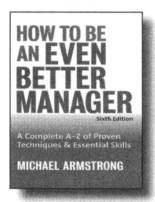

"Written with the benefit of over 30 years' experience."
—**Business Executive**

Paperback 352 pages
0 7494 4262 X

"Covers everything you need to know from the job description to the golden handshake."
—**Human Resources**

Paperback 1008 pages
0 7494 4105 4

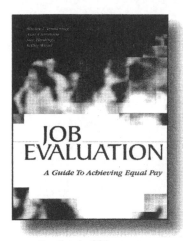

Hardback 224 pages
0 7494 3966 1

Hardback 768 pages
0 7494 3094 X

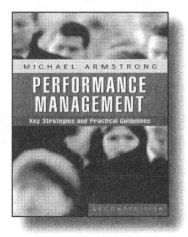

Paperback 272 pages
0 7494 2628 4

Paperback 288 pages
0 7494 3331 0

Paperback 448 pages
0 7494 2899 6

Paperback 256 pages
0 7494 2612 8

Visit
Kogan Page
online

Comprehensive information on Kogan Page titles

Features include:

- **complete catalogue listings, including book reviews and descriptions**

- **sample chapters**

- **special monthly promotions**

- **information on NEW titles and BEST-SELLING titles**

- **a secure shopping basket facility for online ordering**

PLUS everything you need to know about KOGAN PAGE

www.kogan-page.co.uk